Frommer's

KU-330-950

Seville
day BY day™

2nd Edition

by Jeremy Head

WILEY

A John Wiley and Sons, Ltd, Publication

Contents

14 Favorite Moments 1

1 The Best Full-Day Tours 5
The Best in One Day 6
The Best in Two Days 12
The Best in Three Days 16

2 The Best Special-Interest Tours 21
Art Old & New 22
New World Adventures 28
Churches & Convents 32
Gastronomic Seville Tapas 36
Things to Do with Kids 40

3 The Best Neighborhood Walks 45
Santa Cruz 46
Centro 52
Triana 58
Alameda 62
La Macarena 66

4 The Best Shopping 69
Shopping Best Bets 70
Seville Shopping A to Z 73

5 The Great Outdoors 81
Seville on Two Wheels 82
Parks & Pavilions 88

6 The Best Dining 93
Dining Best Bets 94
Seville Restaurants A to Z 99

7 The Best Nightlife 111
Nightlife Best Bets 112
Seville Nightlife A to Z 116

8 The Best Arts & Entertainment 123
Arts & Entertainment Best Bets 124
Arts & Entertainment A to Z 127

9 The Best Lodging 133
Lodging Best Bets 134
Seville Hotels A to Z 138

10 The Best Day Trips 145
Itálica 146
Carmona 150
Córdoba 154

The Savvy Traveler 159
Before You Go 160
Getting There 162
Getting Around 163
Fast Facts 164
Seville: A Brief History 168
Seville's Architecture 169
Useful Phrases 172
Menu Terms 173

Index 176

UK Publisher: Sally Smith
Production Manager: Daniel Mersey
Commissioning Editor: Mark Henshall
Development Editor: Mark Henshall
Content Editor: Erica Peters
Photo Research: Jill Emeny
Cartography: Jeremy Norton

Wiley also publishes its books in a variety of electronic formats. Some
content that appears in print may not be available in electronic books.

British Library Cataloguing in Publication Data

A catalogue record for this book is available from the British Library

ISBN: 978-0-470-74989-0 (pbk), ISBN: 978-0-470-97329-5 (ebk)

Typeset by Wiley Indianapolis Composition Services

Printed and bound in China by RR Donnelley

5 4 3 2 1

A Note from the Editorial Director

Organizing your time. That's what this guide is all about.

Other guides give you long lists of things to see and do and then expect you to fit the pieces together. The Day by Day guides are different. These guides tell you the best of everything, and then they show you how to see it in the smartest, most time-efficient way. Our authors have designed detailed itineraries organized by time, neighborhood, or special interest. And each tour comes with a bulleted map that takes you from stop to stop.

Hoping to wander through the beautiful Moorish royal palace of the Alcázar, get caught in the passion and emotion of Flamenco or munch tapas among Seville's pretty, cobbled squares and tinkling fountains? Planning to admire the city's romantic artworks, bar crawl its boho areas or enjoy its peaceful parks? Whatever your interest or schedule, the Day by Days give you the smartest routes to follow. Not only do we take you to the top attractions, hotels, and restaurants, but we also help you access those special moments that locals get to experience—those "finds" that turn tourists into travelers.

The Day by Days are also your top choice if you're looking for one complete guide for all your travel needs. The best hotels and restaurants for every budget, the greatest shopping values, the wildest nightlife—it's all here.

Why should you trust our judgment? Because our authors personally visit each place they write about. They're an independent lot who say what they think and would never include places they wouldn't recommend to their best friends. They're also open to suggestions from readers. If you'd like to contact them, please send your comments our way at feedback@frommers.com, and we'll pass them on.

Enjoy your Day by Day guide—the most helpful travel companion you can buy. And have the trip of a lifetime.

Warm regards,

Kelly Regan

Kelly Regan, Editorial Director
Frommer's Travel Guides

About the Author

Jeremy Head is a travel writer, photographer and broadcaster based in Brighton, UK. Over the past decade or so, his travel writing and photographs have appeared in most of the UK's national newspapers and specialist travel magazines. He also recently spent a summer wearing covert camera gear as an undercover reporter for ITV's Holidays Undercover. His obsession with Seville began with a weekend break in 2000 and he has been going back for more ever since. (Maybe it's the wine?) As well as writing and completely updating this second edition of the Day by Day guide to Seville he took pretty much all of the pictures. You can find out what he's currently up to by reading his blog: www.travelblather.com. If you've got comments about this guidebook – good or bad – feel free to email him. He'd be very interested to hear from you: seville@jeremyhead.com

Acknowledgments

A book is never really written by just one person. The advice, opinions and friendship of a whole bunch of people have helped make *Seville Day by Day* far, far better than anything I could have achieved alone. Thanks very much to you all: David Cox and Luis Salas at reallydiscover.com, Jeff Spielvogel at exploreseville.com, Eduardo Blanco at differentspain.com, Markus Christmann at sevilla5.com, Francisco Naranjo and the team at the Alminar Hotel, Carlos Amarillo at rentabikesevilla.com, Saida Segura and the excellent front of house team at the Seville Tourist Board, Amanda Corbett at the Seville Provincial Tourist Board, Céline Rambaud at the Seville Film Office, the Seville Hotels Association, Manolo Carmona, John Harrop, Christine Gesthuysen, David Garcia, Aurora Ortega, Kurt Grötsch, Tamsin Hemingray and everyone at iCrossing UK, Mark Henshall, Tim Locke, Karen Head.

This book is dedicated to the memory of my brother, Stephen David Head.

An Additional Note

Please be advised that travel information is subject to change at any time—and this is especially true of prices. We therefore suggest that you write or call ahead for confirmation when making your travel plans. The authors, editors, and publisher cannot be held responsible for the experiences of readers while traveling. Your safety is important to us, however, so we encourage you to stay alert and be aware of your surroundings.

Star Ratings, Icons & Abbreviations

Every hotel, restaurant, and attraction listing in this guide has been ranked for quality, value, service, amenities, and special features using a star-rating system. Hotels, restaurants, attractions, shopping, and nightlife are rated on a scale of zero stars (recommended) to three stars (exceptional). In addition to the **star-rating system,** we also use a `kids` **icon** to point out the best bets for families. Within each tour, we recommend cafes, bars, or restaurants where you can take a break. Each of these stops appears in a shaded box marked with a coffee-cup-shaped bullet ☕ .

The following **abbreviations** are used for credit cards:

AE	American Express	**DISC**	Discover	**V**	Visa
DC	Diners Club	**MC**	MasterCard		

Travel Resources at Frommers.com

Frommer's travel resources don't end with this guide. Frommer's website, **www.frommers.com**, has travel information on more than 4,000 destinations. We update features regularly, giving you access to the most current trip-planning information and the best airfare, lodging, and car-rental bargains. You can also listen to podcasts, connect with other Frommers.com members through our active-reader forums, share your travel photos, read blogs from guidebook editors and fellow travelers, and much more.

A Note on Prices

In the "Take a Break" and "Best Bets" sections of this book, we have used a system of dollar signs to show a range of costs for 1 night in a hotel (the price of a double-occupancy room) or the cost of an entree (main course) at a restaurant. Use the following table to decipher the dollar signs:

Cost	Hotels	Restaurants
$	under $100	under $10
$$	$100–$200	$10–$20
$$$	$200–$300	$20–$30
$$$$	$300–$400	$30–$40
$$$$$	over $400	over $40

How to Contact Us

In researching this book, we discovered many wonderful places—hotels, restaurants, shops, and more. We're sure you'll find others. Please tell us about them, so we can share the information with your fellow travelers in upcoming editions. If you were disappointed with a recommendation, we'd love to know that, too. Please write to:

Frommer's Seville Day by Day, 2nd Edition
Wiley Publishing, Inc. • 111 River St. • Hoboken, NJ 07030-577

14 Favorite
Moments

14 Favorite **Moments**

Map Area

CENTRO

SANTA
CRUZ

TRIANA

1	Parque María Luisa
2	Alcázar
3	Carriage hire
4	Giralda
5	Hotel Doña María
6	Barrio Santa Cruz
7	Casa de la Memoria
8	Arab baths
9	Casa Morales
10	Capillita de San José
11	Calle Sierpes
12	Museo de Bellas Artes
13	El Tremendo
14	The Alameda

Previous page: Plaza de España.

Sevillians will tell you there's no need to go anywhere else—their city has it all. And, you know, after going back time and again, I completely agree with them. Whatever you're looking for—delicious dining to suit all pockets, jaw-dropping cultural treasures, funky and stylish shopping, non-stop nightlife—Seville has it in abundance. Here are just a few of my favorites. It was a real struggle to keep the list to a manageable size.

❶ Cycle around Parque María Luisa. Seville's largest park (*parque*) is an unrushed tree-, ornament- and shrub-filled space. There are wide, smooth paths too, perfect for a relaxed pedal. Hire a bike in the park or use one of the Seville city bikes. *See p 41.*

❷ Wander the Alcázar. Seville's royal palace is a feast of romantic Moorish archways and patios, beguiling and beautiful. The gardens are delightfully cool and colorful too. *See p 10.*

❸ Clip-clop through the old town in a horse-drawn carriage. Many of the carriages pulled along by the splendid horses here date back to the 18th century. An idyllic way to see the city. *See p 42.*

❹ Look out across the city from the Giralda. The cathedral's ornate bell tower is one of the city's signature sights, but it also offers some of the widest views across Seville from the top. *See p 8.*

Ornate arches in the Alcázar.

❺ Sip a cocktail on Hotel Doña María's roof terrace. This is a great spot to end the day. Enjoy a sundowner long drink and take in the views of the cathedral. *See p 141.*

❻ Get lost in Barrio Santa Cruz. The old Jewish quarter is the heart of the tourist district, a warren of white-washed houses, cobbled squares

See the city from a horse-drawn carriage.

Flamenco is a dance of passion and excitement.

and tinkling fountains. Best enjoyed early evening or early morning when it's not too busy or hot. *See p 9.*

7 **Get caught up in the passion of flamenco.** The essence of romantic Seville, good flamenco is enthralling, almost engulfing with its charged emotion and rhythm, and Casa de la Memoria's intimate patio is an authentic setting. *See p 130.*

8 **Wallow in a Moorish-style bathhouse.** Aire de Sevilla's ornate plunge pools, steam rooms and massages are a great way to get seriously relaxed. Morning or early afternoon is best as it can get quite busy. *See p 14.*

9 **Munch tapas surrounded by noise at lunchtime.** Tapas is the quintessential Sevillian lunch experience and Casa Morales, an old corner bar, is a classic spot to try some. Stand at the bar so it's easy to order and enjoy the hubbub around you, which peaks at around 1:30pm. *See p 108.*

10 **Discover dazzling church interiors.** The Catholic desire to overwhelm the believer reaches its zenith in the phantasmagoric gold-leaf swirls, eerily lifelike statues and huge dimensions of the altarpieces in many churches—even smaller

places of worship like Capillita de San José. *See p 53.*

11 **Browse the shops in Calle Sierpes.** The *paseo*, or evening stroll, is an institution here. Locals love to promenade the classy shopping streets in the cool of the evening, seeing and being seen—and doing a little shopping if the mood takes them. *See p 57.*

12 **Admire the romantic artworks at the Museo de Bellas Artes (Museum of Fine Arts).** The 17th-century Sevillian greats Murillo, Valdés Leal and Zurbarán are all well represented in this, one of Spain's best-stocked fine-arts museums. *See p 27.*

13 **Sink an ice-cold beer at a busy street bar.** There's debate aplenty about just which bar serves the coldest beers in town. My vote is El Tremendo, a no-nonsense street bar where you stand on a busy corner surrounded by gossiping locals. *See p 117.*

14 **Bar crawl in the Alameda.** The city's boho alternative area is a long, wide tree-lined boulevard with bars and clubs overflowing onto the pavement. Cool cafes, noisy dives, funky dance bars—there's something for everyone. *See p 63.* ●

The Best **in One Day**

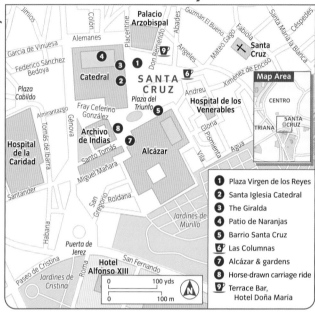

1. Plaza Virgen de los Reyes
2. Santa Iglesia Catedral
3. The Giralda
4. Patio de Naranjas
5. Barrio Santa Cruz
6. Las Columnas
7. Alcázar & gardens
8. Horse-drawn carriage ride
9. Terrace Bar, Hotel Doña Maria

Seville has fine monuments aplenty, but its unique atmo-sphere is what keeps me coming back. A first day takes in the two most famous sights, the immense cathedral with its tremen-dous works of art and the beguilingly beautiful royal palace, the Alcázar; but much of the enjoyment is about wandering the ancient streets and squares and soaking up the scenery, adapting a little to the rhythms of the local ways of life. START: **Walk to Plaza Virgen de los Reyes. Nearest tramstop: Archivo de Indias.**

① **Plaza Virgen de los Reyes.** More than any other, this square (*plaza*) evokes all things Sevillian, a perfect spot to start exploring Seville. At its center is an early 20th-century fountain by José Lafita (around 1865–1925), with water burbling from gar-goyles at its center. Crane your neck upwards and admire the massive height of the cathedral tower, the Giralda, and take a walk down the line of horses and carriages waiting for

their fares. The horses are immacu-lately groomed. On the north side of the square is the Palacio Arzobispal (Archbishop's Palace) with its ornate baroque facade. Opposite is the whitewashed convent known as the Convento de la Encarnación, founded in 1591.

② ★★★ **Santa Iglesia Catedral (Seville Cathedral).** Dominating the city skyline, Seville's cathedral is

Previous page: The Casa de Pilatos has an exquisite main patio.

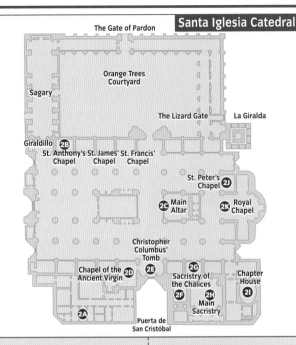

Santa Iglesia Catedral

The Gate of Pardon

Orange Trees Courtyard

Sagary

The Lizard Gate

La Giralda

Giraldillo **2B**

St. Anthony's Chapel St. James' Chapel St. Francis' Chapel

St. Peter's Chapel **2J**

2C Main Altar

2K Royal Chapel

Christopher Columbus' Tomb

Chapel of the Ancient Virgin **2D** **2E**

2G Sacristy of the Chalices

Chapter House **2I**

2F **2H** Main Sacristy

2A

Puerta de San Cristóbal

2A The cathedral's small **art gallery** contains works by legendary Sevillian painters **Murillo** and **Zurbarán** (p 24). **2B** The **Chapel of St. Anthony** features more of their vast canvases. A piece of *The Vision of St. Anthony* by Murillo (1617–82) was stolen in 1874 and subsequently recovered and stitched back—you can just see the join toward the bottom right. *Saints Justa and Rufina* by Zurbarán (1598–1664) shows the city's patron saints protecting the Giralda. **2C** The golden central **altarpiece** is the world's largest, containing over 2,000 statues illustrating 45 scenes from the Bible. **2D** The *mihrab*, the niche in the mosque's wall that faced Mecca, was located in what is now the **Chapel of the Ancient Virgin**. **Christopher Columbus** (1451–1506), the city's most famous adventurer, prayed for protection here before his second

voyage in 1493. **2E** His extravagant **tomb** is found here, held aloft by figures of four knights representing the Spanish kingdoms of Castile, Aragon, Navarra and Léon. **2F** The **Sacristy of the Chalices** features *Saints Justa and Rufina* painted by **Goya** (1746–1828) and, behind you and above the door *St. John the Baptist* by **Zurbarán**. **2G** The sculpture of *Cristo de la Clemencia* in the **Chapel of St. Andrew** is by Montañés (1568–1649). **2H** The ornate **monstrance** in the **Main Sacristy**, used to display consecrated bread, contains 200 kg of silver. **2I** The oval **Chapter House** has a seat for each of the original 117 canons of the Seville diocese. The ceiling decoration is by Murillo. **2J** **St. Peter's Chapel** features a series of paintings by Zurbarán. **2K** The **Royal Chapel** contains the body of St. Ferdinand.

Seville's cathedral is the third-largest in the world.

built on the site of a 12th-century mosque. After the Christians reconquered the city in 1248, they were determined their cathedral would outdo any Moorish monument preceding it. The result is the world's third-largest cathedral after St. Peter's in Rome and St. Paul's in London—an incredible jungle of Gothic spires and buttresses. ⏲ *1 hr. Plaza Virgen de los Reyes.* ☎ *954 214 971. www.catedralsevilla.org. 8€ adults, children under 12 free, free entry Sun. Mon–Sat 11am–5pm, Sun & holidays 2:30pm–6pm. July & Aug Mon–Sat 9:30am–4pm, Sun & holidays 2:30–6pm. Audio guide 3€.*

❸ ★★★ **kids** **The Giralda (cathedral tower).** Like many of Seville's churches, this tower is adapted from the minaret of the mosque it replaced. The 12th-century minaret originally had four shiny globes on top but these fell during an earthquake and were replaced in 1568 with a Renaissance belfry with 25 bells and the weather-vane, El Giraldillo (hence the name Giralda), depicting a woman representing the Christian virtue of Faith. Despite being 91m high, it's an easy climb—there are no steps, just gentle ramps, built so that the *muezzin* could ride his horse to the top when it was time for him to make the call to prayer. The views of the city and the cathedral's remarkably complex buttresses are tremendous. Seville's foremost landmark is often depicted protected by the city's patron saints, Justa and Rufina. ⏲ *40 min. You can only climb the Giralda if you have paid for a visitor ticket to the cathedral.*

❹ **Patio de Naranjas.** Another very tangible remnant of the mosque, this orange-tree-shaded patio with a fountain at its center was the original ablutions courtyard for the mosque, where the faithful would wash before prayers. You exit the cathedral complex through the Puerta del Pedron, the old mosque gateway, where you can clearly see Moorish decoration (the Muslim style characteristic of the Middle Ages in much of southern Spain).

The cathedral gates clearly show the Moorish heritage.

The iron cross at the center of Plaza Santa Cruz marks the site of an old church.

5 ★★★ Barrio Santa Cruz. The city's old Jewish quarter is a maze of narrow passageways flanked by whitewashed houses with flower-filled window boxes. It's the center of the tourist district. It can get a bit full of tour groups, and staff in the restaurants can get a bit grouchy, but there's plenty of scope for a souvenir-shop browse or a cool beer on a terrace. For a relaxed wander, take Romero Murube and turn right into Plaza Doña Elvira with its tinkling fountain and specialty boutiques. Exit via Vida and wander along unspoilt Callejón del Agua up to Plaza Santa Cruz. Exit along Santa Teresa, and continue along Mesón del Moro to Mateos Gago. Las Columnas (**6**) is on a corner on the left. There's a detailed tour of Barrio Santa Cruz on p 46.

Get into the Local Rhythm

Seville gets seriously hot in summer, and the culture of the siesta remains embedded in local life. Most shops and many monuments close for a long lunch between 2pm and 5pm. It's not a bad idea to follow the locals' lead and rest too. Seville wakes up again in late afternoon and keeps going until the very small hours. To enjoy the city at its best it's worth taking it easy when the day is at its hottest and staying out later. It's completely normal to eat dinner at 10:30pm or 11pm.

Those Allowed to Remain

When Seville was reconquered by the Christian King Fernando III in 1248, the defeated Moorish leaders left the city (the Moors being the Muslims who originated from north Africa). But many of the local populace remained and converted, nominally at least, to Christianity. They were known as Mudéjar—literally 'those allowed to remain'. Their architecture, gardens and food were ideally suited to the climate, and Christians adopted many elements of their culture. Moorish craftsmen were employed to build churches and civic buildings. This Mudéjar architecture, a combination of Moorish and Christian styles, remains all over the city—most notably in the Alcázar, but also in many smaller churches. The influence continued into the 20th century in updated form. Many buildings created for Seville's great 1929 Ibero-American Exposition (p 89) borrow Mudéjar features.

6 ★★★ Las Columnas. A buzzing bar, by far the most authentic in the area, Columnas is a great intro to tapas. Tapas are small dishes to go with a beer or cold sherry—there are menus on boards either side of the bar. Order loud and clear at the bar if it's busy. Take your phrasebook—you'll need it! *Rodrigo Caro 1.* ☎ *954 213 246. $.*

The craftsmanship on display at the Alcázar.

7 ★★★ Alcázar & gardens. This romantic royal palace is Seville at its most exotic and enticing. Pedro I, king of Castile, who built it in the 14th century, was known as Pedro the Cruel, but he must have had a softer side. His complex of courtyards and patios is graced with the deftest of carvings and a fragrant, shady garden. Pedro used Moorish craftsmen from Granada to craft this ultimate homage to Moorish architecture, at a time when Seville had long been reconquered by the Christians. The result is an exquisite blend of Moorish and Christian influences known as the Mudéjar style (see box above). The delicate carved arches of the Patio de las Doncellas (the Maidens' Patio), the dazzling dome and stalactite stucco ceiling of the Salon de Embajadores (the Ambassadors' Hall) and the restful gardens are the highlights. Carlos V's later Gothic additions also feature intricate tilework and carved ceilings. King Juan Carlos I and his Queen Sophia still stay here when visiting Seville, and the royal apartments can be visited on a separate pre-booked tour. ⏱ *2 hr. Patio de Banderas.* ☎ *954 502 323. www.patronato-alcazarsevilla. es. 7.50€ adults, children under 12 free. Oct–Mar daily 9:30am–5pm. Apr–Sept daily 9:30am–7pm. Audio tour recommended 3€.*

8 ★★ **kids Horse-drawn carriage ride.** Early evening, when the day is a little cooler, is the perfect time to hop into a carriage for a trot around the city. It's a quintessential Seville experience. Most drivers speak a little English and will point out the sights. The standard tour takes you to Parque Maria Luisa to see the Plaza de España and other buildings from Seville's 1929 Ibero-American Exposition and back to the historic center. There's a fixed fee for the standard tour, but less scrupulous drivers may try to charge more. Hold your ground! ⏱ *1 hr. Pick-up points at Plaza Virgen de los Reyes & Plaza del Triunfo.* ☎ *954 924 015. 36.06€ per carriage (43.27€ during Holy Week; 86.54€ during April Fair).*

The Alcázar's delightful gardens.

9 ★★★ **Terrace Bar, Hotel Doña María.** Finish the day with a cool sundowner cocktail on one of Seville's most attractive roof terraces. The service is friendly, and the views of the floodlit cathedral delightful. *Don Remondo 19.* ☎ *954 224 990. $$.*

See the sights by horse-drawn carriage.

The Best **in Two Days**

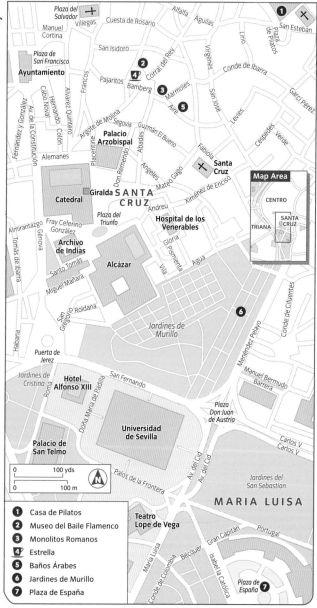

Plaza del Salvador
Manuel Cortina
Villegas
Cuesta de Rosario
Alfalfa
Águilas
San Esteban
Plaza de Pilatos
1

Plaza de San Francisco
Ayuntamiento
San Isidoro
Corral del Rey
Lirio
Virgenes
Conde de Ibarra
Gatcí Pérez

Francos
Pajaritos
Bámberg
2
4 Estrella
3
Marmoles
San José
Levies
Céspedes
Verde

Argote de Molina
Segovia
Guzmán El Bueno
Aire
5

Alvarez Quintero
Hernando Colón
Cabo Noval
Av. de la Constitución
Fernández y González

Placentine
Abades
Angeles
Fabiola
Santa Cruz
×

Alemanes
Don Remendo
Mateo Gago
Ximénez de Enciso

Giralda S A N T A
Catedral
C R U Z
Andreu

Fray Ceferino González
Plaza del Triunfo
Hospital de los Venerables

Almirantazgo
Génova
Tomás de Ibarra
Archivo de Indias
Santo Tomás
Miguel Mañara
Gloria
Pimienta
Vilia
Agua

Alcázar

San Gregorio Roldana

Jardines de Murillo
6
Conde de Cifuentes
Menéndez Pelayo

Habana
Puerta de Jerez
Jardines de Cristina
Hotel Alfonso XIII
Roma
Doña María de Padilla
San Fernando

Manuel Bermudo Barrera
Plaza Don Juan de Austria

Universidad de Sevilla
Av. del Cid
Av. del Cid
Carlos V
Carlos V

Palacio de San Telmo
Palos de la Frontera
Jardines del San Sebastian

0   100 yds
0   100 m
N

Teatro Lope de Vega
M A R I A   L U I S A
Gran Capitán
Portugal

María Luisa
Conde de Colombia
Bécquer
Isabel la Católica
Plaza de España
7

Map Area
CENTRO
TRIANA
SANTA CRUZ

1 Casa de Pilatos
2 Museo del Baile Flamenco
3 Monolitos Romanos
4 Estrella
5 Baños Árabes
6 Jardines de Murillo
7 Plaza de España

The highlights of day two include a palace that exudes an extraordinary atmosphere of calm, an introduction to flamenco and an Arabic bathhouse. If you want to go to these baths, booking is recommended, and remember your swimsuit. You might want to book a flamenco show this evening as well (p 129). START: **Plaza de Pilatos. Bus: C5 or walk.**

1 ★★★ Casa de Pilatos. Still inhabited by the Dukes of Medinaceli, this is one of Seville's finest palaces and I love it. The name 'Pilate's House' probably refers to the fact that one of its owners—the first Marquis of Tarifa—made a pilgrimage to the Holy Land in 1518. He came back from his two-year trip so enthused with the ancient Greek- and Roman-inspired 'classical' architecture of Renaissance Italy that he set about creating a new interior for his palace, inspired by the Roman governor Pontius Pilate's house in Jerusalem. The result is a harmonious mixture of styles—Mudéjar, Renaissance and Gothic. The main patio has a fountain imported from Genoa, and Roman and Greek marble busts in each corner, Mudéjar-style tiles and arches at ground level and Gothic balustrades and arches above. Rooms leading off the patio are similarly ornate, in particular the Salon de Pretorio and Gabinete de Pilatos—both with intricate coffered ceilings and Mudéjar tiles and walls—and the tiny chapel with its Gothic vaulted ceiling. The gardens are a tranquil series of fragrant bushes, vast trees and a fountain. The upper level, which contains family portraits, antique furniture and more vaulted ceilings, is reached by climbing a tiled staircase with golden dome above; this part can only be visited on a half-hourly guided tour. ⏱ *1 hr. Plaza de Pilatos 1.* ☎ *954 225 298. 5€ ground floor & gardens, 8€ upper floor as well. Ground floor: Mar–Sept 9am–7pm daily (6pm Oct–Feb); upper floor: 10am–2pm, 4–5:30pm. No credit cards.*

The tranquil patio at the Casa de Pilatos.

2 ★★★ Museo del Baile Flamenco. This ranks among my top recommended museums in Seville—that's assuming you like hi-tech displays using video and touch screens. Spain's most celebrated flamenco dancer, Cristina Hoyos, is artistic director. Five rooms of audiovisual displays in six different languages (including English) chart the history and development of the dance and its connection with the soul of Andalusia. Particularly informative are the demonstrations of the different styles of dance in room two, showing the unique colors and emotions of each technique. There are displays of outfits worn by famous dancers: one belonging to Antonio Gades—his waist size seems impossibly small—and Cristina Hoyos's outfit from the opening ceremony of the Barcelona Olympics. Upstairs galleries feature the paintings of Colita (influenced by the

On the Street

The Spanish for street is calle—sometimes abbreviated to C/ and often left out completely. I've chosen to leave it out in service details at the end of each tour stop as it's simply not necessary. Occasionally I do use it when describing tour start points or locations within the description, just to make clear that I am referring to a street and not a site or place.

Spanish artist Miró) and there are more displays in the basement. Dance classes take place here too; even complete beginners can participate. There are also nightly flamenco shows (p 130). The museum is housed in an old town house with a relaxing patio. ⏱ *1 hr. Manuel Rojas Marcos 3.* ☎ *954 340 311. www.museoflamenco.com. 10€, 6€ concessions. Family & group rates available on demand. 9am–7pm daily. All credit cards accepted.*

❸ **Monolitos Romanos.** These three vast columns hewn from single blocks of granite are some of the few reminders that Seville's founders were Roman. They are the only remaining parts of what is thought to have been a vast temple to the goddess Diana, erected in the 1st

Costumes on display at the Flamenco Museum.

century A.D. The two columns that now guard the Alameda square were taken from here. Notice how much lower ground level was in Roman times compared to the modern streets around it. *Mármoles.*

❹ ★★ **Estrella.** A seriously authentic tapas bar tucked down a side street. There's a small restaurant if you want to sit down. The tapas menu is available in English and includes traditional favorites and a few more exotic recipes. Try the langostinos con aguacate—avocado stuffed with large prawns. *Estrella 3.* ☎ *954 561 426. $.*

❺ ★★ **Baños Árabes (Arab Bathhouse).** Here's a perfect way to relax when the day is at its hottest. This bathhouse is a modern sanctuary built inside a 16th-century town house palace. It features pools of different temperature, hydro and salt baths, and massage and relaxation rooms, all decorated in Moorish style with vaulted wood ceilings and candlelit lamps. Bath entry and a short massage costs 32€. Other treatments are available. You can relax with a cup of fragrant tea in the teahouse on the first floor too. Avoid the evening sessions, when it gets rather busy. Reservations are essential. Swimsuits mandatory. ⏱ *2 hr. Aire 15.* ☎ *955 010 024. www.aire desevilla.com. Daily 10am–midnight.*

The Plaza de España's ornate colonnades.

6 ★ **Jardines de Murillo.** Originally the orchards of the Alcázar, these gardens were donated to the city in 1911. Today they're a shady respite from the sun. Look for the monument to one of Seville's most famous citizens, Christopher Columbus (1451–1506). A lion stands on two columns, a front paw on a globe. Halfway down is a bronze of Columbus's flagship, the *Santa María*.

7 ★★★ **Plaza de España.** If you're planning to host a great exhibition, you want your own pavilion to be star of the show. Seville's great Ibero-American Exposition of 1929 (p 89) left it with a host of remarkable buildings. The Plaza de España—the name given to a spectacular colonnaded crescent and erected as the Spanish pavilion—is the boldest of the lot. Aníbal González, Seville's most famous 20th-century architect, took inspiration from the Mudéjar and Renaissance styles of earlier centuries; the result is a truly unique series of richly decorated curves and exotic towers. Each region of Spain is depicted with a tiled panel along the walls of the colonnades. Be careful not to get sunburned here: there's little shade.

Getting Around Town

Seville's old town came into being long before the car, and by far the best way to navigate its narrow streets is on foot. The historic center is pretty compact and lends itself well to walking. The modern tramway is handy for getting along Avenida de la Constitución. The only bus route through the old town is the C5—often served by a dinky electronic micro-bus—which stops at most major monuments (see map on inside cover). Taxi ranks can be found on Plaza Nueva outside the Hotel Inglaterra, Calle Alemanes right next to Starbucks, and Puerta de Jerez outside Hotel Alfonso XIII.

The Best **in Three Days**

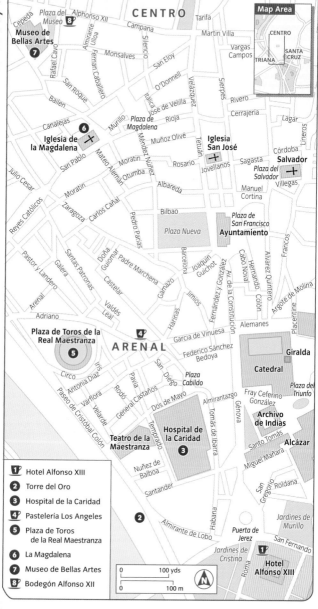

1. Hotel Alfonso XIII
2. Torre del Oro
3. Hospital de la Caridad
4. Pastelería Los Angeles
5. Plaza de Toros de la Real Maestranza
6. La Magdalena
7. Museo de Bellas Artes
8. Bodegón Alfonso XII

Day three concentrates on sights in the Arenal quarter, taking in Seville's grandest hotel, the iconic Torre del Oro, two spectacular churches, the famous bullring and the city's excellent Fine Arts Museum. START: **Puerta de Jerez. Tram: San Fernando. Bus: AC, 21, 22, 23, 41, 42.**

1 ★ **Hotel Alfonso XIII.** King Alfonso XIII ordered Seville's most opulent hotel to be built to house visiting heads of state for the great 1929 Exposition. It remains one of Seville's most select hotels. Even if you can't afford to stay, you can admire the interior decor while sipping a drink in the Bar Alfonso or on the San Fernando patio. *San Fernando 2.* ☎ *954 170 00. $$.*

2 ★★★ **kids Torre del Oro.** Built in 1220 by the Moors as part of the city wall constructed to protect Seville against Christian invaders, the 'tower of gold' is one of Seville's most iconic landmarks. Its 12 sides—one for each of the different winds that the Moors gave names to—make it unique. The turret on top is more recent, added in 1760. Originally another tower was sited across the river and a huge chain would be stretched between them

The Torre del Oro formed part of the old city walls.

to stop ships sailing upriver. It sounded like a good idea, but it didn't work. The Christian fleet easily broke the chain during the reconquest of the city in 1248. Theories differ about how the tower got its name. One is that here was where

NO8DO: Seville's Strange Motto

Seville's motto appears all over the city—from ornate carvings on municipal buildings to drain covers. It consists of two syllables, *No* and *Do*, with a skein of wool between them which looks rather like the figure 8. It's a play on words. The Spanish for skein is *medaja*. In the 11th century during the Christian reconquest of Andalusia, King Alfonso the Wise decided the warring had gone on long enough and made a truce with the Moors. But his hot-blooded son Sancho rebelled and started a civil war. Most of Spain sided with the king's rebel son, but not Seville. In thanks to Seville, King Alfonso declared '*No ma dejado*,' which means 'You did not desert me.' The phrase stuck and the motto was devised: *No Madeja Do*.

The courtyard and fountain, Hospital de la Caridad.

New World riches were stored, another that the tower was covered with golden tiles in Moorish times. It has been variously used as a light-house, private lodgings and a hiding place for Pedro the Cruel's mistress. Today, it houses a small naval museum with two floors of maps and curios, including a model of the *Santa María*, one of the ships which Columbus sailed to America. Climb to the top and you see what a great vantage point it is—handy for taking photos of the city skyline. Most entertaining is the audio guide, which features a schmaltzy encoun-ter between two students as the

backdrop for the tour. 'If you see her, dear visitor, you'll recognize her by the loving way her eyes fol-low the contours of the now naked stronghold!' murmurs the besotted student. Unintentionally hilarious, but good nonetheless. ⏱ *30 min. See p 31,* **8**.

3 ★★★ **Hospital de la Cari-dad.** Founded in 1674, this charity hospital still cares for the elderly and infirm as it has always done, but it's the hospital's church which makes it worth a stop. It contains some of Seville's most sumptuous baroque sculpture and painting, worthy of any museum, but it gets few visitors. Paintings include can-vases by many of Seville's greatest 17th-century painters, including seven by Murillo and two fascinat-ing works by Juan de Valdés Leal (p 24). The altarpiece features an incredibly lifelike 17th-century carv-ing by Pedro Roldán. ⏱ *45 min. See p 23,* **1**.

4 ★★ **Pastelería Los Angeles.** This classic street-corner bakery and bar does great coffee, yummy pastries and delicious *tostadas* (toasted buns) with ham and tomato. *Adriano 2.* ☎ *954 228 146.* $.

The Hospital de la Caridad's ornate altarpiece.

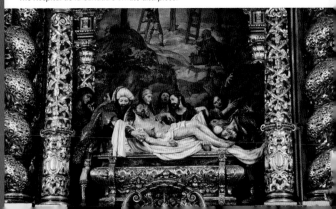

⑤ ★★ Plaza de Toros de la Real Maestranza.

Seville is often referred to as the birthplace of modern bullfighting and its 14,000-seater bullring is a beauty. While it isn't the country's biggest, aficionados claim it's the most atmospheric. Even if you don't much like the idea of bullfights, you may like to take a guided tour of the arena and museum (in Spanish or English). It traces the origins of the sport from bull-less jousting competitions to today's complex theatrical spectacle, with displays of costumes, paintings and stuffed bulls' heads. The first thing that hits you when you walk into the arena is its intimacy. Apparently its incredible acoustics mean that during a bullfight you can even hear the shallowest snort of a bull's breath. The structure was built between 1761 and 1881 by the Royal Order of Chivalry of Seville. Bullfights had previously been staged in temporary arenas in town squares—disorganized affairs involving numerous bulls released among horsemen and men on foot all at the same time. Most poignant is the story of Juan

Seville's bullring is one of Spain's finest.

Belmonte (1892–1962), the modern-day founder of the sport, and his childhood friend and rival José Gomez Ortega (1895–1920). They developed a new form of bullfight—man to man—just two matadors and six bulls in the bullring. Ortega was killed during one such fight at the

Going to a Bullfight

In Spanish it's not thought of as a bullfight: it's a *corrida* or run; a show of bravery as a man lets a bull charge him and maneuvers it around his body. There are three acts, or *tercios*. In the *tercio de varas* the matador and picadors—horsemen with lances—test out the bull to gauge its intelligence. In the *tercio de banderillas* long darts are used to pierce its back, weakening its neck muscles. In the *tercio de muleta* the matador makes passes at the bull with the cape, ultimately killing it, planting his sword between its shoulder blades to pierce its heart. This 'moment of truth' is the most dangerous. If he misses he will be gored. If he is accurate, the bull will drop dead. Sometimes there's much bloodshed. Aficionados say it's a spectacle of pageantry, passion and poignancy. Bullfights are not for the faint-hearted. Six bulls are dispatched in each show and the horses occasionally get gored too. See p 131 for tickets. The parliament of Catalonia has voted to ban bullfighting — the first region in Spain to do so. The ban takes effect in January 2012.

age of just 25. Belmonte continued to fight but was never the same after the death of his friend. ⏱ *1 hr. Paseo de Colón 18.* ☎ *954 224 577. 6€. 9:30am–7pm daily by guided tour only, every 20 min. No credit cards. (See previous page for information about watching a bullfight.)*

⑥ ★★ La Magdalena. A vast baroque church, this is one of Seville's most spectacular. It was designed by Leonardo de Figueroa and completed in 1709. It has a stunning domed chancel with extravagant frescoes and a hugely ornate golden altarpiece. Two side chapels echo earlier Mudéjar chapels on the same site with Moorish domes. The Capilla de la Quinta Angustia was where the famous Sevillian painter Murillo (p 24) was baptized in 1618, while the Capilla de Dulce Nombre de Jesús has a strikingly realistic statue of Christ's body being taken down from the cross. ⏱ *20 min. San*

San Jerónimo Penitente by Florentine Torrigiano at Museo de Bellas Artes.

Pablo 10. ☎ *954 229 603. Mon–Sat 8am–11am, 6:30–8:30pm. Sun 8am–1:30pm, 6:30–8:30pm.*

⑦ ★★★ Museo de Bellas Artes. Housed in the former convent known as the Convento de la Merced Calzada, Seville's Fine Arts Museum is arranged around three classically Sevillian cloistered patios. It's one of the finest collections in Spain—particularly of the 17th-century Seville School of artists. ⏱ *1½ hr. See mini tour on p 27.*

☕ ⑧ Bodegón Alfonso XII. Just up the road from the Museo de Bellas Artes, this neighborhood bar offers a wide range of tapas with an English menu. Tapas can be ordered at the tables or the bar and the bartenders are really friendly. If you like garlic and salsa, don't miss the patatas a la brava. *Alfonso XII 33.* ☎ *954 211 251. $.* ●

La Virgen de Las Cuevas by Francisco de Zurbarán at Museo de Bellas Artes.

Art Old & New

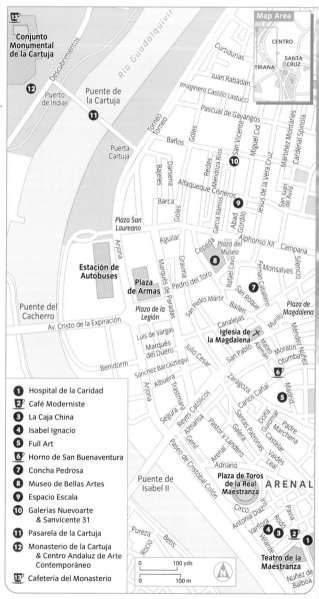

1 Hospital de la Caridad
2 Café Moderniste
3 La Caja China
4 Isabel Ignacio
5 Full Art
6 Horno de San Buenaventura
7 Concha Pedrosa
8 Museo de Bellas Artes
9 Espacio Escala
10 Galerías Nuevoarte & Sanvicente 31
11 Pasarela de la Cartuja
12 Monasterio de la Cartuja & Centro Andaluz de Arte Contemporáneo
13 Cafetería del Monasterio

Previous page: The Alcázar.

Seville's artistic heyday was the 17th century when the great Sevillian painters, Murillo, Valdés Leal and Zurbarán were painting. This tour features many of their works, some contemporary galleries and the Contemporary Art Museum. If you've not already visited the cathedral you should do so as it houses many works by Seville's great painters (see p 6). START: **Calle Temprado. Bus: AC, B2, C4. Nearest tram: Archivo de Indias.**

❶ ★★★ Hospital de la Caridad. This charity hospital still cares for the elderly and infirm as it did when founded in 1674. It has a colorful history. It was built on land which belonged to the brotherhood of Santa Caridad, who dedicated themselves to burying abandoned corpses washed up on the riverside. A new hospital and church were commissioned in 1661 by Miguel de Mañara, the playboy son of a wealthy landowner. It's often said that the character of Don Juan was based on him, but at the age of 34 he had a vision of his own death and gave up his philandering ways and joined the brotherhood. He might have adopted a pious lifestyle, but I reckon he must have still had a flamboyant side. The church contains some of Seville's most sumptuous baroque sculpture and painting, worthy of any museum. Mañara commissioned his friend Murillo, one of Seville's most famous painters (see

below), to paint 11 canvases on the theme of Mercy. Seven survive today. He also commissioned works by Juan de Valdés Leal, whose two morbidly fascinating paintings, *The End of the World's Glories* and *In The Blink of an Eye*, above and opposite the entrance, are considered his finest. The altarpiece features an incredibly lifelike carving of the burial of Christ, by another celebrity craftsman of the day, Pedro Roldán. ⏱ *30 min. Temprado 3.* ☎ *954 223 233. 5€. Mon–Sat 9am–1:30pm, 3:30–7pm, Sun 9am–12:30pm. Audio guide included. No cards.*

❷ ★★ Café Moderniste. Great ambience and good coffee and tostadas (toasted bread with toppings such as cheese and ham) await at this corner cafe-bar which is vaguely Art Deco in style and usually busy with locals. *Dos De Mayo 28. No phone. $.*

Sculpture of Christ the Charity, *by Roldán, in the Hospital de la Caridad.*

Seville's Painting Greats

The triumvirate of Sevillian 17th-century painters produced some of the city's favorite and most memorable works of art. Bartolomé Estéban Murillo (1618–1682) painted sentimental religious images which became immensely popular during the Romantic era in the late 19th century. Juan de Valdés Leal (1622–1690) adopted a more aggressive and realistic style for his depictions of saints, and I find them more appealing. Francisco de Zurbarán (1598–1664) was more realistic still, happily accepting commissions to paint portraits of living people. His paintings of monks in the Cartuja monastery are remarkably lifelike.

The Cartuja monastery was once a ceramics factory.

❸ ★ La Caja China. This arched, airy exhibition space is perfect for the contemporary works on display by Andalusian artists. Sculpture, painting and photography are on show and exhibitions change regularly. More information on the website. *General Castaños 30.* ☎ *954 219 358. www.lacajachina.net. Mon 10:30am–1:30pm, Tues–Fri 10:30am–1:30pm, 6–9pm, Sat noon–2pm.*

❹ Isabel Ignacio. This one-room gallery opened in 1989 and hosts contemporary art exhibitions from up-and-coming artists. Painting, sculpture installations, video: the website details the latest exhibition. *Velarde 9.* ☎ *954 562 555. www. galeriaisabelignacio.com. Mon 6–9pm, Tues–Fri 11am–1:30pm, 6–9pm, Sat 11am–2pm (closed Sat June–Aug).*

❺ Full Art. This two-room gallery on the ground floor (first door to the right) hosts seven exhibitions a year of modern art by Spanish contemporary artists. Works are primarily painting, sculpture and photography and many are for sale. Latest and past exhibitions are on the website,

which has an English version. *Madrid 4.* ☎ *954 221 613. www.fullart.net. Mon–Fri 11am–2pm, 6–9pm, Sat 11am–2pm.*

❻ ★ Horno de San Buenaventura. There are several more of these traditional pastry shops dotted around Seville. They're all fantastic, selling all sorts of yummy cakes and tarts. There's a cafe area at the front. Order at your table from one of the helpful waiting staff. Take the tiny passageway immediately to the left of the shop when you leave. *Carlos Cañal 28.* ☎ *954 223 372. Daily 8am–9:30pm. $.*

❼ ★★★ Concha Pedrosa. Concha's mission is to provide a space for new local artists to display and sell their work. The gallery opened in 1992 and exhibitions change regularly. The quality of the work is consistently high. There's more information on the website. *Fernán Caballero 11.* ☎ *954 226 536. www. conchapedrosa.com. Tues–Fri noon–2pm, 6–9pm, Sat noon–2pm.*

8 ★★★ **Museo de Bellas Artes.** Housed in the former Convento de la Merced Calzada, Seville's Fine Arts Museum (see floor plan and mini tour, p 26) is arranged around three cloistered patios. It's one of the finest collections in Spain—particularly of the 17th-century Seville School of artists. ⏱ *1½ hr. Plaza del Museo 9.* ☎ *954 786 500. 1.50€; free for E.U. passport holders. Tues 3–8pm, Wed–Sat 9am–8pm, Sun 9am–2pm. Closed Mon. Bus C3, C4.*

9 ★★ **Espacio Escala.** This small gallery displays items from the 5,000-piece collection of Cajasol Bank which is worth 13 million euros and still growing. When I visited there were video installations in the four rooms, but all disciplines are featured, usually contemporary in style. *Cisneros 5.* ☎ *954 373 241. Mon–Fri 11am–2pm, 5–9pm, weekends 11am–2pm.*

10 **Galerías Nuevoarte & Sanvicente 31.** These two contemporary galleries stand almost opposite each other. Exhibitions change regularly and works are for sale. *Galería Nuevoarte. San Vicente 32.* ☎ *954 915 668. Mon–Fri 5:30–9pm, Sat 11am–2pm. Galería Sanvicente 31.* ☎ *954 908 424. Mon–Fri 11am–2pm, 5:30–9pm, Sat 11am–2pm.*

11 ★ **Pasarela de la Cartuja.** One of five bridges built for Expo 92, Seville's great 1992 exhibition. As you cross, look right to see the two most celebrated: the arched Puente de la Barqueta and, behind, the angular Puente del Alamillo (the Harp) by one of Spain's best modern architects, Santiago Calatrava. Next, cross the road to reach the rear entrance to Cartuja monastery.

12 ★★ **Monasterio de la Cartuja & Centro Andaluz de Arte Contemporáneo.** There's little historic art in the monastery, as it was more recently a ceramics factory (p 86). It was built in the 15th century and those striking paintings of the monks by Zurbarán in the Museo de Bellas Artes once adorned its walls. The grounds are very pleasant and Andalusia's Contemporary Art Museum in the cloisters features exhibitions by international artists. ⏱ *45 min. Avda Américo Vespucio 2.* ☎ *955 037 070. www.caac.es. 3.01€; free for E.U. passport holders on Tues. Oct–Mar 10am–8pm Tues–Fri, 11am–8pm Sat, 10am–3pm Sun. Apr–Sept open till 9pm weekdays. Closed Mon. Bus C1, C2.*

San Hugo en el Refectorio *by Francisco de Zurbarán at Museo de Bellas Artes.*

Museo de Bellas Artes

GROUND FLOOR

Room III
8A
Room IV
Room V
8B
Room II
Room I
PLAZA DE LAS CONCHAS
PLAZA DEL ALJIBE

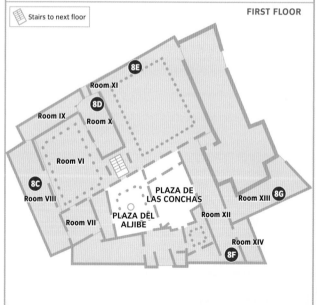

FIRST FLOOR

Stairs to next floor

8E
Room XI
8D
Room IX
Room X
Room VI
8C
Room VIII
Room VII
PLAZA DE LAS CONCHAS
PLAZA DEL ALJIBE
Room XII
Room XIII
8G
Room XIV
8F

8A The **Renaissance Collection** in rooms II, III and IV includes an almost frighteningly lifelike sculpture of *San Jerónimo Penitente* by Italian Florentine Torrigiano (1472–1578), a graphic painting of the *Day of Judgement* by Martin de Vos and an anatomically gruesome sculpture of the *Head of John the Baptist* by Gaspar Núñez Delgado, who worked in Seville between 1576 and 1606. **8B** The spectacularly domed space of **Room V** is the perfect backdrop for the collection of vast canvases by Seville's most famous painter, **Bartolomé Estéban Murillo.** His romanticized depictions of saints and the Holy Family were hugely popular at a time when Seville was beset by misfortunes. *Saints Justa and Rufina Holding the Giralda* is among his best-known works. **8C** I prefer the more dynamic portrayals by his contemporary **Juan de Valdés Leal** in **Room VIII.** **8D** Zurbarán's depictions of **monks at the Cartuja monastery** (where this tour ends) are striking in their realism **(Room X).** Later rooms include depictions of old Seville. **8E** **Room XI** has eight fascinating views of **Seville** by Domingo Martínez (1699–1749). They were originally hung in the Royal Tobacco Factory. **8F** **Room XII** features a large, intimate portrait of the *cigarreras,* the girls who rolled cigars in the factory, by Gonzalo Bilbao Martínez (d 1938). **8G** **Room XIII** has vivid portraits of **bullfighters and flamenco dancers** by José García Ramos (d 1921).

13 **Cafetería del Monasterio.** Service can be a bit haphazard at this modern cafe, but the location in an attractive courtyard is pleasant and the *tostadas* go well with a coffee. There's lots of space for kids to run about. *Monasterio de la Cartuja.* ☎ 954 460 426. 8am–8pm.

Las Cigarreras *by Gonzalo Bilbao Martinez at Museo de Bellas Artes.*

New World Adventures

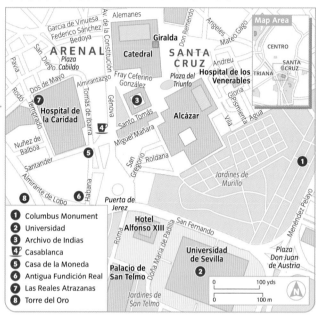

- **1** Columbus Monument
- **2** Universidad
- **3** Archivo de Indias
- **4** Casablanca
- **5** Casa de la Moneda
- **6** Antigua Fundición Real
- **7** Las Reales Atrazanas
- **8** Torre del Oro

S eville's golden age was the 16th century. Spain was entrusted by the Pope with converting the Native Americans, and granted a monopoly on trade with the New World. Astonishing wealth plundered from the Americas poured into Spain, and Seville was the gateway for these riches. This tour takes in the sites and people involved in the great New World adventure. START: **Jardines de Murillo. Tram to Prado de San Sebastián and cross back over Avda Menéndez Pelayo, or bus C3, C4.**

1 Columbus Monument. More than anyone, Christopher Columbus (Cristóbal Colón in Spanish) embodies the spirit of Seville's expeditionary adventures, so it's fitting to start with his monument. A lion stands on top of two columns, a front paw on a globe—symbolizing the extent of the Spanish empire. Halfway down is a bronze of the Santa María, his flagship for his first voyage to the Americas in 1492. The names of King Fernando and Queen Isabella

are inscribed on either side. There's a bust of Columbus at its base. *Jardines de Murillo.*

2 ★★ Universidad (university). One of the most important discoveries in the New World was tobacco. The university is housed in the former Royal Tobacco Factory where, in its heyday, several thousand *cigarreras* (cigar girls) rolled three-quarters of Europe's cigars by hand. Constructed in the 18th century, it was the second-largest building in Spain. The cigar girls had a reputation for loose morals, and became the subject of many a male traveler's daydreams. In 1845 French writer Prosper Mérimée was so seduced by the atmosphere here that he made it the setting of his novel *Carmen*. The French composer Georges Bizet used this story to create perhaps the most popular opera of all time in 1875. The moat and watchtowers around the perimeter make clear how important the king's lucrative tobacco monopoly was. Wander the patios and you still get a sense of the factory. Look for busts of Columbus and Cortés (see below) on the portal of the main entrance. ⏱ *15 min. San Fernando 4.* ☎ *954 551 000. Free. Mon–Sat 8am–8:30pm.*

3 ★ **Archivo de Indias.** Built between 1584 and 1598, the Archivo was originally a traders' market where New World deals were sealed and wares sold. In 1785, Carlos III, with remarkable foresight, had all documents relating to the Spanish Indies colonies collected here. The result is an archive of more than 80 million

The ornate exterior of the Archivo de Indias.

The old crest of the Royal Tobacco Factory.

documents, including letters from the likes of Columbus, Cortés and Magellan (see below). You can enter a small section of the Archivo. There are temporary exhibitions on the ground floor and, up a vast red marble staircase, you'll find displays of documents, a portrait of Cortés and two of Columbus. The first is opposite the top of the staircase and shows Columbus with his hand on a globe, the words in Latin *Non Sufficit Orbis* ('the world is not enough') written around it. It's highly inaccurate: Columbus is wearing clothes that were fashionable when the portrait was painted, more than 100 years after his death. There's a simpler portrait on the wall to the right between two of the windows. Here he is in a sober black smock. In fact, no one knows what Columbus looked liked; even this likeness is painted from descriptions given to the painter by his son. ⏱ *20 min. Avda de la Constitución.* ☎ *954 211 234. Mon–Sat 10am–4pm, Sun 10am–2pm. Free.*

Great Adventurers

Seville was the starting point for many who found fame and fortune in the great New World adventure. Christopher Columbus (Cristóbal Colón) set sail west across the Atlantic looking for a new route to the Indies. He didn't find India, but he did find the Americas, arriving in the Bahamas in 1492. Hernando Cortés was one of the young men who followed in Columbus' footsteps, intent on making his fortune. The Spanish had already reached Mexico, but it was Cortés who set sail to conquer the country against the orders of his commanding officer, subduing and virtually wiping out the mighty Aztec empire. Portuguese adventurer Ferdinand Magellan set out from Seville in 1519 to circumnavigate the world. He only got as far as the Philippines, where he died in battle, but his ship, the *Victoria*, continued and completed the voyage.

4 ★★★ **Casablanca.** A slightly upmarket tapas bar: the tapas might be a bit more pricey, but they're worth every cent. The King of Spain, Juan Carlos, often samples a few when he's in town. The tapas of the day is always good. *Adolfo Rodríguez Jurado 12.* ☎ 954 224 114. $.

5 **Casa de la Moneda.** The old mint dates from 1585 when Seville was at the height of her powers. There was so much silver and gold flooding into the city from the New World that coins for the whole of Spain were minted here. In the second half of the 16th century, Spanish theologians, alarmed at the newly apparent phenomenon of inflation, blamed Seville's imports of

The Casa de la Moneda dates back to 1585.

CASA E LA MONEDA

PLVS ULTRA

AÑO 1585

huge amounts of silver from the so-called Indies for devaluing Europe's currencies. They had invented the idea of a 'money supply', still important in economics today, though modern theories suggest there were other contributory factors, notably population pressure and state-sponsored devaluation. The mint was being refurbished at the time of writing. If it's open, walk through the archway down the cobbled courtyard, otherwise walk around it, taking the small road to the left and then first right. *Adolfo Rodríguez Hidalgo 3.*

6 **Antigua Fundición Real.** This building housed the old royal foundry, where the New World silver and gold were melted down before being forged into new coins to be stored at the Casa de La Moneda. There was little interest in what was being smelted, and often priceless statues and jewelry were melted down to make currency. The building is now a small contemporary theater, called Fundición (foundry). *Habana 18.* ☎ *954 225 844. www. fundiciondesevilla.es (see p 131).*

⑦ ★ Las Reales Atrazanas. The royal shipyards were built by Alfonso X in 1252 in El Arenal, a sandy area by the river, outside the city wall. They remained a hive of boat-building and renovation activity well into the 16th century. There were originally 17 docks, lying at right angles to the river so that ships could be repaired and re-launched easily. Seven of the docks have been excavated, forming an impressively large vaulted space, reached through a huge set of doors. Eventually the river silted up and the docks were used for storing munitions, as a Customs house and as a fishing market. (Closed for restoration works at time of writing.) *Temprado 1.*

⑧ ★★★ kids Torre del Oro. The 'tower of gold' was also built long

The Torre del Oro dates back to 1220.

before Seville's golden age, by the Moorish Almohads in 1220. See p 17. *Paseo de Colón.* 🕐 *30 min.* ☎ *954 222 419. 2€. Free Tues. Tues–Fri 10am–2pm, weekends 11am–2pm. Closed Aug. No cards.*

The entrance to the royal shipyards.

Churches & Convents

Map Area
CENTRO
SANTA CRUZ
TRIANA

Juzgado
Pedro Miguel
San Blas
Inocentes
Convento de Santa Isabel
Maravillas
Mallol
Enladriadas
Iglesia de San Marcos
8 †
Castellar
Santa Paula
Convento de Santa Paula
7
Socorro
Enladriadas
Sol
Amparo
Feria
9
10
Espíritu Santo
Palacio de las Dueñas
Dueñas
Jeromino Hernandez
Gerona
Sor Ángela de la Cruz
Bustos Tavera
Sol
6
Plaza Ponce de León
Plaza de la Encarnación
Doña María Coronel
San Felipe
2
4
5 Santa Catalina
Imagen
Apodaca
Azafrán
Plaza San Pedro
1
Plaza del Cristo de Burgos
Alhóndiga
Francisco Camón Mejías
Santiago
Escartín

0   100 yds
0   100 m

1 Iglesia de San Pedro
2 Convento de Santa Inés
3 Palacio de las Dueñas
4 El Rinconcillo
5 Iglesia de Santa Catalina
6 Iglesia de los Terceros
7 Convento de Santa Paula
8 Iglesia de San Marcos
9 Iglesia de San Juan de la Palma
10 La Plazoleta

Seville's neighborhood churches (iglesias), chapels (capillitas) and convents (conventos) reveal a rich seam of the city's history and culture. Often sober exteriors belie ornate decoration inside. The Macarena area has a church on almost every corner, but it can be difficult to get access. Opening hours are for Mass rather than for tourists. Chances are a few will be closed, but you shouldn't do too badly if you start off around 9am or 7pm. **START: Plaza San Pedro. Bus: C5, 10, 11, 12, 15, 20, 24, 27, 32.**

1 ★ **Iglesia de San Pedro.** St. Peter looks down from his vantage point above the entrance to the church, the keys of Heaven grasped tightly in his right hand. This doorway is baroque and dates from 1624, but you can clearly see older

Spot the tiny bird and you'll get married.

Mudéjar elements in the windows and tower of the church. One of the tile paintings to the right of the doorway depicts Purgatory. According to a local legend, if you can spot the bird hidden in the painting you'll get married (it's there, I found it). Inside, don't forget to look up at the colorful geometric patterned ceiling. ⏱ *15 min. Plaza San Pedro.* ☎ *954 229 124. Mon–Sat 8:30–11:30am, 7–8:30pm, Sun 9:30am–1:30pm, 7–8:30pm.*

② ★★ **Convento de Santa Inés.** A short stroll down the road to the right of the entrance to the church, duck through the small gate into the courtyard of the convent if it's open. It was built on the site left by Doña María Coronel in the 14th century. The church has an interesting carving of a lamb above the door. Inside there's an eye-catchingly gilded altarpiece, an ornate baroque ceiling and Mudéjar tiling. The nuns have their own section, separated from the church by a huge iron trellis. It's like looking into a scene from a play. To the left of the entrance to the church is a small room with a rotating shelf in the wall, where you can often buy cakes and biscuits. ⏱ *10 min. Doña María Coronel 5. Cakes available Tues–Sat 9am–1pm, 4–6:30pm. Church open 7pm weekdays for Mass.*

The gateway to the Palacio de las Dueñas.

Iglesia de Santa Catalina.

③ Palacio de las Dueñas. Keep an ear out for the sounds of nuns' singing wafting through the open windows of the convent as you walk on toward this 15th-century Mudéjar palace, which is the private residence of the Dukes of Alba. You can see their coat of arms on the tile decoration above the gateway. Inside there's a lemon-tree-lined garden. *Dueñas.*

④ ★★★ **El Rinconcillo.** Legend has it tapas were first created in this atmospheric old bar which dates back to 1670. Dusty old bottles line the shelves behind the bar, and the walls are tiled in traditional fashion. Tapas are good and the service friendly. Spinach with chickpeas is a favorite. Your bill is chalked up on the bar top. *Gerona 40.* ☎ *954 223 183. $.*

⑤ Iglesia de Santa Catalina. A 14th-century Mudéjar church, the Gothic portal was taken from Santa Lucía, another church, and added in 1930. At the time of writing it was closed for restoration. If you do get inside, look for the beautiful

The belfry at Convento de Santa Paula.

horseshoe arch inside this entrance and see if you can find the statue of Santa Lucía, patron saint of the blind. *Plaza Ponce de Léon.* ☎ *954 217 441.*

⑥ ★★★ Iglesia de los Terceros.

The facade of this church has a distinctly Latin American feel. The church was once owned by Franciscan monks and its interior is a feast of 17th-century baroque detailing with a large vaulted dome. Upper galleries were presumably for important people to celebrate Mass without mixing with the commoners below. Most remarkable are the life-sized statues of Jesus and the disciples at the Last Supper around the main altar. Full color and extremely detailed, you almost expect them to move. Side chapels along the nave are similarly ornate, some with colorful Mudéjar tilework. ⏱ *15 min. Sol 10. Mon–Fri 6–9pm, Sat 11am–1pm, 7–9pm, Sun 11:30am (for Mass).*

⑦ ★★★ Convento de Santa Paula.

This is one of Seville's few enclosed religious complexes that welcomes visitors. The convent dates from 1475 and is still home to around 40 nuns. Enter through the door marked number 11 on Calle Santa Paula. You'll probably have to knock. Steps lead into two galleries crammed with religious artifacts. The windows of the second look onto the nuns' cloister. The nuns make jams and marmalades, which you can buy in a room near the exit. Ring the bell by the brick doorway to the left of number 11 to visit the convent church, reached through a garden. The church is a blend of Gothic, Mudéjar and Renaissance features, the nave has an elaborate carved roof and there are statues of St. John the Evangelist and St. John the Baptist. ⏱ *20 min. Santa Paula 11.* ☎ *954 536 330. Usually open Tues–Sun 10am–1pm.*

The tower of the Iglesia de San Marcos was once the minaret of a mosque.

Iglesia de San Juan de la Palma.

❽ ★ Iglesia de San Marcos.
This church's tower is based on a minaret from an ancient mosque and looks rather like the Giralda at the cathedral. Two baroque statues of Christ and St. Mark inside are worth admiring. St. Mark was probably carved by Juan de Mesa (1583–1627). The unusual horseshoe arches in the nave are quite unique. ⏱ *10 min. Plaza de San Marcos.* ☎ *954 502 616. Mon–Sun 7:30–8:30pm.*

❾ Iglesia de San Juan de la Palma. The nave of this typical parish church is Mudéjar in style with Moorish geometric tiles on the walls and columns, and a carved altarpiece with the Madonna at its center, thought to have been made at the workshop of the celebrated sculptor Pedro Roldán (1624–99).

The adjacent image of St John the Evangelist dates from 1760. More interesting are the side chapels. One, with a baroque domed ceiling and several very old-looking paintings, including a large canvas of *The Last Supper* on the back wall, has a macabre depiction of Purgatory between its two entrance doorways. ⏱ *10 min. Feria 2. Mon–Fri 7:30–8pm (Mass at 8pm), Sun 10:45am–12:45pm (Mass at 11am & 12:30pm).*

❿ La Plazoleta. This friendly tapas bar on the square to the right of the church is a shady spot to relax with a drink or tapas. Specials include chicken with dates and salsa, and baked goat's cheese and marmalade. Service can be slow. *Plaza San Juan de Palma. No phone. $.*

Gastronomic Seville Tapas

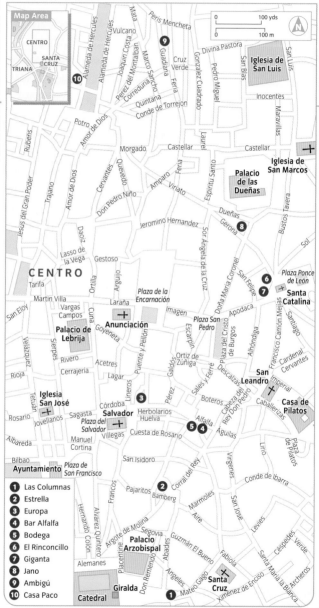

Map Area

CENTRO

SANTA
CRUZ

TRIANA

0   100 yds
0   100 m

1 Las Columnas
2 Estrella
3 Europa
4 Bar Alfalfa
5 Bodega
6 El Rinconcillo
7 Giganta
8 Jano
9 Ambigú
10 Casa Paco

Grazing on tapas in Seville isn't just eating. It's a way of life. Sampling small portions rather than eating three courses makes perfect sense in a hot climate. Locals move from one bar to another, choosing a dish or two in each. It's social, fun and very Sevillian. This tour takes you to some of my favorite bars and introduces you to the city's best bar-hopping areas. Start early for Seville—say 9pm—before places get too busy. Most bars are open daily. Few take credit cards so have cash handy. START: **Walk to Calle Mateos Gago. Nearest bus: C5.**

① ★★★ **Las Columnas.** Santa Cruz, the tourist center of town, is not the best place for quality and value but Las Columnas is an exception. It's a classic tapas bar, often really busy with people spilling out onto the pavement, but the bar staff are friendly. Try to get a spot at the bar to get the chance of quick service. It's very normal for locals to eat standing up rather than sitting at a table. Deep-fried zucchini (courgette) with honey is one of my favorites. Your bill is chalked up on the bar top in front. *Rodrigo Caro 1.* ☎ *954 213 246.*

② ★★ **Estrella.** A seriously authentic tapas bar with lots of tables outside, down a side street. The menu is available in English and includes traditional favorites and more exotic dishes like *langostinos con aguacate*—avocado stuffed with large prawns. Very popular with locals. *Estrella 3.* ☎ *954 561 426.*

③ ★★★ **Europa.** Some of the most delicious tapas in Seville are served in this traditional old corner bar. The menu is in English and the staff really helpful. There's lots of table space outside in the square too. Stand-out dishes for me are the deep-fried langoustine—with just a hint of lime in the batter and the aroma of fresh mint in the *alioli*, and melt-in-the-mouth liver on toast with red berry reduction. *Siete Revueltas 35.* ☎ *954 217 908.*

④ ★★ **Bar Alfalfa.** The oddest-shaped bar in town is stuck precariously between two streets at a junction that's genuinely triangular. It beats me how they manage to turn out such good tapas in their tiny kitchen. Go for the specials chalked

Despite its tiny dimensions Bar Alfalfa turns out delicious food.

Legend has it that tapas were invented at El Rinconcillo.

up on the blackboard. They do great bruschetta-style toasted bread and the aubergine in balsamic vinegar is lip-smacking. Wash it down with a glass of Manzanilla sherry if you're bored with wine and beer. *Candilejo 1.* ☎ *654 809 297*. Or else try:

⑤ Bodega just opposite, which does the best *montaditos* (tiny sandwiches) in town. *See p 109.*

⑥ ★★★ El Rinconcillo. The area around Plaza de los Terceros is great for tapas bars. Above all, try Rinconcillo. Legend has it tapas were first created in this little-changed bar, which dates back to 1670. Take a stool at the bar, order a *tinto de verano* (a refreshing mix of red wine and lemonade) and a tapa or two. The old chaps who

Tapas Tips

According to most stories, the original tapa was a small dish that the barman placed on top of your glass to keep the flies off it. Hence the name, which means lid. There are four sizes of tapa: a *pincho* (little more than a mouthful), a *tapa* (a small saucerful), a *media-ración* (half a plateful) and a *ración* (a plateful). Not all of these will always be offered. Some dishes will only be available as *raciónes* or *medios raciónes*. You may also see *montaditos* on the menu—they're small sandwiches. The tapas list is displayed on a menu at the bar or on a board on the wall. It's normal to order one or two and see how you go rather than ordering lots in one go. Settle the bill once you're ready to leave. For a list of common tapas see p 174.

Waiter!

You might think you've done the hard part finding a table, but it's sometimes really difficult to get the attention of busy waiting staff. Locals seem to glide in, order almost as they sit down and get served while you sit trying desperately to catch the waiter's eye. There's not much of a sense of waiting your turn in Seville, so wave a hand and call out as the waiter passes, no matter how stressed they look. A great alternative is to stand or perch at the bar. Here you're close to the bar staff so service is never a problem and you're right in the thick of the action, which is always great fun.

serve behind the bar look as if they've been there as long as the bar itself, but they're a friendly bunch. *Gerona 40.* ☎ *954 223 183.* Or else try: ❼ **Giganta** for top-notch food and friendly service. *See p 110.*

❽ ★★★ **Jano.** Another stand-out tapas bar serving gorgeous food. Claudia, the owner, trained at Seville's prestigious Alabardero cookery school. She also speaks great English. My favorite dishes here are deep-fried camembert with tomato marmalade, and honey-stuffed squid in salsa verde—or else try the slow-cooked pig's cheek in basil sauce. It's all good! *Doña María Coronel 17.* ☎ *954 214 804.*

❾ ★★ **Ambigú.** You're into the Macarena neighborhood now, well off the tourist trail, and this place is a typical local tapas bar with tables on the pavement. You'd walk past without batting an eyelid, but the food is surprisingly original. Last time I was here we had basmati rice with prawns, and potatoes in green bean dressing. Both were delicious. You sometimes have to wait at the bar for a table; your name is added to a list by the barman. *Feria 47.* ☎ *954 381 015.*

❿ ★★ **Casa Paco.** You've reached the up-and-coming Alameda area, full of funky bars and boho brasseries. Paco's is an old favorite which still turns out authentic, great-value tapas. It's seriously popular so you may have to wait for a table. To get back to your hotel, it's fairly easy to hail a taxi on the Alameda, or ask bar staff to order one. This is a slightly shadier part of town, so keep your wits about you if you choose to walk: it's a straight-line, 15-minute stroll back to the center along Amor de Dios, then Sierpes. *Alameda de Hércules 23.* ☎ *954 900 148.*

Deep-fried camembert with tomato marmalade at Jano.

Things to Do with Kids

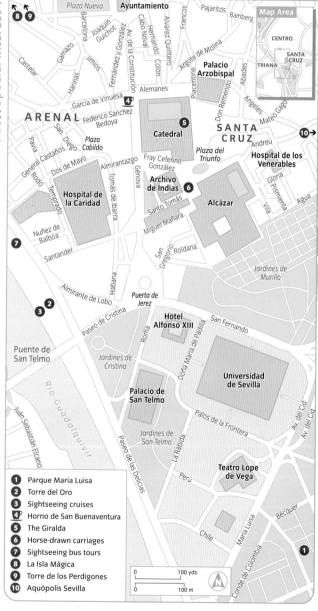

1. Parque Maria Luisa
2. Torre del Oro
3. Sightseeing cruises
4. Horno de San Buenaventura
5. The Giralda
6. Horse-drawn carriages
7. Sightseeing bus tours
8. La Isla Mágica
9. Torre de los Perdigones
10. Aquópolis Sevilla

0   100 yds
0   100 m

There's plenty to keep junior sightseers happy in Seville despite the lack of attractions solely for children. I include this tour more as a round-up of activities than a point-by-point tour. You won't want to do all these in one day, so cherry-pick the best activities to suit the ages of those taking part. START: **Parque María Luisa. Bus: C2, 1, 20, 31, 33, 36.**

1 ★★★ Parque María Luisa.
Seville's largest park is a shady respite from the heat of the sun and perfect for kids to let off steam. It's far more than an open patch of grass. There are unusual trees and plants from all over the world, and monuments and enclosures to explore. In the center there's a lake with a gazebo (the Isleta de los Patos) and nearby there's Monte Gurugu, a mini-mountain with a waterfall. You can climb to the top or walk through the tunnel underneath. You can also hire bicycles and four-person pedal carts at the entrance next to the Plaza de España and in the Plaza de América. They're great fun. ☎ *663 811 043. www.cyclotouristic.com. From 7€ for 30 min.*

Sightseeing cruises depart from the Torre del Oro.

2 ★★ Torre del Oro. The 12-sided 'tower of gold' was built by the Moorish Almohads in 1220. It was part of the city wall built to protect Seville against Christian invaders. Climb to the top and you see what a great vantage point it was (and is), with its sweeping

Hire a bike in the Parque María Luisa.

views. Today it houses a small naval museum full of maps and curios—ideal for older children to explore. It's big enough to keep them amused for a while, but not so large they'll lose interest. There are old cannons, shark skins, sextants and quadrants, and a model of one of the ships in which Columbus's expedition reached America. *Paseo de Colón.* ☎ *954 222 419. 2€. Free on Tues. Mon–Fri 10am–2pm, 11am–2pm weekends. Closed Aug.*

❸ ★★ Sightseeing cruises.

Taking to the water on a cruise boat is another fun way to see the city skyline and the numerous bridges that span the river, in particular Santiago Calatrava's remarkable harp-shaped Puente del Alamillo, built for the 1992 Expo. Boats depart every half-hour, and the trip lasts an hour with commentary in six languages. *Paseo Alcalde Marqués del Contadero.* ☎ *954 561 692; 954 211 396. www.crucerostorredeloro.com. Adults 16€, children under 14 free. Daily 11am–7pm Nov–Feb; 11am–11pm Mar–Oct.* Older kids will enjoy messing about in boats themselves.

Kids will enjoy a carriage ride.

You can hire pedalos and canoes just along from where the cruise boats depart, from the Pedalquivir floating bar. *10€ per hr for a two-person pedalo. 11:30am–9pm. Kids under 13 free.*

❹ ★★ Horno de San Buenaventura.

Kids' eyes will pop at the array of yummy sweets and pastries behind the bright counters of this fab traditional pastry shop. There's a cafe area at the front. Order at the counter. *Avda de la Constitución 16.* ☎ *954 221 815. Daily 8am–9:30pm. $.*

❺ ★★★ The Giralda.

Despite being 91m high, the cathedral's ornate bell tower is an easy climb—there are no steps, just gentle ramps, so even smaller children should make it the top if they have a bit of stamina. You can break up the climb by stopping to look at seven chambers inside the tower featuring displays relating to its history, including an old clock mechanism from 1764, Islamic artifacts, ropes and pulleys used to shift the huge blocks of stone used to construct its base and old bells from the tower. There are also lots of places to stop as you climb to look out and admire the views of the city and the cathedral's remarkably complex buttresses. Once at the top you can look up at the 25 bells. Chances are you'll hear them ringing too. You can only climb the Giralda if you've paid for a visitor ticket to the cathedral. *Plaza Virgen de los Reyes.* ☎ *954 214 971. www.catedralsevilla.org. 8€ adults, children under 12 free. Mon–Sat 11am–5pm. Sun & holidays 2:30–6pm. July & Aug Mon–Sat 9:30am–4pm, Sun & holidays 2:30–6pm.*

❻ ★★ Horse-drawn carriages.

Clip-clopping across Seville's ancient cobbles is a really exhilarating experience, no matter your age, and what's particularly pleasing for parents is that both the horses and the old carriages are well looked after. Most drivers will point out the sights although few speak English. There's a fixed fee for a carriage (p 163). The standard tour takes you from outside the cathedral or the Alcázar to Parque María Luisa to see the Plaza de España and other buildings from Seville's 1929 Ibero-American Exposition, and back to the historic center. There are other pick-up points elsewhere in the city, in particular in Parque María Luisa. ⏱ *1 hr. Plaza Virgen de los Reyes.* ☎ *954 924 015. 36.06€ per carriage.*

❼ Sightseeing bus tours.

Though they don't get that close to the city's landmarks, it's great fun just traveling for a while on the open top of one of the city's double-decker tour buses. Two companies offer similar itineraries that skirt the old city walls, cross the river to Cartuja—stopping at Isla Mágica (see below)—and return along the riverbank. They also offer add-on tours through the Triana neighborhood

The Gateway to America log flume at La Isla Mágica.

across the river. Both offer multi-language descriptions on headphones. The level of detail is pretty slim, but it's a good way of orienting yourself or resting tired legs. On sunny days bring hats, sunglasses

See the sights from an open-top double decker.

There's a camera obscura at the top of the Torre de los Perdigones.

World of the Maya, which has a vertiginous spinning slide ride; the Gateway to America, with its big dipper and log flume; and Amazonia, which features a hanging roller coaster, like riding a chairlift only much, much faster. Little ones are catered for with small boat ponds and radio-controlled boats, and there's often live entertainment in the cafes and restaurants. There's also a show spectacular two or three times daily (depending on the season) based around the galleon, with roaring cannons, flashing cutlasses, pirate queens and ships boarded from the rigging. *Pabellón de España, Isla de la Cartuja.* ☎ *902 161 716. www.islamagica.es. 25–28€ adults, 18–20€ children for a full day. Children under 4 free. Family & half-day tickets available. Daily 11am–11pm (summer), to 10pm (spring), to 9pm (fall). Free parking. Bus C1, C2.*

⑨ ★★ Torre de los Perdigones. This 45m-high tower has a *camera obscura* inside and is great for older kids. From this vantage point you can home in on what's going on across the city via the combination of mirrors and lenses based on an invention of the Greek philosopher Aristotle in the 4th century B.C. *Resolana.* ☎ *954 909 353. 4€, 2.50€ concessions. Daily 10am–1:30pm, 4–5:30pm. Access every 30 min in groups of up to 10.*

⑩ ★★ Aquópolis Sevilla. Perfect for cooling down and letting off steam in summer, this large water-park set in the Barrio de las Delicias, to the east of the center, has kamikazi slides, water flumes and more. There are quieter pools for younger water babes too. *Avda del Deporte.* ☎ *954 406 622. www.aquopolis.es. Adults 19.95€, children (3–10 years) 14.95€. May–Sept noon–7pm daily; July/Aug noon–8pm. Bus L22, L55.* ●

and sunscreen as there's no shade on top. You can hop off and on all day long from four different pick-up points: Plaza de España, Torre del Oro, Isla Mágica, Monasterio de la Cartuja. ⌚ *1 hr. 16€ adults, 7€ children. Children under 5 free. 10am–6pm (winter), 8pm (spring), 10pm (summer). Buses depart every 20 min. Sevillatour,* ☎ *902 101 081. www.sevillatour.com. Sevirama,* ☎ *954 560 693. www.busturistico. com.*

⑧ ★★ La Isla Mágica. Seville's theme park is said to be the only one in the world within a city's limits, and it's a sprawling place of water and jungles. It uses the city's golden age of New World discovery as its theme. Older kids could almost argue that it's educational! The different zones include Sevilla, Port of the Indies, where you can boat on the lake or take a 70m plunge and then come to a stomach-churningly abrupt halt; Quetzal,

Santa Cruz

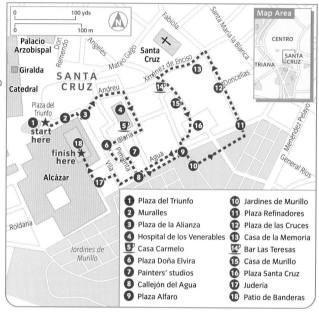

① Plaza del Triunfo	⑩ Jardines de Murillo
② Muralles	⑪ Plaza Refinadores
③ Plaza de la Alianza	⑫ Plaza de las Cruces
④ Hospital de los Venerables	⑬ Casa de la Memoria
⑤ Casa Carmelo	⑭ Bar Las Teresas
⑥ Plaza Doña Elvira	⑮ Casa de Murillo
⑦ Painters' studios	⑯ Plaza Santa Cruz
⑧ Callejón del Agua	⑰ Judería
⑨ Plaza Alfaro	⑱ Patio de Banderas

The city's old Jewish quarter is a warren of passageways and whitewashed houses bedecked with flower baskets. This is quintessential Seville and the main tourist area. If you find parts a little overwhelming with the crowds, take a few steps to one side and you'll find quiet courtyards and tinkling fountains, particularly if you set out early. This walk is circular. START: **Walk to Plaza del Triunfo. Nearest tram: Archivo de Indias.**

① ★ **Plaza del Triunfo.** Separating the cathedral from the royal palace, this square was built in gratitude for the city's survival of the great earthquake of 1755, which destroyed much of Lisbon but had little impact on Seville, merely making the Giralda's bells peal. This miraculous escape was attributed to the city's devotion to the Virgin Mary. Next to the building known as the Archivo de Indias (the Archive of the Indies; see p 29) there's a baroque column in her

honor. At the square's center is a statue of the Virgin of the Immaculate Conception. At midnight on December 8 local minstrel groups gather around the statue to sing and pay her homage. Turn your back on the cathedral and exit the square to the left of the gateway along Joaquín Romero Murube.

② ★ **Muralles.** This street hugs the old Moorish city's stone wall, which completely encircled Seville. It

Previous page: Fountain in the Alcázar's gardens.

The tree-lined Plaza del Triunfo.

proved insufficient protection from the Reconquistadors who re-claimed Seville for the Christians and ousted the Moors in 1248. This is one of the few stretches that remain. Much of the rest was pulled down during 19th-century redevelopment.

❸ Plaza de la Alianza. There's a fountain in the middle of this square. Exit the far side along Rodrigo Caro, and turn right down Pasaje de Andreu, which has souvenir shops selling Arabic-inspired wares. Turn right down Jamerdana. **Morales Ortega** on the corner (Jamerdana 2) is an antiques shop full of curiosities. Look out for Hosteria del Laurel as you enter the next square—it was the setting for the opening scene in Cervantes' play of 1605, *Don Juan*. See p 49, ⓫.

❹ ★★★ Hospital de los Venerables. This was built as a nursing home for old and sick priests at the initiative of a local canon in 1676. It's been restored as a cultural center and its tree-lined patio with sunken fountain is one of Seville's most unusual. Even though it's in the

middle of the tourist district it rarely gets busy. There's an informative audio guide included with the ticket. The hospital was designed as a functional place of healing but the church is a feast of baroque painting and sculpture. Look out for creepy bone relics in glass cases built into some of the side altars—supposedly to give protection. The *trompe l'oeil* ceiling mural of the Triumph of the Cross in the sacristy is thought to be Juan de Valdés Leal's last work before he died. I sometimes lie on my back on the floor to get a sense of the clever perspective. A room off the patio contains a permanent exhibition of works by the great Sevillian painter **Diego Velázquez** (1599–1660), with detailed descriptions in English, while upper floors and the cellar provide space for temporary art exhibitions. ⏱ *1 hr. Plaza de los Venerables 8.* ☎ *954 562 696. www. focus.abengoa.es. 4.75€, 2.40€ concessions. Free Sun afternoons. Open 10am–2pm, 4–8pm daily.*

❺ Casa Carmelo. Turn right out of Venerables and you'll find this cafe-bar just down Gloria. The tapas are a bit predictable, but the service

Ornate ceiling decoration at Hospital de Los Venerables.

is far friendlier than elsewhere here in tourist-land. One of the rooms is lined with old bottles, another has a collection of ancient televisions. When you're ready continue down Gloria to the next square. *Gloria 6.* ☎ 954 225 332. $.

6 ★★ Plaza Doña Elvira. This is one of Santa Cruz's most character-istic squares. Splash water on your face from the fountain if you're feeling the heat. Take the tiny street marked Susona—a left turn if you come down Gloria. According to leg-end, Susona was a beautiful Jewish girl who fell in love with a Christian. Her father was a powerful figure in the Jewish community and was plotting against the Christian Inquisition. She betrayed him and she and her family were killed. Full of remorse, she asked that when she died her skull be placed in the street as a reminder of the effects of her

Washington Irving stayed in Barrio Santa Cruz.

treachery. Look for the skull painted on a tile on house number 10A (called Las Cadenas) on your right. It's just below the left-hand upper window.

7 ★ Painters' studios. Look left as you get to the T-junction with Pimienta. You'll see El Patio del Arte, where an artist sometimes sits at his easel. His pretty oil paintings are for sale. The street gets its name ('pepper street') from a leg-end about a Jewish spice merchant who had problems obtaining pepper. A Christian told him to believe in Christ and next morning he woke to find a pep-per tree growing outside his door. The spice merchant was converted to Christianity. You need to turn right out of Susona so if you've been to the artist's gallery double back and walk down the street to the T-junction.

8 ★★ Callejón del Agua. Turn left along this street, which trans-lates as 'water alley' and is shaded by climbing plants growing on frames above. It's named after the watercourse that ran along the top of the wall in Moorish times. Look for the plaque on the left commem-orating Washington Irving (1783–1859), who stayed here and wrote his romanticized descriptions of Andalusia in *Tales of the Alhambra* (1831). Through the gate next to the plaque is a flower-bedecked patio.

9 Plaza Alfaro. If you look at the stately house ahead, you'll see it has a balcony. This was apparently the inspiration for a scene between two young lovers in Rossini's opera

Artists sometimes sit painting outside their studios.

The Barber of Seville. Turn right into the gardens.

⑩ ★★ Jardines de Murillo. These gardens (*jardines*) were the old orchards and vegetable plots of the king's royal palace, the Alcázar. Today they're a nice place to escape the heat of the sun. They were donated to the city in 1911 and named after the famous Sevillian painter Murillo (p 24). We visit his house later on this walk. Have a wander in the shade or sit awhile. Then keep left, following the city walls. Continue across the small road into the next small section of the park. As you cross look at the wall: you can clearly see the old pipes that ran through it carrying water in Moorish times.

⑪ Plaza Refinadores. In the center of this square you'll see a statue of Don Juan. Seville's legendary seducer has featured in many novels and operas down the ages—most notably Mozart's opera *Don Giovanni.* Much of the story takes place around Santa Cruz. An inscription on one side of the statue reads, 'Don Juan, there was no other man like him.' The *refinadores* or 'refiners' who worked here smelted iron and steel to make weapons. Continue across the square and take the tiny narrow passageway called Mariscal.

⑫ Plaza de las Cruces. Tucked away from the tourist crowds, this quiet 'square of the crosses' is named after the three crosses at its center, set on three far more ancient Roman columns. Wander along a dead end off to the left down Doncellas if you're feeling inquisitive. These dead ends were put here in Moorish times to make it harder for would-be invaders to find their way. (And they certainly work—it's easy to get lost around here!) There's a more solemn history to these dead ends, however. It

Statue of legendary seducer Don Juan in Plaza Refinadores.

was where many Jewish people killed in the great purge of 1391 met their end. There's more information about this later on this walk. Continue across the square down another narrow passage and turn left into Ximénez de Enciso.

⑬ ★★ Casa de la Memoria. If you glance left as you walk down this street you might see open windows looking onto a small chair-lined courtyard. This restored 18th-century patio is the stage for one of the most pleasant flamenco evenings I've encountered in Seville, featuring local young award-winning musicians and dancers. There aren't many seats, so if you fancy going, step inside the next doorway and buy tickets. Performances are daily at 9pm and at 7:30pm or 10:30pm depending on the time of year. *Ximénez de Enciso 28.* ☎ *954 560 670. www.casadela memoria.es. 15€ adults, 13€ students & seniors, 9€ children.*

⑭ ★★ Bar Las Teresas. At the busiest crossroads in the Barrio, this tapas bar is surprisingly authentic. It's been here since 1870. Inside you'll find huge hams hanging from the ceiling, and dark wood tables.

The Casa de Murillo.

Tapas prices are on signs on the shelves behind the bar. Try a glass of chilled sherry or a Cruzcampo beer. *Santa Cruz 2.* ☎ *954 213 069. $.*

⑮ Casa de Murillo. Turn left down Santa Teresa and you find the

house where Seville's best-known painter lived. His sentimental paintings of the Madonna were an inspiration to churchgoers of the 17th century (p 24). At the time of writing, there were plans to turn the house into a museum. For now, if the door is open, step inside and view the patio. ⏱ *5 min. Calle Santa Teresa 8.* ☎ *954 229 415. Mon–Fri 10am–2pm, 4–7pm.*

⑯ ★★ Plaza Santa Cruz. This is another of my favorite squares, with its orange-tree-lined center. The wrought-iron cross marks the spot where a church once stood. It was Murillo's local church and he was buried in it. It was destroyed in 1820 during the French occupation, the only reminder a plaque on the end house. Exit Plaza Santa Cruz to the bottom right and you're back in Plaza Alfaro. Retrace your steps back along Callejón del Agua, past Pimienta to the bottom and into Plaza del Agua. Turn left out of Agua into another narrow passageway which leads to Judería.

Wandering the tiny streets of Santa Cruz.

There are few reminders of the Barrio's Jewish history.

17 ★ **Juderia.** Seville's Jewish community once numbered 4,000 and most lived in the tiny streets and squares you've been walking around. After the reconquest of Seville from the Moors in 1248, the three populations—Jews, Christians and Muslims—lived in relative prosperity and harmony. The Jewish population flourished in the 13th and 14th centuries, many holding government positions like King Alfonso X's treasurer, Zulema Pintadura. The Jewish quarter had its own inner wall to protect it, but ultimately this contributed to its downfall. In 1391, Spain underwent a surge in Catholic fanaticism. A radical local priest, Ferrán Martínez, Archdeacon of Écija, stirred up the local Christians by proclaiming it was the Jews who killed Christ. A rabble was organized to murder Seville's Jewish inhabitants. Hemmed in by these walls, only a handful escaped. One of the few signs of the Jewish influence left today is this street name. To the right is one of the claustrophobia-inducing low gateways that terrified families must have tried to escape through. It might look like a blind alley, but there's a low archway that leads around a corner to bring you out into one of Seville's largest squares. Originally this was an escape route to the safety of the royal palace built by King Alfonso X.

18 ★★ **Patio de Banderas.** This wide, orange-tree-lined square is one of Seville's most elegant, with the Giralda (p 8) overlooking it. The 'patio of the flags' gets its name from the military maneuvers that were practiced here. If you exit the patio at the top end you'll find you're where we started.

Distant views of the Giralda from the Patio de Banderas.

Centro

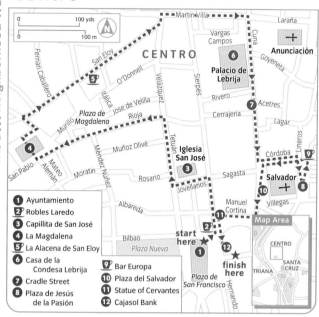

0 — 100 yds
0 — 100 m

CENTRO

① Ayuntamiento
② Robles Laredo
③ Capillita de San José
④ La Magdalena
⑤ La Alacena de San Eloy
⑥ Casa de la Condesa Lebrija
⑦ Cradle Street
⑧ Plaza de Jesús de la Pasión
⑨ Bar Europa
⑩ Plaza del Salvador
⑪ Statue of Cervantes
⑫ Cajasol Bank

Anunciación

Palacio de Lebrija

Iglesia San José

Salvador

start here ★

finish here ★

Plaza Nueva

Plaza de San Francisco

Map Area

CENTRO
SANTA CRUZ
TRIANA

Central Seville offers a little of everything: this walk particularly evokes the 16th and 17th centuries as it takes in baroque churches, the ornate city hall and a private house (casa) turned eclectic museum, illustrating the Countess of Lebrija's passion for hoarding antiquities. If you fancy denting the credit card you can browse in the prime shopping streets in town. START: **Plaza de San Francisco. Bus: C5. Tram: Plaza Nueva.**

① ★★ **Ayuntamiento.** Seville's city hall is almost two buildings in one. The current neoclassical entrance, dating from 1891, overlooks Plaza Nueva, centered on a statue of Fernando III (1201–52), who liberated the city from the Moors. Walk around to the other side of the building in Plaza de San Francisco and you'll find the older and far more ornamental 16th-century facade, built between 1527 and 1534: this is one of the best examples of the ornate Plateresque

style—so called because it imitated the intricate craftsmanship of local silversmiths (*plato* means silver in Spanish; see p 170). Its frieze tells the story of the city, chronologically arranged left to right, from its founding (by Hercules and Caesar, according to legend). This frieze begins either side of the first ornate archway, but two-thirds of the way along, it stops, and the remaining facades are blank, because the city fell on hard times during construction and work was never completed.

Hercules on the ornately carved facade of the Ayuntamiento.

More recently some of the blank facades have had new statues added to them. Can you spot the likeness of Grace Kelly—added to commemorate her visit to Seville for the Feria de Abril in 1966—on the last carved section? The interior can be visited as part of a group tour in Spanish only. Highlights are the intricately restored, beautifully ornate ceilings, and works of art by Velázquez and Zurbarán. ⏱ *45 min. Plaza Nueva 1.* ☎ *954 590 101. Free. Tues–Thurs, tours at 5:30pm & 6pm. Closed July/Aug. ID required.*

2 ★★ **Robles Laredo.** Here you can sit on a street corner, perfect for watching the world go buy, and sample Laura Robles' sumptuous cakes—indulgent creations in chocolate and cream. My favorite is the Stracciatela, with cherries soaked in a local liquor called Miura. *Sierpes 90.* ☎ *954 293 232. $.*

3 ★★★ **Capillita de San José.** This little chapel squeezed between Seville's two main shopping streets comes as a complete contrast to the celebrations of Mammon around it. It's one of Seville's most complete baroque places of worship. I was literally stopped in my tracks the first time I saw the altarpiece. It's a feast of ornate golden carving, the Madonna at its center picked out with subtle separate lighting. ⏱ *10 min. Jovellanos 10. Mon–Fri 9am–12:30pm, 8am–8:30pm, Sat 10am–12:30pm, 7am–8:30pm, Sun 9:30am–1pm, 7–8:30pm.* On leaving, continue down Jovellanos and turn right into Tetuán. As you wander, look out for the old tiled advertisement for Studebaker automobiles at Tetuán 9 on the right. It dates back to 1924 and is one of the best-preserved of its kind in Seville.

Take a break at Robles Laredo.

Capillita de San José.

body being taken down from the cross. ⏱ *20 min. San Pablo 10.* ☎ *954 229 603. Mon–Sat 8–11am, 6:30–8:30pm, Sun 8am–1:30pm, 6:30–8:30pm.*

⑤ ★★ La Alacena de San Eloy. More of a wine bar than a tapas bar, the Alacena serves excellent wines by the glass and fabulous serrano ham and cheese. Once you've found what you like, you can purchase many of these gourmet products at their shop next door. *San Eloy 31.* ☎ *954 215 580. $.*

④ ★★ La Magdalena. One of Seville's most spectacular churches, La Magdalena was designed by Leonardo de Figueroa and completed in 1709. It has a large domed chancel with extravagant frescoes and an immensely ornate altarpiece. Moorish-style domes or *cupolas* on two side chapels are clues that there were previously Mudéjar chapels on the same site. The great Sevillian painter Murillo (p 24) was baptized in the Capilla de la Quinta Augustia in 1618. The Capilla de Dulce Nombre de Jesús (the Chapel of the Sweet Name of Jesus) has a remarkably lifelike statue of Christ's

⑥ ★★★ Casa de la Condesa Lebrija. Off the tourist trail, this house gets far fewer visitors than it should. The Countess of Lebrija was an enlightened antiquarian who traveled the world—something single women didn't generally do in the 19th century. Her home is testament to her life. She remodeled this 15th-century house, adding artifacts discovered at the Roman ruins in nearby Itálica (p 146) together with curios from her travels. The relocated Roman marble floors are some of the most complete in Europe. The main patio's exceptionally well-preserved

The ornate staircase at Casa de la Condesa Lebrija.

Plaza de Jesús de la Pasión features in a novel by Cervantes.

mosaic, found in an olive grove in 1914, features Cyclops in the center with four female heads depicting the seasons at the corners. Look for the portrait of the Countess in the first room on the right off the main patio. She's in fancy dress, wearing an Egyptian costume. The main staircase to the upper level is an extravagant combination of Mudéjar tilework and coffered ceilings. The upper level can be visited on a half-hourly guided tour—the guide speaks English—which includes the book-lined library, the Arabic-style tea room and the dining room with its 240-piece dining set made by the English pottery firm Spode. 🕐 *1 hr. Cuna 8.* ☎ *954 227 802. www.palaciodelebrija.com. 4€ ground floor, 8€ includes upper floor tour. Mon–Fri 10:30am–7:30pm (July–Aug 9am–3pm), Sat & Sun 10am–2pm (July–Aug closed Sun).*

7 Cradle Street. Calle Cuna ('cradle street') retains its original identity today. Although it's now a smart shopping street, many of the shops sell children's and babies' clothes. Perhaps rather appropriately there are also a lot of wedding dress shops.

8 ★ Plaza de Jesús de la Pasión. This square is also known as Plaza del Pan ('bread square') to locals because in the distant past the city's bread ovens were outside the city and fresh bread was brought here to be sold. It features in Cervantes' novel *Rinconete y Cortadillo*. In Moorish times shops butted right up against the old mosque walls—now the Iglesia de Salvador. Look carefully at the shops running along the rear of the church and you can see they have vaulted ceilings typical of a Moorish medina, and reused Roman pillars supporting their roofs—as was the custom for Moorish buildings. The jeweler's shop M. Serrano Navarro at number 11 is a good example.

9 ★★★ Bar Europa. This corner bar, on the left as you enter the square, does some of the most innovative tapas in Seville. How about pâté toasts with chocolate and orange jus? There are tables in the square if you prefer to sit outside. *Siete Reveultas 35.* ☎ *954 221 354. $.*

Roman treasures on show at Casa de la Condesa Lebrija.

Plaza de San Francisco was once the site of public heresy trials.

⑩ ★★★ Plaza del Salvador.
This square is a favorite for locals for a beer, a tapa and a chat, particularly at Saturday lunchtime. Overlooking the square, the huge Iglesia del Salvador is second only in size to the cathedral. It's one of the city's most popular churches, and predates the cathedral. Converted from the 9th-century mosque of Ibn Addabas in 1672, it has an exquisitely restored baroque exterior. Inside there's a baroque altarpiece and

The city motto crops up everywhere, including lampposts.

carvings including *Señor de la Pasión* by Juan Martínez Montañés (1568–1649), but it's the scale of the place that really impresses me. Vast sandstone pillars support a huge domed roof. These proportions were the result of the Christian conquerors' desire to outdo their Moorish predecessors by building bigger and higher than they did. You can clearly see signs of the old mosque. The small courtyard to the left was the patio where Muslims carried out their ablutions, and at the far end excavations have revealed the ground level of the mosque. Here archeologists found hundreds of tombs of babies who had died at the orphanages that once existed on nearby Calle Cuna. The bell tower was the mosque's minaret. It's inhabited today by a bell-maker. If you plan to see the cathedral, buy a joint entrance ticket here. This saves lining-up time and is cheaper than buying separate tickets. ⏱ *30 min. Plaza del Salvador.* ☎ *954 211 679. www.colegialsalvador.org. 3€. Mon–Sat 11:30am–5:30pm, Sun 3–7pm.*

⑪ Statue of Cervantes. Exit the square at the bottom left corner. To the right there's a narrow street called Carceles ('prison street'),

What's in Store?

This neighborhood is the city's traditional shopping district. It's nice and condensed, perfect for unhurried purchasing when the day's not too hot. Calle Sierpes and parallel Calle Velázquez (which changes its name to Tetuán about halfway down) have a great mixture of clothing retailers and traditional Sevillian stores, while Plaza Nueva which precedes them has a clutch of high-end designer shops featuring, among others, Carolina Herrera and local favorites Victorio & Lucchino. See Chapter 4 for full shopping information.

where the buildings either side were once jails. One of the most famous inmates was the playwright Cervantes. There's a statue of him on the right. A soldier of fortune, Cervantes became a tax collector for the navy in 1587. He entrusted some of the taxes he'd collected to a merchant who absconded with the money (or else he spent it himself—the details are sketchy). Cervantes was imprisoned by King Philip II for five years for failing to pay up. It was during this time that he began writing. Among his works are, of course, *Don Quixote*.

⓬ ★ **Cajasol Bank.** You're back at the Ayuntamiento. Just opposite, across Plaza de San Francisco, step inside the door of the bank to admire the meticulously restored patio. Plaza de San Francisco has a sinister history. It was the site for *auto-da-fés*, public trials held by the Inquisition. Those found guilty of heresy against the Catholic church were burned alive. You can learn more about the Inquisition at the Castillo de San Jorges museum in Triana (p 60). *Plaza de San Francisco 1. Mon–Fri 9am–5pm.*

Look out for this tile advertisement for Studebaker autos.

Triana

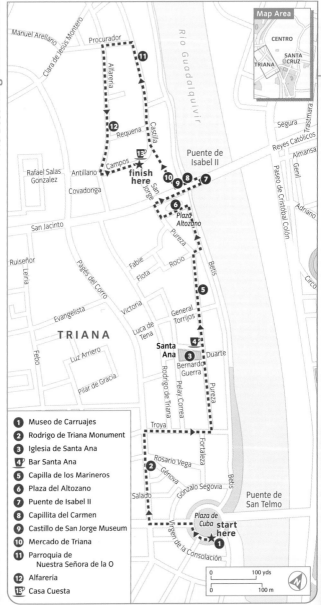

Map Area

CENTRO

SANTA CRUZ

TRIANA

1 Museo de Carruajes
2 Rodrigo de Triana Monument
3 Iglesia de Santa Ana
4 Bar Santa Ana
5 Capilla de los Marineros
6 Plaza del Altozano
7 Puente de Isabel II
8 Capillita del Carmen
9 Castillo de San Jorge Museum
10 Mercado de Triana
11 Parroquia de
   Nuestra Señora de la O
12 Alfarería
13 Casa Cuesta

Many of Seville's flamenco artists, sailors and bullfighters hail from Triana. It retains its working-class roots and remains the center of the city's ceramics trade. Calle Betis, on the riverbank, is moving upmarket, with trendy restaurants and busy bars offering some of the best views of the city. Visitors often don't make it across the river here, but it's well worth the trip. START: **Museo de Carruajes.** Bus: C3, 42, 5.

1 ★ **kids** **Museo de Carruajes.** Housed in the old Los Remedios convent, the carriage museum contains 19 horse-drawn carriages from down the centuries. My favorites both have connections with Britain: a dinky London-to-Bath Royal Mail coach and a George IV Phaeton—a version of the popular carriage designed specifically for the fat British monarch so he could get in more easily. Some descriptions are in English, but unfortunately not all. ⏱ *30 min. Plaza de Cuba.* ☎ *954 272 604. 3.60€ adults, 2.40€ concessions. Mon–Thurs 9am–2pm, 4:30–7:30pm.*

An old fire carriage at the Museo de Carruajes.

2 **Rodrigo de Triana Monument.** Many of the sailors who crewed the ships to the New World came from Triana. Best known of all of them, Juan Rodrigo Bermejo (1469–?), is honored with this statue. On October 12, 1492, while in the crow's nest of Christopher Columbus's ship, *La Pinta*, he was the first to catch sight of the Americas. His cry of '*Tierra*' (Land!) is engraved at the statue's base.

3 ★★ **Iglesia de Santa Ana.** The oldest church in Triana was built by Alfonso X (1221–84) in 1276, shortly after the Christian reconquest of the city. He dedicated it to St. Anne, the Mother of the Virgin Mary,

The Iglesia de Santa Ana is Triana's oldest church.

The Capillita del Carmen at the Triana end of the Puente de Isabel II.

☎ 954 332 645. Mon–Sat 9:30am–1pm, 5:30–9pm, Sun 9:30am–1pm.

for curing him of an eye disease. Today it's a focal point for the *cofradias*, the religious brotherhoods of the district. The delicately carved and painted 16th-century altarpiece, the double row of carved choirstalls which date from 1620 and the ornate silver monstrance from 1726 are highlights. According to local legend, children baptized in the font here—the Pila de los Gitanos—were bestowed with the gifts of flamenco singing and dancing. ⏱ 15 min. Pureza 84. ☎ 954 270 885. 7:30–9pm daily.

4 ★ **Bar Santa Ana.** This local bar on a corner has a good range of tapas and interesting pictures of bullfighters, the Virgin Mary and her mother, the Santa Ana of the name, on the wall behind the bar. If it's hot try a tinto de verano—red wine and lemonade, really refreshing. *Pureza 82.* ☎ *954 272 102. Mon–Sat 7:30am–1am, Sun 7:30am–5pm. $.*

5 ★★★ **Capilla de los Marineros.** This little church was built between 1759 and 1815 as a sailors' chapel. Many of the men who set out on voyages of discovery said their final prayers before departure here. The interior is one of Seville's most memorable, with a statue of the Esperanza de Triana—the Virgin of Hope—shimmering in silver ornamentation. One of the most important processions during Holy Week takes place when she's paraded through the town. There's a strikingly realistic statue of Christ carrying the cross here too. After your visit, double back and turn left down to the riverbank for great views of the city. ⏱ 15 min. Pureza 53.

6 **Plaza del Altozano.** As you enter this busy square, there's a modern statue of Juan Belmonte (1892–1962), one of the best-known bullfighters in Seville's history, 50m to the right. Walk round onto the bridge and you pass another statue, of a woman flamenco singer with a guitar, celebrating Triana's many renowned dancers.

7 ★ **Puente de Isabel II.** Before this iron bridge was built in 1854, the only way to cross the river was on a pontoon bridge of boats moored side by side. It's one of just a handful of ironwork structures in the city. If it looks vaguely familiar that could be because it's a copy of the Carousel Bridge in Paris, designed by Gustav Eiffel of Eiffel Tower fame.

8 ★ **Capillita del Carmen.** This tiny chapel was built by Seville's most acclaimed architect, Aníbal González, in 1926. He also built the **Plaza de España** for the 1929 Exposition (p 15). Locals call it the 'cigarette lighter' because of its odd two-tower structure. You can just see small statues of Santa Justa and Santa Rufina—the city's patron saints—in the plinth on top of the dome, holding a replica of the Giralda. These two Christians worked in the Triana potteries in the 3rd century, and were thrown to the lions by the city's Roman rulers after refusing to worship the pagan god Venus. They're often shown with the Giralda, as local legend says they protected it from the earthquake of 1755.

9 ★ **Castillo de San Jorge Museum.** When the modern market was being built, the remains of the Castilla de San Jorge (St. George's Castle) were discovered here, and these have been turned into a museum. You enter it just to the right of the market entrance. The castle dates from 1171 and has a sinister history: it was the headquarters of the Spanish Inquisition in the 16th century. Suspected deviants from the Catholic faith were dragged here up Callejón de la Inquisición, a passage leading to the river as you exit the rear of the market, after being brought across the river. It's all that survives in Seville of what was the most feared institution in Spain. The museum features video exhibits, descriptions of the castle and a walk around what's left of the ruins beneath the market. ⏱ *30 min. Plaza del Altonzano.* ☎ *954 332 240. Free. Mon–Fri 11am–6:30pm, Sat 10am–3pm.*

🔟 ★★ **Mercado de Triana.** It's in a modern building these days, but a market (*mercado*) has stood here since 1823 and it's one of the city's most lively, with colorful stalls selling bright fruit, fresh fish, vegetables and meat.

⓫ ★★ **Parroquia de Nuestra Señora de la O.** Inside this 17th-century church are sculptures by Pedro Roldán (1624–99), Seville's greatest sculptor of his age: St. Anne, St. Joachim, Mary the Virgin, and Jesus bearing the cross. The

Triana is the city's main producer of ceramics.

Fresh vegetables at the Mercado de Triana.

belfry is decorated with locally made tiles. ⏱ *15 min.* ☎ *954 337 539. 10am–1pm, 6–9pm daily.*

⓬ ★★ **Alfarería.** For centuries 'ceramics street' has been the center of Seville's ceramics industry. Clay from the river has been used since Roman times and until relatively recently fumes from its many kilns used to fog the Triana air. They've been moved out of the city to guard against the risk of fire, but you can still sometimes see artists decorating pots and tiles. In particular, Antonio Compos at number 22 sometimes has his workshop door open so you can see him at work. Cerámica Montalván has an intricately detailed tiled exterior and several rooms of antique-style pottery (it's at number 23 along the street across Antillano). Cerámica Santa Ana, down Antillano (San Jorge 31), has a colorful tiled facade and workshop.

⓭ ★★ **Casa Cuesta.** A few doors down from Cerámica Santa Ana, this traditional old tapas bar has been here since 1880. There's a long list of tapas with daily specials too. I like the pans de la casa—bread with various toppings. There's also a good restaurant if you're hungrier. *Castilla 1.* ☎ *954 229 718. www.casacuesta. net. $.*

Alameda

1 Plaza de San Lorenzo
2 Café Bar Sardinero
3 Templo de Nuestro
   Padre Jesús del Gran Poder
4 Alameda de Hércules
5 República

6 Diablito
7 Convento de Santa Clara
   & Torre de Don Fadrique
8 Monasterio de San Clemente
9 Centro de las Artes de Sevilla
10 Torre de los Perdigones

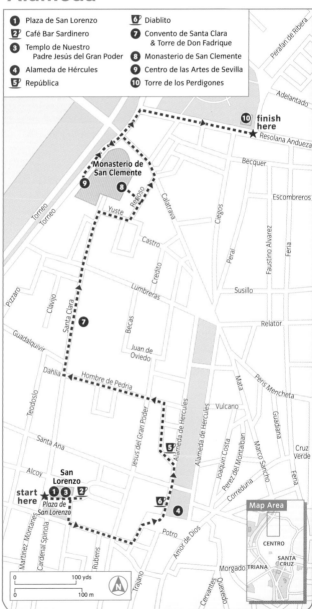

This little-visited district is well off the tourist trail. It has two impressive convents, attractive squares perfect for a coffee in the shade, an art gallery and a 45m tower with a *camera obscura* that makes an entertaining visit for curious kids. Visiting the convents takes persistence and they're open on different days so you can't see both. I recommend booking ahead. If you don't speak Spanish ask your hotel to do it for you. **START. Walk to Plaza de San Lorenzo. Nearest bus: B2, C3, C4, 13, 14.**

① ★★★ **Plaza de San Lorenzo.** The prettiest square in Seville? For me, it's definitely a candidate—with the red walls and marble frontispiece of the church overlooking a shady square of orange trees. The church's interior features an odd statue of San Lorenzo on the main altarpiece: bizarrely, he's holding a grill. Martyred under the persecution of Roman Emperor Valerian in the year 258, it's said that San Lorenzo was burned or 'grilled' to death. Legend has it he was so strong-willed that instead of giving in to the Romans and releasing information about the Church, he simply shouted as he died, 'I am done on this side! Turn me over and eat.' ⏱ *15 min. Daily 8:30–10:45am, 7–8:45pm, except Sun 8:30–9:30am, 11:45am–1:45pm, 7:30–8:45pm.*

San Lorenzo is one of Seville's prettiest squares.

② ★★ **Café Bar Sardinero.** This local bar on Plaza de San Lorenzo is a hive of activity. Pensioners sit chatting, mums nurse babies, kids play hide-and-seek—it's a perfect spot for people-watching. Order and pay at the little window if you sit outside. *Plaza de San Lorenzo 15.* ☎ *954 389 424. Mon, Tues, Thurs, Sun 7am–midnight. Closed Aug.*

③ ★★ **Templo de Nuestro Padre Jesús del Gran Poder.** Just to the right of the church you'll find this more modern temple.

Inside is one of the most revered and moving sculptures in the city: a depiction of Christ carrying the cross. You can walk round behind the sculpture and, as many of the devotees do, touch the end of the cross. It's the work of one of Seville's foremost sculptors, Juan de Mesa (1583–1627), whose statue is outside in the middle of the square. ⏱ *15 min. Plaza de San Lorenzo 13.* ☎ *954 915 686. Daily 8am–1:30pm, 6–9pm (Fri 7:30am–10pm).*

Statues of Caesar and Hercules look down on the Alameda de Hércules.

❹ ★★ Alameda de Hércules.

One of Seville's liveliest squares, the Alameda is the hub of a district that's very much on the up. A long tree-lined square now surrounded by cool bars and cafes, it was designed in 1574 by the Count of Barajasi, who drained what was swampland and planted trees. At one end he installed two columns from a Roman temple discovered in the center of Seville. He crowned them with statues of Julius Caesar and Hercules, the supposed founders of the city. In the latter half of the 18th century, two more columns were placed at the other end of the square, topped with statues of lions bearing shields. It's a pleasant place for a stroll or a coffee, and buzzing with life at night.

There are lots of places I would recommend on the Alameda. Two of my favorites are funky cafe-bar ❺ **República** *(Alameda de Hércules 27.* ☎ *954 909 435. $)*, which does great cakes and has friendly staff,

and ❻ **Diablito** *(Alameda de Hércules 7.* ☎ *954 377 461. $)*, right in front of the columns, with Hercules and Caesar looking down on you.

❼ ★★ Convento de Santa Clara & Torre de Don Fadrique.

Founded in the Middle Ages, at the time of writing this convent was undergoing major renovation, which will take years. In the meantime you can take a guided visit on Saturday mornings, wearing a hard hat and picking your way through supporting trusses and round piles of rubble. I found it fascinating. There's an ancient orange-tree-lined courtyard with a fountain, a tiled refectory and a larger cloistered patio. It's all in pretty bad shape, with much of it supported by scaffolding. The Mudéjar-style church features an altarpiece by Juan Martínez Montañés (1568–1649). Hidden inside another courtyard is the Torre de Don Fadrique, a tower which formed part of the defences for a palace, built by Fernando III, which pre-dated the convent. It's quite a mixture of styles—if you look at the windows you see a

The Torre de Don Fadrique's different styles of window.

The shady courtyard at Monasterio de San Clemente.

smaller Romanesque one below a larger, more ornate Gothic one. The tour (in Spanish only) includes a slide show about the 3 million euro renovation project, including the painstaking work of restoring the 5,000 tiles around the main patio by hand. ⏱ *1 hr. Santa Clara 40.* ☎ *954 379 905. Free. Visits (Sat 9am–2pm) must be booked in advance (*☎ *660 555 284, Mon–Fri mornings only); numbers are limited.*

8 ★★ **Monasterio de San Clemente.** Tradition has it that this is the oldest monastery in Seville, founded in the 13th century. Enter by the gateway on Calle Reposo. The nuns will invite you in and sell you their cakes (not the cheapest in Seville, but they're for a good cause). You may have to ask to see the church. It helps if you speak Spanish. Alternatively get your hotel to call ahead for you. The church is a trove of art and architecture, with a colorful Mudéjar ceiling, a baroque altarpiece featuring St. Clemente and frescoes by Lucas Valdés (1661–1725). There are descriptions in Spanish. ⏱ *20 min. Reposo 9.* ☎ *954 378 040. Mon 10am–12:45pm, 3:30–5:45pm. Reservations suggested.*

9 ★ **Centro de las Artes de Sevilla.** This small, airy exhibition space is round the other side of the Monasterio de San Clemente on Torneo, the main road. It houses regularly changing contemporary art exhibitions, video installations, theater and more. ⏱ *20 min. Torneo 18. No phone. Free. Tues–Sat 11am–2pm, 6–9pm, closed Sun & Mon.*

10 ★★ **kids Torre de los Perdigones.** This 45m-high tower has a *camera obscura* inside. From this vantage point you can home in on what's going on across the city via the combination of mirrors and lenses based on an invention of the Greek philosopher Aristotle in the 4th century B.C. (see p 44 for kids' tour). ⏱ *30 min. Resolana.* ☎ *954 909 353. 4€, concessions 2.50€. Daily 10am–1:30pm, 4pm–5:30pm. Access every 30 min in groups of up to 10.*

La Macarena

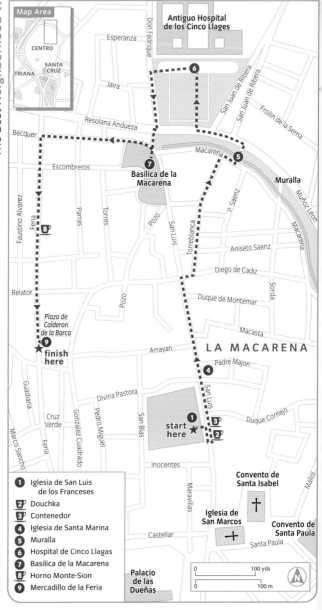

Map Area

CENTRO

SANTA CRUZ

TRIANA

Antiguo Hospital de los Cinco Llages

Esperanza

Don Fadrique

Jaira

San Juan de Ribera

San Juan de Ribera

Froilin de la Serna

Resolana Andueza

Becquer

Escombreros

Macarena

⑥

⑦

Basílica de la Macarena

Muralla

Muñoz Léon

Macarena

P. Saenz

Faustino Alvarez

Feria

Parras

Torres

Pozo

San Luis

Torreblanca

Aniseto Saenz

Sorda

⑧

Relator

Diego de Cadiz

Duque de Montemar

Macasta

Pozo

Plaza de Calderon de la Barca

⑨ finish here

★

LA MACARENA

Arrayan

Padre Majon

④

San Luis

Guadiana

Cruz Verde

Feria

Gonzalez Cuadrado

Pedro Miguel

Divina Pastora

San Blas

Marco Sancho

① start here ★

③

②

Duque Cornejo

Inocentes

Maravillas

Convento de Santa Isabel

Iglesia de San Marcos

Castellar

Convento de Santa Paula

Santa Paula

Mallol

① Iglesia de San Luis de los Franceses
② Douchka
③ Contenedor
④ Iglesia de Santa Marina
⑤ Muralla
⑥ Hospital de Cinco Llagas
⑦ Basilica de la Macarena
⑧ Horno Monte-Sion
⑨ Mercadillo de la Feria

Palacio de las Dueñas

0   100 yds
0   100 m

N

La Macarena is one of my favorite neighborhoods, a time-warp of tiny squares, narrow streets, parish churches and old-fashioned local shops. This is real Seville, away from the tourists, and it has remained unchanged for decades. But that's slowly changing as developers upgrade the houses. You might see the slogan 'Stop especulación' ('stop speculative building') graffitied on some of the walls. START: **Walk to Calle San Luis. Nearest buses: C1, C2, C3, C4, 10, 13, 14.**

1 ★★★ Iglesia de San Luis de los Franceses. With an exterior smothered in baroque statues and swirls, San Luis is one of this walk's highlights. It's no longer a functioning church and is owned by the town council, which means its opening hours are rather more visitor-friendly than other churches. It has one of Seville's most extravagant baroque interiors—a jaw-dropping multitude of twisting columns and gilded carvings. Depictions of saints and angels look down at you from the huge painted dome. Reputedly the skulls that some of the statues in the altarpieces are holding are genuine human remains. ⏱ *15 min. San Luis.* ☎ *954 389 902. Free. Open Tues–Thurs 9am–2pm, Fri, Sat 9am–2pm, 5–8pm. Closed Sun, Mon & Aug.*

2 Douchka *(San Luis 46.* ☎ *655 753 768. $)* and **3 ★★ Contenedor** *(San Luis 50.* ☎ *954 916 333. www.contenedorcultural.com. Tues–Sat 4pm–midnight. $)* come as a bit of a surprise in such a down-at-heel district. Douchka is a trendy teahouse; Contenedor is a chilled-out cafe with great, rather eclectic live music in the evenings. Douchka serves flapjacks and cookies, while Contenedor does nice tapas.

4 Iglesia de Santa Marina. This is a typical Mudéjar-style church, with a tower that looks like it could once have been a minaret. The brickwork interior is very plain, but there are informative labels in English describing the various statues,

Seville was once surrounded by walls, but only a few sections remain today.

arches and towers. ⏰ *10 min. San Luis 60. Mon–Fri 11am–1pm.*

⑤ ★★ Muralla. Moorish Seville was completely surrounded by a fortified wall (*muralla*) which originally had more than 100 towers. It dates from the 12th century and was built with a patrol walkway along the top. Most of it was torn down as the city expanded in the 19th century, but here an evocative 400m stretch remains with seven towers—one an unusual octagonal design. Walk through the gate opposite Macarena 24 for better views.

⑥ ★ Hospital de Cinco Llagas. Across the busy road, the present-day Andalusian Parliament building was once Europe's largest hospital. The 'hospital of five wounds,' founded in 1500, was originally located inside the city in Barrio Santa Cruz. In 1540 work began on a new hospital to be sited here outside the city walls. Completed in 1613, the south front has an impressive baroque central portal by Asensio de Maeda (around 1547–1607). The parliament debating chamber has been converted from a Mannerist-style church built by Hernán Ruiz II

The belfry at the Basílica de la Macarena.

(1500–69) in 1560. *Parlamento de Andalucía.* ☎ *954 592 100. Visits (free) by written application only.*

⑦ ★★★ Basílica de la Macarena. The Virgen de la Esperanza Macarena, the much-adored 17th-century statue of the Virgin Mary which gives this district its name, sits above the main altar in this church, surrounded by a cascade of gold and silver. During the pulsating festivities of Semana Santa, the Virgin is paraded through the streets.You can see her unbelievably ornate processional platforms laden with baroque cherubs and dripping with gold and silver in the museum to the left of the church. There are also interesting descriptions of the history of the processions in English. The scale of their extravagance is simply incredible. There's also a small shop selling rather tacky Virgin mementos, and a handy Seville tourist board information desk. ⏰ *1 hr. Bécquer 1.* ☎ *954 901 800. Church: free. 9am–2pm, 5–9pm daily. Museum: 5€. 9:30am–1:30pm, 5–8:30pm daily (closed Sun afternoons). No cards.*

⑧ ★ Horno Monte-Sion. This is a traditional Macarena bakery and pastry shop. No airs and graces, just tasty cakes and pastries arrayed in long glass cabinets. There's a small seating area at the back; order at the counter first. *Feria 148.* ☎ *954 370 248. 7am–12:30pm, 4:30pm–9pm (closed afternoons June–Aug). No cards.*

⑨ ★★ Mercadillo de la Feria. Feria's little market is one of the city's nicest. In an old whitewashed building, it's packed with stalls selling local produce, all painstakingly laid out. Fresh fish, cheese, meat and vegetables are all on offer. It's a great place for taking photographs. *Feria. 7am–1pm daily except Sun & Mon.* ●

Shopping Best Bets

Best **English Bookstore**
★★ FNAC, *Avda de la Constitución 8 (p 73)*

Best **Gentleman's Milliner**
★★★ Maquedano, *Sierpes 40. (p 79)* and Padilla Crespo, *Adriano 18B (p 79)*

Best **Sexy Shoes**
★★★ Pilar Burgos, *Tetuán 1 (p 80)*

Best for **Watch Addicts**
★ El Cronómetro, *Sierpes 19–21 (p 78)*

Best **Inexpensive Trendy Womenswear**
★★★ Mango, *Velázquez 7–9 (p 76)* and ★★★ Zara, *Plaza Duque 1 (p 76)*

Best **Grown-Up Boys' Toys**
★★ Heracles, *Villegas 1 (p 76)*

Best **Pretty Frocks & Shoes**
★★★ HAND, *Adriano 22 (p 76)* and ★★★ Bimba & Lola, *Rioja 5 (p 76)*

Best **Upmarket Menswear & Womenswear**
★★★ Carolina Herrera, *Plaza Nueva 8 (p 76)*

Best **Stylish Designer Jewelry**
★★ Tous, *Sagasta 7 (p 78)*

Best **Flamenco Music Shop**
★★ Compás Sur, *Cuesta del Rosario 7-F (p 79)*

Best **Kids' Clothes Store**
★★ Nanos, *Álvarez Quintero 5 (p 75)*

Best **Flamenco Finery**
★★★ Juan Foronda, *Sierpes 79 (p 78)*

Best **Sevillian Women's Fashion**
★★ Agua de Sevilla, *San Fernando 3 (p 75)*

Best **Religious Paraphernalia**
★★★ Cerería del Salvador, *Plaza del Salvador 8 (p 78)*

Best **Sexy Handbags**
★★ Toscana, *Plaza Nueva 3 (p 80)*

Best **Department Store**
★★★ El Corte Inglés, *Plaza del Duque (p 75)*

Best **Chic Designer Clothes**
★★★ Victorio & Lucchino, *Plaza Nueva 10 (p 77)*

Best **Silverware**
★ Casa Ruiz, *Sierpes 68 (p 73)*

Best **Old-Fashioned Food Store**
★★★ El Reloj, *Arfe 18 (p 79)*

Best **Antiques Browsing**
★★★ Popularte, *Pasaje de Vila 4 (p 73)*

Best **Elegant Ceramics**
★★★ La Cartuja de Sevilla, *Avda de la Constitución 16 (p 74)*

Best **Value Fun Souvenirs**
★★ Bazar Isbilia, *Ximénez de Enciso 11 (p 77)*

Best **Leather Goods**
★★ El Caballo, *Antonia Díaz 7 (p 80)*

Best **Gourmet Food Store**
★★★ La Alacena Tienda, *San Eloy 31 (p 78)*

Traditional orange wine is a local specialty. Previous page: Traditional sombreros at Padilla Crespo.

Santa Cruz & Arenal Shopping

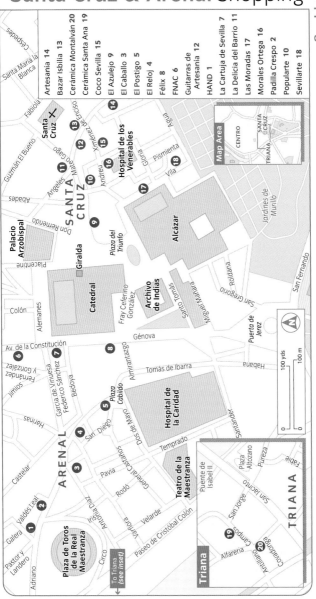

Artesanía 14
Bazar Isbilia 13
Cerámica Montalván 20
Cerámica Santa Ana 19
Coco Sevilla 15
El Azulejo 9
El Caballo 3
El Postigo 5
El Reloj 4
Félix 8
FNAC 6
Guitarras de Artesanía 12
HAND 1
La Cartuja de Sevilla 7
La Delicia del Barrio 11
Las Moradas 17
Morales Ortega 16
Padilla Crespo 2
Populaarte 10
Sevillarte 18

Map Area

CENTRO

SANTA CRUZ

TRIANA

Santa María la Blanca
Céspedes
Fabiola
Guzmán El Bueno
Santa Cruz
Encina
Ximénez de Enciso
Agua
Gloria
Pismienta
Vila
Jardines de Murillo

Abades
Angeles
Mateos Gago
Andreu
SANTA CRUZ
Hospital de los Venerables
Don Remedio

Placentine
Palacio Arzobispal
Giralda
Plaza del Triunfo
Alcázar
San Gregorio
San Fernando

Colón
Alemanes
Catedral
Fray Ceferino González
Archivo de Indias
Santo Tomás
Miguel Mañara
Roldana
Puerta de Jerez

Av. de la Constitución
Fernández y González
García de Vinuesa
Federico Sánchez
Bedoya
Génova
Tomás de Ibarra
Almirantazgo
Habana

Jimios
Harinas
ARENAL
Plaza Cabildo
San Diego
Dos de Mayo
Hospital de la Caridad
Temprado
Santander

Castelar
Valdés Leal
Galera
Pastor y Landero
Adriano
Plaza de Toros de la Real Maestranza
Circo
Antonia Díaz
Iniesta Díaz
Pavia
Rodó
General Castaños
Varflora
Velarde
Teatro de la Maestranza
Paseo de Cristóbal Colón

To Triana (see inset)

Triana
TRIANA
Puente de Isabel II
San Jorge
San Jacinto
Plaza Altozano
Pureza
Fábile
Antillano
Covadonga
Alfarería
Campos

N

0   100 yds
0   100 m

Centro Shopping

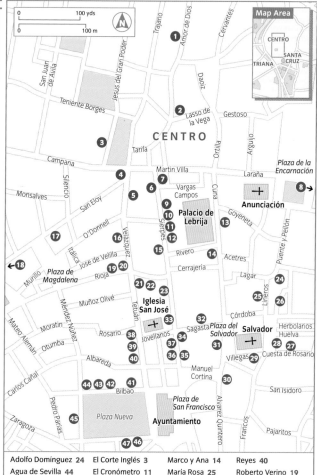

Adolfo Domínguez 24	El Corte Inglés 3	Marco y Ana 14	Reyes 40
Agua de Sevilla 44	El Cronómetro 11	María Rosa 25	Roberto Verino 19
Belmondo Bazaar 2	Festa 6	Martian 37	Santana 28
Beta 12	Foto Supra 15	Massimo Dutti 20	Siete Revueltas 33 26
Bimba & Lola 22	Heracles 29	MaxMara 47	Toscana 46
Boarderking 10	Juan Foronda 34	Nanos 30	Tous 32
Camper 39	La Alacena Tienda 17	Nervión Plaza 8	Uterque 21
Carolina Herrera 45	La Jaboteca 13	O'Kean 41	V&L Vintage 35
Casa del Libro 16	L'Occitane 33	Papelería Ferrer 7	Victorio & Lucchino 43
Casa Ruiz 36	Loewe 42	Pilar Burgos 38	Visionlab 9
Cerería del Salvador 31	Mango 5	Plaza de Armas 18	Zara 4
Compás Sur 27	Maquedano 23	Record Sevilla 1	

Seville Shopping **A to Z**

Antiques

Casa Ruiz CENTRO Silver in all its antique styles is the specialty in this traditional shop: animals, ships and jugs along with rings and necklaces. *Sierpes 68. No phone. AE, DC, MC, V. Bus: C5. Tram: Plaza Nueva. Map p 72.*

★★ **Morales Ortega** ARENAL This place is full of diverse artifacts: ancient ceramics, old paintings, Arabic coffee pots and pewter and postcards are just some of the curiosities on show. *Jamerdana 2.* ☎ *954 223 606. MC, V. Bus: 1, C3, C4, 23. Map p 71.*

★★★ **Popularte** SANTA CRUZ Another trove of pots, signs, door knockers and more in a U-shaped little shop in Santa Cruz that could require a prolonged browsing session. *Pasaje de Vila 4.* ☎ *954 229 444. AE, DC, MC, V. Bus: 1, C3, C4, 23. Map p 71.*

★ **Siete Revueltas 33** CENTRO If you want a 2,000€ 18th-century table or the like, this is the place. The informed owner speaks English if you ask him nicely. *Siete Revueltas 33.* ☎ *954 228 493. No cards. Bus: C5. Map p 72.*

Books

★ **Beta** CENTRO This is the best of Beta's eight branches. It's housed in an old theater reached through a short passageway, which doesn't hint at the remarkable two-floor auditorium inside, stacked with books, including a couple of shelves of English stock. *Sierpes 25.* ☎ *954 293 724. MC, V. Bus: B2, C5. Map p 72.*

★ **Casa del Libro** CENTRO The Casa also has a range of English books and is ideally located in the main shopping district. English books are at the back of the shop. *Velázquez 8.* ☎ *954 502 950. MC, V. Bus: B2, C5. Map p 72.*

★★ **FNAC** ARENAL This cool modern French chain right next to the cathedral sells books in English (top floor), CDs, software and more on four floors. *Avda de la Constitución 8.* ☎ *954 596 517. AE, DC, MC, V. Tram: Plaza Nueva. Map p 71.*

Cameras & Photo-Developing

Foto Supra CENTRO A convenient place for getting films and digital prints developed, you can also pick up memory cards, films and compact cameras here, but serious enthusiasts should try Santana, below. *Sierpes 22.* ☎ *954 563 803. AE, DC, MC, V. Bus: B2, C5. Map p 72.*

★ **Santana** CENTRO This is the place for a new lens, extra filter or tripod. Manuel and Joaquín have the latest Canon and Nikon DSLR gear too, if you're feeling like a splurge. Essentials like memory cards and

Popularte is a trove of interesting antiques.

The Shopping Fine Print

Spain still respects time-honored traditions. Sundays are not big shopping days, though this is slowly changing, especially in malls and larger stores. The traditional closing for siesta during midday is undergoing some revision, but most smaller stores still shut between 2pm and 4pm (and then stay open until 8pm or 9pm). Sales (*rebajas*) are held twice annually, starting in July and again in January. Discounts are often up to 50%. For information on sales tax and rebates for non-E.U. residents, see p 166.

batteries are also stocked. *Plaza de la Pasion 3.* ☎ *954 225 492. AE, DC, MC, V. Bus: C5. Map p 72.*

Ceramics & Pottery

★ **Cerámica Montalván** TRIANA The Montalván family has been making traditional ceramics since the 19th century. Their old shop features a tiled shopfront and workshop space. *Alfarería 23.* ☎ *954 333 254. www.ceramicamontalvan.com. MC, V. Bus: B2, C3, 43. Map p 71.*

★★ **Cerámica Santa Ana** TRIANA The best of a cluster of Triana ceramics shops, this lovely tile-fronted shop is great for typical Triana pottery, including house numbers, pots, vases and decorated tiles. *San Jorge 31.* ☎ *954 333 990. MC, V. Bus: B2, C3, 43. Map p 71.*

★★ **El Azulejo** SANTA CRUZ Unsurprisingly with a name that means 'tile', this place specializes in ceramics. They are all hand-painted—some in modern styles, others more traditional—and very distinctive wares. *Mateos Gago 10.* ☎ *954 220 085. AE, DC, MC, V. Bus: C5. Map p 71.*

★★ **El Postigo** ARENAL This small arts and crafts market offers an interesting selection of bowls, jewelry and tiles, most at the less expensive end of the scale, by local artists. *Arfe.* ☎ *954 560 013. AE, DC, MC, V. Bus: C5. Tram: Archivo de Indias. Map p 71.*

★★★ **La Cartuja de Sevilla** ARENAL Delicate chinaware of the highest quality is sold here from the famous Cartuja china factory,

Local pottery is a good buy at El Postigo.

originally set up by Englishman Charles Pickman in 1839. *Avda de la Constitución 16.* ☎ *954 214 155. www.lacartujadesevilla.es. V. Tram: Archivo de Indias. Map p 71.*

Martian CENTRO Good-value vases, bowls and jugs in the three traditional styles—patio Sevilliano (floral), cerámica clasica and monterai (rustic hunting scenes)—make handy souvenirs or inexpensive presents. *Sierpes 74.* ☎ *954 213 413. AE, DC, MC, V. Bus: C5. Tram: Plaza Nueva. Map p 72.*

★★ **Sevillarte** SANTA CRUZ On a photogenic square, this place specializes in china figurines, in particular the Spanish Lladro brand. There's also a branch at Sierpes 66. *Vida 17.* ☎ *954 500 005. www.sevillarte.com. AE, DC, MC, V. Bus: 1, C3, C4, 23. Map p 71.*

Children
★★ **Marco y Ana** CENTRO You'll find this shop on Cradle Street which, unsurprisingly, has many children's shops. This one stands out for its locally produced handmade clothes for newborns to older toddlers, such as cute lace sun bonnets and crocheted booties. *Cuna 24.* ☎ *954 213 038. AE, DC, MC, V. Bus: B2, C5. Map p 72.*

★★ **Nanos** CENTRO This small Spanish boutique chain sells gorgeous and pricey babies' and kids' clothes with a slightly vintage feel. Fabulous designer quality—which comes at a price. *Álvarez Quintero 5.* ☎ *954 215 872. www.nanos.es. AE, DC, MC, V. Bus: B2, C5. Map p 72.*

Cosmetics & Perfumes
★★ **Agua de Sevilla** CENTRO Originally a perfume store, Agua still creates its own unusual fragrances, based around Sevillian orange blossom. These days its three outlets (the others are at San Fernando 3 and Roderigo Caro 16) sell luxury women's fashionware which is contemporary and stylish with a Sevillian flavor. *Plaza Nueva 9.* ☎ *954 213 145. AE, DC, MC, V. Bus: C5. Tram: Plaza Nueva. Map p 72.*

La Jaboteca CENTRO This super scented soap shop sells all kinds of fragrances—coconut, rose, incense and more, and the staff are friendly. *Cuna 9.* ☎ *954 213 606. AE, MC, V. Bus: B2, C5. Map p 72.*

★★ **L'Occitane** CENTRO This French chain sells soaps, shampoos, lotions and creams fragranced with natural herbs and essences from Provence, great as presents or a little indulgence. *Sierpes 50b.* ☎ *954 210 882. www. loccitane.com. AE, MC, V. Bus: C5. Tram: Plaza Nueva. Map p 72.*

Department Stores & Shopping Centers
★★★ **El Corte Inglés** CENTRO Spain's favorite department store has several branches around the main shopping district. You can buy just about anything here, from toothpaste to flamenco costumes. Perfect for finding something in a hurry. Open daily until 10pm including Sundays. *Plaza del Duque.* ☎ *954 571 440. AE, DC, MC, V. Bus: B2, C5, 13, 14. Map p 72.*

Nervión Plaza NERVION This large commercial and entertainment center is ideal for escaping the summer heat or the winter rain. It's a short taxi or bus ride from the old center. *Avda Luis de Morales.* ☎ *954 989 131. Bus: C1, C2, 22, 23, 32, 70. Map p 72.*

★ **Plaza de Armas** ARENAL The old railway station has been attractively converted into a small shopping center with boutiques selling clothes, cellphones and gifts. There's also a well-stocked grocery store and several restaurants, McDonald's among them. *Plaza la Legion.* ☎ *954 908 282. Bus: B2, C4, 43. Map p 72.*

Fashion, Designwear & Accessories

★ **Adolfo Domínguez** CENTRO Smart, upmarket men's and women's contemporary fashion in a stunningly ornate old building. Stylish and quite pricey. *Cuidad de Londres, Cuna 30.* ☎ *954 213 067. www. adolfodominguez.com. AE, DC, MC, V. Bus: B2, C5. Map p 72. Also at Puente Y Pellon 11.*

★★★ **Bimba & Lola** CENTRO Cool, funky and unique, B&L's range of elegant designer clothes, bags and shoes is just perfect for young, sassy ladies looking for something a little different. *Rioja 58.* ☎ *954 219 375. www.bimbaylola.com. AE, DC, MC, V. Bus: C5. Tram: Plaza Nueva. Map p 72.*

★★★ **Carolina Herrera** CENTRO This gorgeous boutique, all dark wood and soft lighting, sells upmarket, very fashionable menswear and womenswear, including silk ties, leather travel gear, scarves and dresses. *Plaza Nueva 8.* ☎ *954 500 418. AE, DC, MC, V. Bus: C5. Tram: Plaza Nueva. Map p 72.*

Flamenco dresses are still worn on special occasions.

★ **Festa** CENTRO Festa's shops in most major Spanish cities offer stylish, fashionable garb for younger women at great prices. Perfect for picking up a new top to go out in. *Sierpes 6.* ☎ *954 293 380. www. festa.es. AE, DC, MC, V. Bus: B2, C5. Map p 72.*

★★★ **HAND** ARENAL It stands for 'have a nice day'. And you will if you like classy, very feminine dresses and shoes with a vintage vibe. Quality clothes and shoes at reasonable prices. *Adriano 22.* ☎ *954 229 226. AE, DC, MC, V. Bus: C5. Map p 71.*

★★ **Heracles** CENTRO I love this place, but I would because I'm a guy. It sells all sorts of funky, classic boys' toys. Wallets, travel gear, shaving kits, alarm clocks and radios. All a little bit cool and kitsch. *Villegas 1.* ☎ *954 502 022. MC, V. Bus: C5. Map p 72.*

★★★ **Loewe** CENTRO Top-end designer wear for men and women, Loewe's unique clothes, fragrances and accessories are popular with celebrities and royalty. Now part of the LVMH stable, the brand began life as a family business in Spain. (There's also an outlet in Hotel Alfonso XIII.) *Plaza Nueva 12.* ☎ *954 225 253. AE, DC , MC, V. Bus: C5. Tram: Plaza Nueva. Map p 72.*

★★★ **Mango** CENTRO Now a worldwide phenomenon, Mango continues to offer great-value copies of catwalk favorites with high-quality crafting. Several branches in Seville and prices are very reasonable. *Velázquez 7–9.* ☎ *954 223 389. www.mango.es. AE, DC, MC, V. Bus: B2, C5. Map p 72.*

Massimo Dutti CENTRO Unmistakably continental, the clothes at Massimo are stylish and affordable for both men and women. Staff are helpful and friendly. *Velázquez 12.*

HAND has vintage-style clothes and shoes.

☎ 954 225 772. www.massimodutti. com. AE, DC, MC, V. Bus: B2, C5. Map p 72.

★★ **MaxMara** CENTRO Smart, stylish and elegant clothes for the busy modern woman. This is another Spanish brand that's gaining worldwide appeal, but it's several notches up the price and quality scale from Mango and Zara. *Plaza Nueva 3.* ☎ *954 214 825. AE, DC, MC, V. Bus: C5. Tram: Plaza Nueva. Map p 72.*

O'Kean CENTRO A continental-style gentleman's outfitter, selling well-cut and well-crafted suits, jackets, shirts and ties. *Plaza Nueva 13. No phone. AE, DC, MC, V. Bus: C5. Tram: Plaza Nueva. Map p 72.*

★ **Roberto Verino** CENTRO This small shop sells attractive mid-priced bags, scarves and clothes for women; stylish, colorful and sophisticated. Friendly service too. *Rioja 14.* ☎ *954 227 151. AE, DC, MC, V. Bus: B2, C5. Map p 72.*

★★ **V&L Vintage** CENTRO Seville's most famous design duo Victorio and Lucchino have a carefully selected range of more retro-style outfits here. Exquisitely tailored, but designer prices too. *Sierpes 87.* ☎ *954 227 951. AE, DC, MC, V. Bus: C5. Tram: Plaza Nueva. Map p 72.*

★★★ **Victorio & Lucchino** CENTRO Anyone who is anyone in the fashion world has heard of Seville's

most famous design duo. Spanish actress Penelope Cruz modeled for them before Hollywood beckoned. Luxurious, creative and elegant, the craftsmanship is exquisite. There's a small selection of clothes for men too. *Plaza Nueva 10.* ☎ *954 227 951. www.victorioylucchino.com. AE, DC, MC, V. Bus: C5. Tram: Plaza Nueva. Map p 72.*

★★★ **Zara** CENTRO Well-made and affordable copies of catwalk fashions have made Zara a perennial favorite for girls who want to look good without spending a fortune. Various branches elsewhere in Seville too. *Plaza del Duque 1.* ☎ *954 214 875. www.zara.es. Bus: B2, C5. Map p 72.*

Gifts & Souvenirs

★★ **Bazar Isbilia** SANTA CRUZ Although it's at a tiny crossroads in Barrio Santa Cruz, this place isn't tacky or overpriced. Inside on a cool patio it sells cards, flamenco CDs, T-shirts, trinkets and ceramics covering the full price range. *Ximénez de Enciso 11.* ☎ *954 228 523. AE, MC, V. Bus: 1, C3, C4, 23. Map p 71.*

Coco Sevilla ARENAL There's a selection of the usual Moorish-style souvenirs like bowls and light shades here. The proprietor is a friendly Frenchman. *Ximénez de Enciso 28.* ☎ *954 214 532. www. cocosevilla.com. Bus: 1, C3, C4, 23. Map p 71.*

The ornate old facade of El Cronómetro the watchmakers.

Félix ARENAL   Right in front of the cathedral, this is a good place for buying antique and modern posters advertising bullfights and festivals. *Avda de la Constitución 26.* ☎ *954 218 026. AE, DC, MC, V. Tram: Archivo de Indias. Map p 71.*

★ Las Moradas ARENAL   In a little patio, Alicia San Martin's tasteful shop sells Andalusian handicrafts a notch up from much of the tourist tat on sale elsewhere in Santa Cruz. Lots of Moorish elements like bowls, fans, jewelry and light shades too. *Rodrigo Caro 20.* ☎ *954 563 917. Bus: 1, C3, C4, 23. Map p 71.*

Jewelry
★★ Artesanía SANTA CRUZ   A tiny boutique in Santa Cruz, this place sells inexpensive handmade jewelry by local artisans. Necklaces using amber and precious stones are particularly unusual. Prices are very reasonable—around 35€ for a necklace. *Santa Teresa 10.* ☎ *954 563 705. MC, V. Bus: 1, C3, C4, 23. Map p 71.*

★ El Cronómetro CENTRO   All the top brands are here at this distinguished family watchmakers, with its eye-catching old shop front with clocks showing time in London, Paris and elsewhere. Along with the Rolexes and Tags, look out for Spanish brand Cuervo y Sobrinos. *Sierpes 19–21.* ☎ *954 225 028. www. elcronometro.com. AE, DC, MC, V. Bus: B2, C5. Map p 72.*

Reyes CENTRO   This traditional jewelry shop sells older-style pieces as well as classic brand names like Cartier and Mercier. *Tetuán 26.* ☎ *954 228 825. AE, DC, MC, V. Bus: C5. Tram: Plaza Nueva. Map p 72.*

★★ Tous CENTRO   The Tous family's unique designer pieces are contemporary and make creative use of precious stones, silver and gold. It's right at the top end of the price scale. The family store in Barcelona has grown into a worldwide brand. *Sagasta 7.* ☎ *954 211 843. www. tous.es. Bus: B2, C5. Map p 72.*

Local Specialties
★★★ Cerería del Salvador CENTRO   Religious statues, icons and artifacts are big business in Seville and this is the place to buy them. Christ carrying the cross, the Virgin Mary and guardian angels are just some of the models on offer. *Plaza del Salvador 8.* ☎ *954 226 523. AE, DC, MC, V. Bus: C5. Map p 72.*

★★★ El Reloj ARENAL   Brothers Antonio and Francisco run this most delightful old provisions store with an antique facade and shelves and counters stacked with cheeses, hams and canned produce. *Arfe 18.* ☎ *954 222 460. MC, V. Bus: C5. Map p 71.*

★★★ Juan Foronda CENTRO   Juan has been selling *mantones* (shawls) and lace *mantillas* (Catholic headscarves) since 1926. There are several of his lovely old shops dotted around the center selling all manner of Catholic artifacts, flamenco fans and jewelry. *Sierpes 79.*

☎ *954 214 050. www.juanforonda. com. AE, DC, MC, V. Bus: C5. Tram: Plaza Nueva. Map p 72.*

★★★ La Alacena Tienda CEN-TRO   The place to find top-quality local hams, cheeses and wines. A full leg of serrano ham can set you back hundreds of euros, but there's produce in all price ranges. You can sample some in their wine bar next door. *San Eloy 31.* ☎ *954 215 580. MC, V. Bus: B2, C5. Map p 72.*

★★ La Delicia del Barrio SANTA CRUZ   This little store sells all sorts of Andalusian food and drink delicacies: marmalades, orange wine, cheeses, hams and olive oils, all attractively packaged. They'd make handy gifts. *Mateos Gago 15.* ☎ *954 210 629. www.lasdeliciasdelbarrio. com. AE, DC, MC, V. Bus: 1, C3, C4, 23. Map p 71.*

★★★ Maquedano CENTRO   A gentleman's milliner—the ultimate place for hats of all shapes and sizes. Panamas, Primaveras and flat caps adorn the window display. If you're feeling bullish you can even buy a traditional toreador hat. *Sierpes 40.* ☎ *954 564 771. AE, MC, V. Bus: C5. Tram: Plaza Nueva. Map p 72.*

★★ Maria Rosa CENTRO   Another of the city's top flamenco outfitters, María has men's suits and children's flamenco clothes as well as the usual dresses. *Lineros 6.* ☎ *954 222 487. www.mariarosa-sevilla.com. AE, DC, MC, V. Bus: B2. Map p 72.*

★★★ Padilla Crespo ARENAL Owner Manolo's grandfather started this lovely sombrero shop. These typically Sevillian hats are all made on the premises and each is unique. Tom Cruise is one of the many satisfied customers. Manolo speaks good English too. *Adriano 18B.* ☎ *954 564 414. MC, V. Bus: C5. Map p 71.*

★★ Papelería Ferrer CEN-TRO   A charming old-fashioned shop, here since 1856 and selling fountain pens, ink, paper, postcards and maps. *Sierpes 5.* ☎ *954 226 414. MC, V. Bus: B2, C5. Map p 72.*

Music & Musical Instruments

★★ Compás Sur CENTRO   This independent music shop specializes in flamenco and Andalusian music, selling CDs, instruments and sheet music. Owner Rafael really knows his stuff and he speaks some English too. *Cuesta del Rosario 7-F.* ☎ *954 215 662. www.compas-sur.com. AE, DC, MC, V. Bus: C5. Map p 72.*

★ Guitarras de Artesanía SANTA CRUZ   One of Seville's best traditional flamenco guitar shops is, surprisingly, right in the middle of the tourist district. *Meson del Moro 12.* ☎ *954 227 898. MC, V. Bus: 1, C3, C4, 23. Map p 72.*

Record Sevilla ALAMEDA   This place could have come straight out of the movie *High Fidelity*. Used and new CDs and vinyl by the boxload and a few hippie-style clothes are on sale. They buy records and CDs too. *Amor de Dios 27.* ☎ *954 387 702. Bus: 13, 14. Map p 72.*

Optical

★ Visionlab CENTRO   National chain of glasses and contact lens specialists. If you run into problems with your glasses or lenses the helpful staff here should be able to fix you up again. *Sierpes 13.* ☎ *954 560 397. www.visionlab.es. MC, V. Bus: B2, C5. Map p 72.*

Teen Boutiques

Belmondo Bazaar ALAMEDA Stacks of T-shirts, funky bags, cards, candles and sarongs are on display in this typical Alameda boutique. *Amor de Dios 4.* ☎ *954 905 041. MC, V. Bus: 13, 14. Map p 72.*

Market Forces

Seville's markets make a very cultural shopping alternative. The main food market is on Pastor Y Landero but those at Triana (Plaza del Altozano) and Macarena (halfway along Feria) are both good, with bright fresh fruit, fish, cheese and more. All are open from 8am to 1pm daily except Sundays. One of my favorite places for browsing is the street flea market on Feria on Thursday mornings. On Sunday mornings there's a great art market featuring paintings by local artists outside the Museo de Bellas Artes (Plaza del Museo) and a small coin and stamp market in Plaza del Cabildo.

★ **Boarderking** CENTRO As you'd expect with a name like this you'll find all sorts of surfwear, bikinis, T-shirts, skater shoes and hats here. Vans, DC, Burton and Quiksilver are among the brands stocked. *Sierpes 15.* ☎ *954 293 222. www.bkdeluxe.es. MC, V. Bus: B2, C5. Map p 72.*

Shoes & Leatherware

★★★ **Camper** CENTRO Spain's coolest sneakers brand continues to offer trendy, comfortable and hard-wearing shoes for guys and girls, and they're less expensive on home territory. *Tetuán 24.* ☎ *954 222 811. www.camper.com. AE, DC,*

You never know what you'll find at the flea market.

MC, V. Bus: C5. Tram: Plaza Nueva. Map p 72.

★★ **El Caballo** ARENAL Possibly Seville's best leatherware shop, Caballo sells classic handbags, suitcases, belts, wallets and shoes. Another branch is on Plaza Nueva. *Antonia Díaz 7.* ☎ *954 229 539. AE, DC, MC, V. Bus: C5. Map p 71.*

★★★ **Pilar Burgos** CENTRO Pilar specializes in brightly colored, seriously sexy heels. He's a huge hit with the locals who love to dress flamboyantly, but will any of his colorful creations go with your wardrobe? *Tetuán 16.* ☎ *954 562 117. www. pilarburgos.com. AE, DC, MC, V. Bus: C5. Tram: Plaza Nueva. Map p 72.*

★★ **Toscana** CENTRO Flirty, even a little flashy, the handbags here are stylish and flamboyant, with an Italian edge, the kind of piece that makes a bit of a statement. *Plaza Nueva 3.* ☎ *954 564 060. AE, DC, MC, V. Bus: C5. Tram: Plaza Nueva. Map p 72.*

★★ **Uterque** CENTRO Trendy shoes, bags and jewelry for women are the order of the day here. Smart and designer-style garb which is colorful and sophisticated. Friendly service too. *Rioja 7.* ☎ *954 226 339. www.uterque.com. AE, DC, MC, V. Bus: B2, C5. Map p 72.* ●

Seville **on Two Wheels**

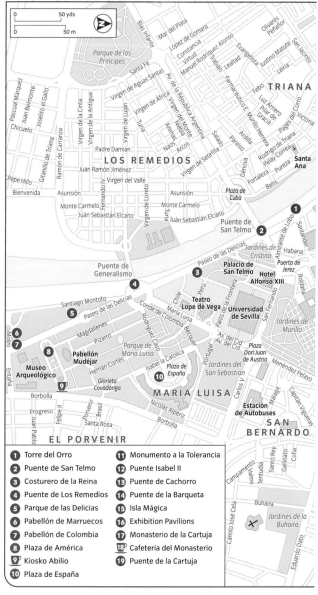

1. Torre del Orro
2. Puente de San Telmo
3. Costurero de la Reina
4. Puente de Los Remedios
5. Parque de las Delicias
6. Pabellón de Marruecos
7. Pabellón de Colombia
8. Plaza de América
9. Kiosko Abilio
10. Plaza de España
11. Monumento a la Tolerancia
12. Puente Isabel II
13. Puente de Cachorro
14. Puente de la Barqueta
15. Isla Mágica
16. Exhibition Pavilions
17. Monasterio de la Cartuja
18. Cafetería del Monasterio
19. Puente de la Cartuja

Previous page: Frog ornaments in Parque María Luisa.

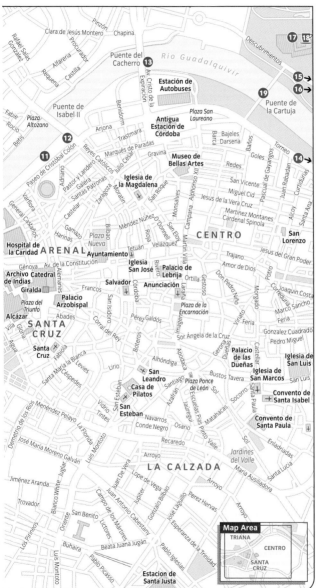

Seville is embracing the bicycle in a big way. There's a well-organized network of cycle paths and a city-wide bicycle loan program which tourists can use too. Hopping into the saddle for a pedal is a great way to see more of Parque María Luisa and to enjoy the riverbank with its imposing bridges, the Cartuja monastery and the pavilions (*pabellones*) built for the 1992 Exposition. This easy 10km (6 miles) ride is completely on the flat. See the section in Savvy Traveler for bike hire and using Sevici, the city bike loan scheme (p 163). START: **Torre del Orro.**

① ★★★ **Torre del Orro.** Start your cycle tour at this tower, one of the city's best-known landmarks (p 17, **②**). Cycle up the slope to the bridge and join the main green cycle path. Seville has a chronic traffic problem and the council is encouraging bike use as much as possible. This path is part of a 77km-long (48 miles), eight-route network.

② **Puente de San Telmo (San Telmo Bridge).** The main road route into Triana across the river takes its name from the Palacio de San Telmo (p 89, **①**), which you can clearly see on the left across the road. The palace once belonged to the Dukes of Montpensier, along with a huge garden. Part of it was donated to the city in 1893 by Princess María Luisa and became a park named after her—Parque María Luisa.

③ ★★ **Costurero de la Reina.** Continuing along the cycle lane you come to the next rotary (roundabout). Across the road, the turreted

building with striped brickwork is known as the Costurero de la Reina (the Queen's Sewing Box). It was a garden lodge which Princess María Luisa liked to visit when this area was part of the gardens of the Palacio de San Telmo. It's now a municipal tourist office housing a free multimedia exhibition on the park's creation and history (p 89). The modernist statue in the middle of the roundabout is the *Glorietta de los Marineros*—a monument to sailors who discovered the New World.

④ **Puente de Los Remedios.** The next bridge you pass is named after the district to which it leads. Los Remedios ('the remedies'), a rather uninspiring area of high-rise apartments, takes its name from a Carmelite convent that once stood there. Until 1964 the bridge could be raised to allow ships to pass.

⑤ **Parque de las Delicias.** Take a right off the cycle lane past the domed Conservatorio Professional

Cycling is increasingly popular with locals.

de Danza (dance academy), previously the Argentina Pavilion for the 1929 Exposition, into this attractive park with several pretty fountains, shady trees and flowery shrubs. It's one of the best tended parts of Parque María Luisa, perhaps because the parks office is situated here: a welcoming spot to lie in the shade for a while. Exit by the gate toward the rear of the park. It may be closed, but it's usually not locked. If it is, backtrack and exit back onto the main cycle path about halfway through the park.

The mosque-like Pabellón de Marruecos.

6 Pabellón de Marruecos and **7 Pabellón de Colombia.** These two pavilions from the 1929 Exposition reflect their cultures. The white-turreted, mosque-like Moroccan pavilion houses more parks offices; the ornately decorated Colombian one is the Colombian consulate. Cross the main road using the pedestrian crossing opposite the Colombia pavilion. Directly opposite is the Pabellón de Brazil. Very different in style, it echoes the Brazilian vogue at the time for modernism. Just to the right is the Pabellón de México.

8 ★★★ Plaza de América. At the far end of Parque María Luisa, the Plaza de América houses two extraordinarily ornate buildings. Facing each other, they are both museums: the Gothic Museo Arqueológico and the neo-Mudéjar Museo de Artes y Costumbres Populares. *See p 91.*

9 Kiosko Abilio. This tapas bar serves tasty montaditos (small rolls with cheese and other fillings) and cool beers. One barman here is a real character—he sometimes sings the orders. *Parque María Luisa, s/n. no phone. 9am–4pm, 8pm–midnight daily. $.* If you want to slurp on the move, continue a little further and pick up a granita crushed-ice drink from one of the booths dotted

around the park. I find lemon is the most refreshing.

10 ★★★ Plaza de España. The high point of the 1929 Exposition, Spain's pavilion is by far the grandest (p 90). Cycle round the main fountain in the middle, dedicated to the man who designed the Plaza de España, Aníbal González (1876–1929)—Seville's most famous architect. Cycle back into the park and straight down Avenida Rodríguez Caso, exiting the park back at the roundabout with the Glorietta de los Marineros. Cross the road back to the main cycle path and continue back the way you came to the Torre del Oro.

11 Monumento a la Tolerancia. Continue past Torre del Oro and the cruise boats along the riverside. You'll see this striking U-shaped monument to the 'universal message of tolerance' by Basque-born sculptor Eduardo Chillida (1924–2002) on the left, close to the next bridge.

12 ★ Puente Isabel II. Often referred to as the Puente de Triana, Seville's first permanent river crossing wasn't built until 1854 (p 60). Previously a pontoon bridge of boats was used—a practical solution because the Guadalquivir river often flooded. Immediately after the bridge, turn left off the cycle path through the shady Jardines de Chapina, keeping an eye out for pedestrians. On exiting the gardens, turn left and continue along the riverbank.

⑬ Puente de Cachorro. You cycle under this bridge with its unusual canopied structure. It's named after one of Seville's most venerated carvings, showing the death of Christ, which is in a church—the Capilla del Patrocinio—just across the river. Shortly after this bridge the sidewalk and road bear right, but you should keep straight on along the riverbank for a pleasant 3km (2 miles) under two more bridges. Look out for artistic graffiti on the walls to the right. Continue on to the next bridge (the bow-shaped Puente de la Barqueta) and immediately after it turn right onto the slope and continue back up to road level to cross it.

⑭ ★★★ Puente de la Barqueta. Five new bridges were built across the river for Seville's great 1992 Expo (see ⑯ below) The Barqueta bridge, which you are crossing now, is in itself a remarkable piece of

The sparkling fountains at Plaza de España

engineering, but it's the harp-shaped Alamillo Bridge just upriver, designed by one of modern Spain's foremost architects, Santiago Calatrava (b. 1951), that is the largest and most striking. Its towering pylon is 142m high and supports a 200m span with 13 pairs of cables.

⑮ ★★ kids Isla Mágica. Seville's theme park uses the city's golden age of New World exploration as its theme. It's built on land developed for the 1992 Expo. Its eight zones include Sevilla Port of the Indies, Amazonia, Pirates' Lair and El Dorado. The biggest thrills are the Jaguar roller coaster and the Anaconda log flume. *Pabellón de España, Isla de la Cartuja.* ☎ *902 161 716. See p 44.* Take the road to the left of the theme park.

⑯ Exhibition Pavilions. Expo 92, Seville's great 1992 exposition, took place from April 20 to October 12, 1992. The theme was The Age of Discovery. Over 42 million people visited the event over six months. Its legacy was less impressive. The city was left with debts of 360 million euros and many of the Expo buildings now lie forlorn and dilapidated. On the left are the curvaceous lines of the Pabellón del Futuro. Turn left after the small bridge onto the green cycle lane. Further along on the left you pass a huge model of the European Saturn 5 space rocket. One of the pavilions is now the local concert hall—the vast Auditorio Municipal. It holds 6,000 people and is the largest open-air concert hall in Europe.

⑰ ★★ Monasterio de la Cartuja. You pass the rear entrance to this monastery on your right. Continue round to the front entrance, keeping the gated gardens on your right. Home to Carthusian monks from the 15th century, the monastery fell on hard times in the 19th

The stylish curves of the Barqueta Bridge.

irrigation channels, so you might like to lock up your bike and stroll around. The monastery also houses the Centro Andaluz de Arte Contemporáneo in the old cloisters, which make an unusual setting for its calendar of eclectic exhibitions by international artists. *Avda Américo Vespucio 2.* ☎ *955 037 070. www. caac.es. See p 28.*

18 **Cafetería del Monasterio.** The cafeteria here has an attractive location in a quiet courtyard and the tostadas (toasted bread with toppings like serrano ham and local cheese) go well with a coffee. Service can be a bit haphazard. *Monasterio de la Cartuja.* ☎ *954 460 426. 8am–8pm.*

19 **Puente de la Cartuja.** Double back to the bridge opposite the rear of the monastery and cross the river. The Puente de la Cartuja is the world's most slender bridge, according to the *Guinness Book of Records*. Rejoin the green cycle path on Tourneo, turning right. Leave the cycle path at the next road, turning right back down to the riverside. Turn left on the sidewalk back along the river, and continue back through the Jardines de Chapina and return to the Torre del Oro.

century. It was bought by a British industrialist, Charles Pickman. He built a ceramics factory here and continued producing pottery until 1980. The monastery was originally built by the Archbishop of Seville, Gonzalo de Mena, after locals saw a vision of the Virgin over a nearby pottery. Columbus also stayed here before he set out for the Americas. There's a statue of him in the grounds. The old monastery buildings retain few original features, but the refectory has an ornate vaulted, carved ceiling and the Capítulo de Monjes (monks' chapterhouse) has had the tombs of the monastery patrons replaced in it. The tranquil gardens are full of fruit trees and

Get on Two Wheels

Non-residents can now use Seville's urban bike-loan scheme, called Sevici. You just need a Visa or MasterCard. Follow the instructions (in English as well as Spanish) on the booths beside the many designated bike-park points. The first 30 minutes are free. Several companies also offer bike hire and will deliver bikes to your hotel and pick them up again. If you want a bike for several days their rates are usually cheaper. Local operator rentabikesevilla.com (☎ 619 461 491) is recommended. (See the Savvy Traveler section for more about bike hire and Sevici.)

Parks & Pavilions

The Great Outdoors

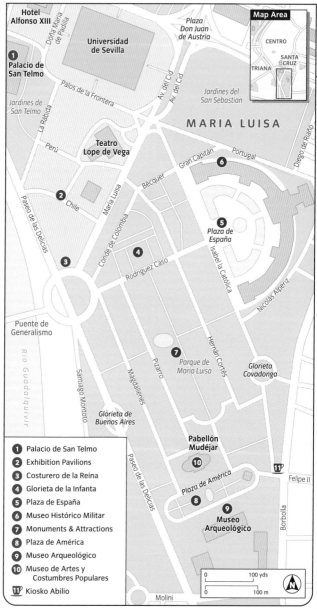

1 Palacio de San Telmo
2 Exhibition Pavilions
3 Costurero de la Reina
4 Glorieta de la Infanta
5 Plaza de España
6 Museo Histórico Militar
7 Monuments & Attractions
8 Plaza de América
9 Museo Arqueológico
10 Museo de Artes y
    Costumbres Populares
🍴 Kiosko Abilio

Seville's largest park is a shady respite from the heat of the sun. It was also the site for the great Ibero-American Exposition which Seville hosted in 1929. The pavilions built for it—in particular the mighty crescent of buildings known as the Plaza de España—are some of the city's most arresting sights, and three house interesting museums. The park is also perfect for kids to let off steam. START: **Bus: AC, B2, C4, 5, 21, 22, 23. Tram: Universidad.**

❶ Palacio de San Telmo. After Europe's first school of navigation was founded in Seville in the 16th century by its chief navigator, Amérigo Vespucci, this establishment continued the tradition. Built in 1682 and named after the patron saint of navigators, it originally served as a university for sailors. In 1843 the Palacio, along with a huge garden, became the residence of the Dukes of Montpensier. Today it's an Andalu-sian government building, undergo-ing renovation at the time of writing. Once completed there will be a per-manent exhibition about the build-ing's history. You can still admire statues of Sevillian celebrities along the roof on Palos de la Frontera— among them Murillo and Velázquez. Their names are inscribed beneath each statue. On Avenida de Roma there's an ornate baroque portal in the Churrigueresque style (p 171), featuring St. Telmo holding a ship and flanked by two saints.

Ornate carvings on the Palacio de San Telmo.

❷ ★ Exhibition Pavilions. Each of the participating nations in the 1929 Exposition had its own pavilion

The 1929 Exposition

The 1929 Ibero-American Exposition, known as the Expo, took place in Seville from May 9, 1929 to June 21, 1930. Participating nations included Argentina, Brazil, Mexico, Chile, Cuba, Peru and Colombia, plus other countries with trade associations with Spain, including Morocco, the U.S. and Portugal. The Expo was intended to boost Andalusia's struggling economy, but the timing could not have been worse. The Wall Street Crash took place soon after it opened and the city was left in debt for the next half-century. Architecturally and culturally, the legacy was more successful. The park's avenues and the pavilion buildings were all created for the Expo.

(*pabellón*). Most are now university buildings or embassies—later in this tour I'll take you inside two of them. As you walk down Avenida de Chile you'll see the Pabellón de Chile (now the School of Applied Arts) and the Pabellón de Uruguay (now the university administration building) on the right, and the Pabellón de Peru (now the Donaña Biological Institute) with its Inca-style carved facade and teak window balconies.

3 ★ Costurero de la Reina (Queen's Sewing Box). The Palacio de San Telmo's huge gardens included this garden lodge, with its colorful striped brickwork, which Princess Maria Luisa, the Duchess of Montpensier, liked to visit. It's now a town tourist office, housing somewhat temperamental multimedia shows about the park's history and the 1929 Exposition. There are handy free brochures detailing themed walks in the park too. ⏱ 15 *min. Paseo de las Delicias 9.* ☎ *954 234 465. Free. Mon–Fri 8:30am–9:30pm, weekends 9:30am–2:30pm.*

4 Glorieta de la Infanta (Monument to the Princess). In 1893 Princess María Luisa donated a large

The Costurero de la Reina is known as the Queen's Sewing Box.

The Pabellón de Peru.

part of the Palacio de San Telmo gardens to the city as a park. Parque María Luisa was laid out by the French landscape designer Jean-Claude Forestier (1861–1930), director of the Bois de Boulogne in Paris. This contemplative bronze statue honors María Luisa as the benefactress of the park.

5 ★★★ Plaza de España. The park was the perfect place to host the 1929 Exposition and the pavilions were all built in or around it. Seville's pavilion needed to be star of the show so the Plaza de España was created as the boldest of statements. Designed by Aníbal González, Seville's foremost 20th-century architect, it's a feast of Mudéjar-style curves and towers. The plaza was used as a backdrop to one of the *Star Wars* movies. Each region of Spain is depicted with a tiled panel along the walls. González insisted on supervising the works to make sure they conformed to his specifications. The result is spectacular. Be wary of the sun here, there's little shade and on bright days it's easy to get sunburned.

6 ★ Museo Histórico Militar (Military Museum). Tucked away inside the colonnade of the Plaza de España, this place will delight military buffs and boys of all ages. It houses an exhaustive array of uniforms, and weapons from swords to torpedoes, collected during Spanish conflicts down the ages, meticulously laid out and labeled. My one disappointment: I couldn't find the gas mask specially designed for a horse! 🕐 *30 min. Plaza de España. ☎ 954 938 283. Free. Tues–Sat 10am–1:30pm, closed Sun & Mon.*

7 ★★★ kids Monuments & Attractions. Walk back into the park the way you came out. Just to the left there's usually a booth where you can hire bicycles and four-person pedal carts, which are great fun. Guided audio tours are also available. There are monuments dotted all around the park too, which kids will enjoy. In the center there's a lake with a gazebo (the Isleta de los Patos or Islet of the Ducks) and further left the Fuente de los Leones (Lions' Fountain) is guarded by ceramic statues of lions. Its design was inspired by the fountain in the Patio de Los Leones in the Alhambra in Granada. A little further on is Monte Gurugu, a rather quirky mini-mountain with a waterfall which kids will enjoy climbing up. *Cycle karts. ☎ 663 811 043.*

www.cyclotouristic.com. From 7€ for 30 min.

8 ★★★ Plaza de América. Three more architecturally impressive exhibition pavilions designed by Aníbal González grace the far side of the park. The Renaissance-style Pabellón Real is now a municipal employment office. The Gothic-style Pabellón de Bellas Artes houses the city's Archeological Museum, and the Mudéjar-style Pabellón Mudéjar contains the Museum of Folk Arts. Details of the museums follow.

9 ★★ kids Museo Arqueológico. This good old-fashioned museum full of exhibits in glass cases is a reminder that you don't need audiovisual wizardry to keep people's attention—just well-displayed finds. Most rooms have introductions in English and there's an English brochure too. The 27 rooms are arranged chronologically, starting in the basement with coverage from Paleolithic Spain through to the beginning of the Roman occupation. Exhibits include Copper Age idols thought to be the oldest representations of divinity in Spain, and copies of the Carambolo treasures, a hoard of 6th-century gold jewelry discovered near Seville in 1958. But the real delight is the Roman galleries on the ground floor. There are several superbly preserved mosaics, in particular the Triumph of Bacchus,

The Museo de Artes y Costumbres Populares.

depicting the god of wine being pulled in a chariot by two tigers, in room 13. Room 20 is an immense oval gallery stuffed with statues—a roll call of some of the greatest Romans, including Trajan, Augustus, Hadrian and Vespasian. Many of the statues and fragments were rescued from nearby Itálica (p 146). The rooms follow on with artifacts from Moorish Spain and Visigoth relics discovered in Córdoba. ⏱ *1 hr. Plaza de América, Parque María Luisa.* ☎ *954 786 474. 1.50€; free for E.U. passport holders. Tues–Sat 9am–8:30pm, Sun & holidays 9am–2:30pm.*

The Gothic exterior of the Museo Arqueológico.

⑩ kids Museo de Artes y Costumbres Populares. Located in the playfully exuberant Mudéjar Pavilion, this museum is devoted to the arts and traditions of Andalusia. Displays include workshop scenes showing local crafts such as leatherwork and ironmongery, and ceramics through the ages—such as finely painted vases from nearby Cartuja. (p 74) The upper floor was being renovated at the time of writing. The displays generally feel a little dated and disorganized, but kids who like exploring will enjoy it. Descriptions are in Spanish, but there's a free brochure in English. ⏱ *1 hr. Pabellón Mudéjar, Parque María Luisa.* ☎ *954 712 391. 1.50€; free for E.U. passport holders.*

Tues–Sat 9am–8:30pm, Sun & holidays 9am–2:30pm.

⑪ Kiosko Abilio. This is a typical tapas bar that serves tasty montaditos (small rolls filled with ham etc.) and cool beers. One barman I've seen here is a real character—he sometimes sings the orders. *Parque María Luisa. No phone. $.* ●

Ornaments and fountains are found all around the park.

Dining Best Bets

Best Classic Tapas
★★★ Casa Morales $ *Garcia de Vinnesa 11 (p 108)*

Best Designer Tapas
★★★ Jano $ *Doña María Coronel 17 (p 109)*

Best Luxury Tapas
★★★ Bar Europa $ *Alameda de Hércules 22 (p 109)*

Best Gourmet Lunch Deal
★★★ Taberna del Alabardero $$ *Zaragoza 20 (p 106)*

Best Wine List
★★★ Enrique Becerra $$ *Gamazo 2 (p 101)* and ★★★ Becerrita $$ *Recaredo 9 (p 100)*

Best Home-Cooked Italian
★★★ Porta Rossa $$ *Arenal 5 (p 105)*

Best Gourmet Dining
★★★ Abantal $$$ *Alcalde José de la Bandera 7 (p 99)* and ★★★ Gastromium $$$ *Ramon Carande 12 (p 102)*

Best Service
★★★ Az-Zait $$ *Plaza de San Lorenzo 1 (p 101)*

Best Hole-in-the-Wall Pizzeria
★★★ La Mia Tana $ *Pérez Galdós 24 (p 103)*

Best Seafood
★★ La Isla $$$ *Arfe 25 (p 102)* and ★★★ Barbiana $$ *Albareda 11 (p 100)*

Best Modern Andalusian
★★★ Salvador Rojo $$ *San Fernando 23 (p 106)* and ★★★ San Fernando 27 $$$ *San Fernando 27 (p 101)*

Best Dessert
★★ Casa Robles $$$ *Álvarez Quintero 58 (p 100)*

Amazing desserts at Casa Robles.

Best Neighborhood Restaurant
★★ Eslava $$ *Eslava 35 (p 101)*

Best Vegetarian
★★ Almanara $ *Alameda de Hércules 85 (p 99)* and ★★ La Habanita $ *Golfo 3 (p 102)*

Best for Romance
★★★ Egaña-Oriza $$$ *San Fernando 41 (p 101)*

Best Family Dining
★★ Al Solito Posto $ *Cuesta del Rosario 15 (p 99)*

Best Coffee & Cake
★★★ Horno de San Buenaventura $ *Avda de la Constitución 16 (p 103)*

Best Burger
★ Foster's Hollywood $ *Plaza de Armas (p 101)*

Best Tagine
★★ As Sawirah $$ *Galera 5 (p 99)*

Best Tex/Mex
★ Texas Lone Star Saloon $ *Placentines 25 (p 106)*

Previous page: Classic tapas at El Rinconcillo.

Alameda Dining

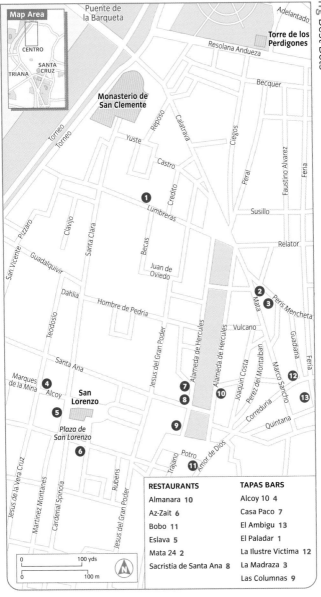

RESTAURANTS

Almanara **10**
Az-Zait **6**
Bobo **11**
Eslava **5**
Mata 24 **2**
Sacristía de Santa Ana **8**

TAPAS BARS

Alcoy 10 **4**
Casa Paco **7**
El Ambigu **13**
El Paladar **1**
La Ilustre Victima **12**
La Madraza **3**
Las Columnas **9**

Centro, Arenal & Santa Cruz

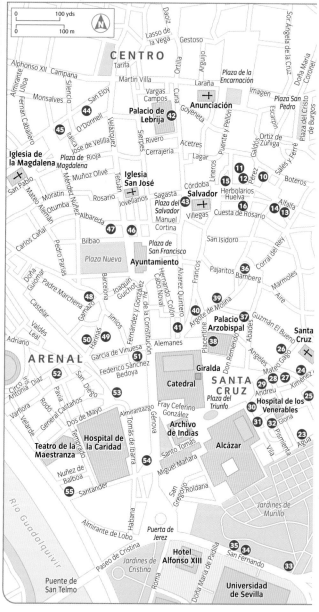

CENTRO

ARENAL

SANTA CRUZ

Iglesia de la Magdalena

Iglesia San José

Palacio de Lebrija

Anunciación

Salvador

Plaza de la Encarnación

Plaza San Pedro

Ayuntamiento

Plaza Nueva

Plaza de San Francisco

Palacio Arzobispal

Santa Cruz

Giralda

Catedral

Archivo de Indias

Alcázar

Hospital de los Venerables

Plaza del Triunfo

Teatro de la Maestranza

Hospital de la Caridad

Río Guadalquivir

Puente de San Telmo

Puerta de Jerez

Hotel Alfonso XIII

Jardines de Cristina

Jardines de Murillo

Universidad de Sevilla

Dining

Fernando 27 **34**
Gastromium **20**
La Albahaca **22**
La Alicantina **43**
La Cueva **31**
La Habanita **11**
La Isla **53**
La Juderia **17**
La Mia Tana **12**
La Nieta de Pepa **30**
La Raza **21**
Luis Barceló **2**
Maccheroni **49**
Mesón Don Raimundo **39**
Modesto **19**
Pozo Luna **50**
Restaurante Horacio **52**
Robles Placentines **40**
Salvador Rojo **35**
San Marco **42**
San Marco Pizzeria **27**
Texas Lone Star Saloon **38**

TAPAS BARS

Ajo Blanco **7**
Bar Alfalfa **13**
Bar Las Teresas **25**
Bodega Belmonte **28**
Bodega Góngora **46**
Casablanca **54**
Casa Carmelo **32**
Casa Morales **51**
Casa Placido **24**
El Rinconcillo **5**
Estrella **36**
Europa **15**
Jano **1**
La Alacena de San Eloy **45**
La Bodega **14**
La Cava del Europa **18**
La Fresquita **26**
La Giganta **6**
La Huerta Mediterránea **3**
Las Columnas **29**
Los Caracoles **10**
Patio San Eloy **44**
Taberna los Terceros **4**

RESTAURANTS

Abantal **9**
Al Solito Posto **16**
Azúcar de Cuba **55**
Barbiana **47**
Becerrita **8**
Casa Robles **41**
Duplex **37**
Egaña-Oriza **33**
El Corral Del Agua **23**
Enrique Becerra **48**

Triana & Lower Arenal Dining

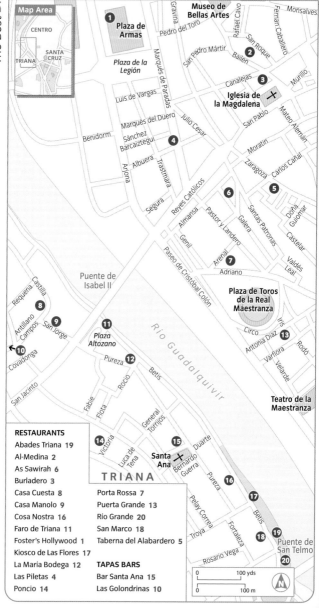

Map Area

CENTRO

SANTA CRUZ

TRIANA

1 Plaza de Armas

Museo de Bellas Artes

Plaza de la Legión

Gravina

Pedro del Toro

San Pedro Mártir

Rafael Cavo

Fernán Caballero

Monsalves

San Roque

Bailén

2

Canalejas

3

Iglesia de la Magdalena

Murillo

Mateo Alemán

San Pablo

Carlos Cañal

Zaragoza

Moratín

Luis de Vargas

Marqués del Duero

Sánchez Barcáiztegui

4

Julio César

San Pablo

Benidorm

Arjona

Albuera

Trastmara

Segura

Reyes Católicos

Almansa

Pastor y Landero

Genil

Galera

Santas Patronas

Doña Guiomar

Castelar

Valdés Leal

6

5

Arenal

7

Adriano

Plaza de Toros de la Real Maestranza

Puente de Isabel II

Requena

Castilla

Antillano Campos

San Jorge

8

9

Covadonga

10

San Jacinto

Plaza Altozano

11

Pureza

12

Rocío

Betis

Río Guadalquivir

Circo

Antonia Díaz

Iris

Rodó

Varflora

Velarde

13

Teatro de la Maestranza

Fabié

Flota

General Torrijos

Victoria

14

Luca de Tena

Santa Ana

15

Bernardo Guerra

Duarte

Pureza

16

Betis

17

Pelay Correa

Troya

Fortaleza

Rosario Vega

18

19

Puente de San Telmo

20

TRIANA

RESTAURANTS

Abades Triana 19
Al-Medina 2
As Sawirah 6
Burladero 3
Casa Cuesta 8
Casa Manolo 9
Cosa Nostra 16
Faro de Triana 11
Foster's Hollywood 1
Kiosco de Las Flores 17
La Maria Bodega 12
Las Piletas 4
Poncio 14

Porta Rossa 7
Puerta Grande 13
Rio Grande 20
San Marco 18
Taberna del Alabardero 5

TAPAS BARS

Bar Santa Ana 15
Las Golondrinas 10

0   100 yds

0   100 m

Seville Restaurants **A to Z**

★★★ **Abades Triana** TRIANA
MODERN/CREATIVE Upscale dining in an airy space with fantastic views across the river. Executive chef Oscar Fernandez serves creative cuisine using local produce. Dishes like cod confit with honeyed asparagus don't come cheap, but are worth it for a special occasion. *Betis 69A.* ☎ *954 286 459. www.abadestriana.com. Entrees 24€–28€. AE, MC, V. Lunch & dinner daily. Closed Mon & Sun eve. Bus: B2, C3, 5, 42. Map p 98.*

★★★ **Abantal** CENTRO *MODERN/ CREATIVE* Michelin-starred chef Julio Fernandez lets his immaculate cuisine speak for itself. My red tuna with peach jus and grilled figs was just mouthwatering. Reservations essential. A little way from the center—so book a taxi. *Alcalde José de la Bandera 7.* ☎ *954 540 000. www. abantalerestaurante.es. Entrees 23€–26€. AE, MC, V. Lunch & dinner daily. Closed Mon. Bus: C3, C4, 24, 27. Map p 96.*

★★ **kids Al Solito Posto** CENTRO *ITALIAN* This modern, good-value Italian restaurant is rightly popular with locals. The usual pizza and pasta dishes are well prepared and service is friendly too. *Cuesta del Rosario 15.* ☎ *954 220 917. Entrees 8€–12€. AE, DC, MC, V. Lunch & dinner Mon–Sat. Closed Aug. Bus: C5. Map p 96.*

★★ **Almanara** ALAMEDA *VEGETAR-IAN* A relative newcomer, this little eatery on the Alameda is totally veggie—pretty unique for Seville—serving a wide range of tapas dishes along with salads and juices in a white funky space. *Alameda de Hércules 85.* ☎ *954 372 897. Entrees 3€–5€. Dinner daily. Closed Mon. Bus: B2, 13, 14. Map p 95.*

★★ **Al-Medina** ARENAL *MOROC-CAN* This reasonably priced Moroccan place serves the usual favorites in a classically Moorish setting. I really enjoyed the lamb tajine, but the veggie couscous was a bit disappointing. Good-value set menu. *San Roque 13.* ☎ *954 215 451. www. restaurantealmedina.com. Entrees 11€–17€. AE, DC, MC, V. Closed Sun eve & Mon. Bus: C5. Map p 98.*

★★ **As Sawirah** ARENAL *MOROC-CAN* Probably the best North African restaurant in town, this place offers tasty tagines and couscous in an attractive courtyard setting suitably decorated with old lamps and terracotta red walls. Good-value tasting menu at 19.90€ too. *Galera 5.* ☎ *954 562 268. Entrees 12€–15€. MC, V. Lunch & dinner daily. Closed Mon & Sun eve. Bus: C5, 40, 43. Map p 98.*

★ **Azúcar de Cuba** CENTRO *CUBAN* The place in Seville for authentic Cuban atmosphere, food and cocktails. Daily menus include dishes like yucca and fried rice. Then there's *mojitos*, and *cubanitos* cigars, so it may be smoky. *Paseo de las*

Beautiful dining spaces at Becerrita.

Delicias 3. ☎ 954 228 668. www. azucardecuba.com. Set menu 32.50€. Lunch & dinner Tues–Sun. Dinner only June–Aug. Bus: B2, C4. Map p 96.

★★★ **Az-Zait** ALAMEDA *ANDALUSIAN/MOZARABE* This romantic, intimate restaurant offers really tasty, imaginative Andalusian dishes with a Moorish twist. The chef is the owner and service is excellent. Recommended. *Plaza de San Lorenzo 1.* ☎ 954 906 475. Entrees 10€–18€. Lunch & dinner Mon–Sat. Closed Aug. Bus: B2, 13, 14. Map p 95.

★★★ **Barbiana** CENTRO *SEAFOOD* This is one of Seville's best seafood restaurants and shellfish is a specialty. Quieter at dinner time; it's often packed out for lunch. *Albareda 11.* ☎ 954 224 402. Entrees 9€–20€. AE, DC, MC, V. Lunch & dinner Mon–Sat. Dinner Sun. Bus: 21, 25, 30, 40, C5. Tram: Plaza Nueva. Map p 96.

★★ **Becerrita** CENTRO *ANDALUSIAN* A family-run restaurant with a modern edge, and classic Sevillian dishes with imaginative twists. Great service and a wine list that runs to 80 pages. *Recaredo 9.* ☎ 954 412 057. Entrees 12€–25€. AE, DC, MC, V. Lunch & dinner Mon–Sat. Lunch Sun. Bus: 1, C3, C4. Map p 96.

Bobo ALAMEDA *INTERNATIONAL* A funky corner restaurant overlooking the Alameda, Bobo offers fresh salads and tasty meals like chicken crepe with goats' cheese. A good selection for veggies too. *Amor de Dios 47.* ☎ 954 909 679. Entrees 6€–9€. MC, V. Lunch & dinner daily. Closed Mon & Sun eve. Bus: B2, 13, 14. Map p 95.

★★ **Burladero** ARENAL *MODERN/CREATIVE* Overseen by two-Michelin-starred Dani Garcia, this famous eatery has had a makeover to create a stylish gastro-bar, serving haute-cuisine tapas and *raciónes*. Cheap eats these aren't—but memorable dining is assured.

Canalejas 1. ☎ 954 507 862. Entrees 9€–12€. AE, DC, MC, V. Lunch & dinner daily. Bus:C5, 40, 43. Map p 98.

★★★ **Casa Cuesta** TRIANA *SPANISH* Across the river in the heart of the pottery district, this offers no-nonsense, good-value Spanish dishes and really tasty tapas in authentic surroundings with few other tourists. *Castilla 1.* ☎ 954 333 335. Entrees 10€–15€. DC, MC, V. Lunch & dinner daily. Bus: 43, C3, B2. Map p 98.

★★★ **Casa Manolo** TRIANA *ANDALUSIAN* A local eatery, with simple decor and unpretentious food. Owner Manolo attracts a diverse crowd of locals with his good selection of meat and fish dishes. *San Jorge 16.* ☎ 954 333 208. Entrees 6€–12€. AE, DC, MC, V. Lunch & dinner daily. Closed Mon. Bus: B2, C3, 43. Map p 98.

★★ **Casa Robles** CENTRO *ANDALUSIAN* Arguably the best-known restaurant in town. Service is very good and food (particularly the ham) is excellent—if pricey. Laura Robles has created her own line of fabulously indulgent desserts and they're a real highlight. *Álvarez Quintero 58.* ☎ 954 563 272. Entrees 18€–28€. AE, DC, MC, V. Lunch & dinner daily. Bus: C5. Map p 96.

Intimate dining rooms at Casa Robles.

★ **Cosa Nostra** TRIANA *ITALIAN*
The Cosa serves typical Italian dishes in a bright, airy space on busy Calle Betis. It's fine for a pizza, and pasta dishes and antipasti are both good. *Betis 52.* ☎ *954 270 752. Pizza 8€. Entrees 9.50€–15€. Open daily. AE, DC, MC, V. Bus: C3. Map p 98.*

★★ **Duplex** SANTA CRUZ *INTERNATIONAL* This hip, friendly bistro serves tapas, couscous, club sandwiches, burgers and more. They also do great-value lunch deals. *Don Remondo 1.* ☎ *954 214 741. Five set lunches 8€–12.50€. Mixed tapas 8€. AE, DC, MC, V. Lunch & dinner daily. Bus: C5. Map p 96.*

Duplex does great-value lunches.

★★★ **Egaña-Oriza** SANTA CRUZ *BASQUE* One of Seville's top-end eateries, with prices to match. The setting here in a mansion overlooking the Murillo Gardens is delightful. Recommended for game dishes. *San Fernando 41.* ☎ *954 227 211. Entrees 20€–30€. AE, DC, MC, V. Lunch & dinner Mon–Fri. Dinner Sat. Closed Sat July/Aug. Bus: C3, C4, 21, 23. Tram: Prado de San Sebastian. Map p 96.*

★ **El Corral Del Agua** SANTA CRUZ *ANDALUSIAN* The Corral has a romantic setting in a converted 18th-century palace patio. Food isn't exceptional, but it's good value and service is friendly. *Callejón del Agua 6.* ☎ *954 224 841. Entrees 15€–18€. AE, DC, MC, V. Lunch & dinner Mon–Sat. Bus: 1, C3, C4, 23. Map p 96.*

★★★ **Enrique Becerra** ARENAL *ANDALUSIAN* Enrique serves traditional dishes with innovative flourishes, using the freshest ingredients. Dining rooms are intimate and relaxed and his wine cellar is well stocked, particularly with sherries. Tapas in the bar here are also excellent. *Gamazo 2.* ☎ *954 213 049. www.enriquebecerra.com. Entrees 12€–22€. AE, DC, MC, V. Lunch & dinner Mon–Sat. Closed Aug. Bus: 21, 25, 30, 40. Map p 96.*

★★ **Eslava** ALAMEDA *ANDALUSIAN/CREATIVE* This small neighborhood dining room next to one of Seville's most popular tapas bars serves simple, well-presented dishes. It's usually less crowded at lunchtime and the *menu del día* (menu of the day) is great value. *Eslava 3–5.* ☎ *954 906 568. Entrees 8€. Lunch & dinner Tues–Sat. Lunch Sun. Closed Mon & Aug. AE, DC, MC, V. Bus: B2, 13, 14. Map p 95.*

★★ **Faro de Triana** TRIANA *ANDALUSIAN* Simple, fresh and reasonably priced food, combined with great views across the river to the city, make for a very pleasant meal at the Faro. *Puente de Isabel II.* ☎ *954 336 192. Entrees 5€–12€. DC, MC, V. Lunch & dinner daily. Closed Mon. Bus: B2, C3, 43. Map p 98.*

★★★ **Fernando 27** CENTRO *ANDALUSIAN/CREATIVE* This is a good one for foodies: high-end modern Andalusian dining—like red snapper with fresh pasta squid ink and lobster bisque. There's a nice terrace too. *San Fernando 27.* ☎ *954 220 966. Entrees 10€–24€. Lunch & dinner daily. Closed Sun & Aug. AE, DC, MC, V. Tram: Universidad. Map p 96.*

★ **Foster's Hollywood** ARENAL *AMERICAN* From the booth seating to the salt shakers you'll feel like you're in the U.S.A. at Foster's. And it's a pretty good imitation, with great giant hamburgers, nachos and chicken wings. Leave room for dessert! *Plaza de Armas, upper level.* ☎ *954 906 078. www.fosters hollywood.es. Entrees 7€–10€. Lunch & dinner daily. AE, MC, V. Bus: B2, C3, B5, 6. Map p 98.*

★★★ **Gastromium** CENTRO *MODERN/CREATIVE* This place's cool, dark interior is the perfect setting for adventurous dishes like cod tempura in cider reduction and wild leaf salad. Tasting menus and tapas at lunchtime. I bet chef Miguel Diaz gets himself a Michelin star soon. Reservations essential. *Ramon Carande 12.* ☎ *954 625 555. www.gastromium.com. Entrees 20€–30€. AE, MC, V. Lunch & dinner daily. Closed Mon & Sun eve. Bus: 31. Map p 96.*

Kiosco de Las Flores TRIANA *SEAFOOD* Idyllically placed on the riverside with a shady terrace. Seafood dishes are good here, but unfortunately when I visited the staff were plain rude. *Cl Betis, s/n.* ☎ *954 274 576. Entrees 12€–20€. MC, V. Lunch & dinner daily. Closed Sun eve & Mon. Bus: B2, C3, 5, 42. Map p 98.*

Eslava serves great tapas at the bar.

★ **La Albahaca** SANTA CRUZ *BASQUE* In an old palace on one of Seville's most unspoilt squares, this was the place for a romantic meal (and hang the expense). However, it's recently changed hands and is taking time to find its feet again. *Plaza de Santa Cruz 12.* ☎ *954 220 714. Entrees 12€–30€. AE, DC, MC, V. Lunch & dinner Mon–Sat. Bus: 1, C3, C4, 23. Map p 96.*

★★ **La Alicantina** CENTRO *ANDALUSIAN* On a bustling square, this is rightly popular for its seafood, particularly shellfish. Try the baked red king prawns. *Plaza del Salvador 2.* ☎ *954 226 122. Entrees 12€– 20€. AE, DC, MC, V. Lunch & dinner Mon–Sat. Lunch Sun. Closed Sun in Aug. Bus: C5. Map p 96.*

La Cueva SANTA CRUZ *ANDALUSIAN* This is one of the better restaurants in the heart of touristy Barrio Santa Cruz, just on Plaza de Dona Elvira. There's plenty of room inside, so it's usually easy to get a table. *Rodrigo Caro 18.* ☎ *954 213 143. Entrees 15€–18€. All cards accepted. Lunch & dinner Mon–Sat. Bus: 1, C3, C4, 23. Map p 96.*

★★ **La Habanita** CENTRO *VEGETARIAN/CUBAN* It can be hard to find, tucked down a side street off Pérez Galdós, but it's well worth the effort. Veggies will love dishes like deep-fried banana balls in tomato sauce, while meat eaters will be happy too. Menu in English; service is friendly, prices reasonable. Gluten-free food also available. *Golfo 3.* ☎ *954 220 202. Entrees 3€–7€. Lunch & dinner daily. Lunch Sun. MC, V. Bus: C5. Map p 96.*

★★ **La Isla** ARENAL *SEAFOOD* Run by a Galician family, much of its delicious seafood is brought in daily from Galicia. Regular favorites include *merluza a la primavera* (hake with young vegetables). *Arfe 25.* ☎ *954 212 631. Entrees 22€–38€.*

AE, DC, MC, V. Lunch & dinner daily. Closed Aug. Bus: C5. Map p 96.

★★ **La Judería** SANTA CRUZ *ANDALUSIAN* La Judería offers good food that's perhaps a little pricey but the service is friendly. Specialties include local baked fish and suckling lamb. They also do a great filet mignon. *Cano y Cueto 13.* ☎ 954 426 456. www.modesto restaurantes.com. *Entrees 17€–25€. AE, DC, MC, V. Lunch & dinner daily. Closed 2 weeks in Aug. Bus: 1, C3, C4, 21, 23. Map p 96.*

★ **La María Bodega** TRIANA *ARGENTINIAN* La María has been here for years, serving up savory cuts of meat, grilled to perfection. There's good seafood and South American desserts like *dulce de leche* pancakes. *Betis 12.* ☎ 954 338 461. *Entrees 9€–15€. DC, MC, V. Bus: C3. Map p 98.*

★★★ **La Mia Tana** CENTRO *ITAL-IAN/PIZZA* The best inexpensive pizza place in Seville, as the line out the door will tell you. It has only 10 or so tables so get here early (or ask for takeout). Pasta dishes, salads and vegetarian options are all good and the service really friendly. *Pérez Galdós 24.* ☎ 954 226 897. *Pizzas 6€–12€. DC, MC, V. Lunch & dinner*

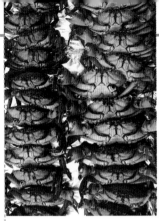

Seafood features on many Sevillian menus.

daily. Dinner only in Aug. Bus: C5. Map p 96.

★ **La Nieta de Pepa** SANTA CRUZ *ARGENTINIAN* One of the less expensive places in the middle of Santa Cruz, La Nieta does tapas as well as good steaks imported from Argentina. They have a shady section of terrace in the Plaza. *Plaza de la Alianza.* ☎ 954 560 726. *Entrees 8€–12€. No cards. Open daily. Bus: 1, C3, C4, 23. Map p 96.*

★ **La Raza** PARQUE MARÍA LUISA *ANDALUSIAN* Among the cool trees and palms of the park, Raza offers the usual steaks and seafood

Cake, Coffee, Ice Cream

Like me, Sevillians have a bit of a sweet tooth, so I couldn't write a dining section without including my favorite pastry and ice cream shops. The lovely Horno de San Buenaventura shops at Carlos Cañal 28 and Avenida da la Constitución 16 are my favorites—with gleaming counters stacked with sugary cakes and sweets. Robles Laredo (Sierpes 90) is perfect for slightly pricier, more modern indulgences, and La Campaña (Sierpes 1) remains ever popular with locals. If you're more of a tea person, the Tetería at the Baños Árabes (Aire 15) does all sorts of fragrant brews. For ice cream, Rayas (Almirante Apodaca 1) is without equal.

Dining at the bar at Las Piletas.

dishes in cool, modern surroundings. *Avda Isabel La Católica 2.* ☎ *954 232 024. Entrees 10€–25€. AE, MC, V. Breakfast, lunch & dinner daily. Bus: C2, C2, 1, 5, 34. Map p 96.*

★★ **Las Piletas** ARENAL *ANDALUSIAN* It's no surprise that this high-ceilinged shrine to everything bullfighting is good for meat lovers, with excellent grilled lamb, oxtail and steaks. *Marqués de Paradas 28.* ☎ *954 220 404. Entrees 7€–15€. AE, DC, MC, V. Breakfast, lunch & dinner daily. Bus: B2, B5. Map p 98.*

★ **Luis Barceló** MACARENA *ITALIAN* A small, friendly, family-run and -owned restaurant: he cooks, she serves the tables. It's good food that's worth paying a bit more for. *Gerona 31.* ☎ *954 223 263. Entrees 14€. MC, V. Dinner daily. Closed Mon. Bus: C5, 20, 24, 32. Map p 96.*

★★ **Maccheroni** ARENAL *ITALIAN* On a side street behind Plaza Nueva, this bright, modern Italian place is run by a family from central Italy and they pride themselves on their tiramisu. Lasagna, pizza and pasta are also good. *Harinas 13.* ☎ *954 501 015. Entrees 7€–10€. MC, V. Lunch & dinner daily. Closed Mon eve, Tues & last 2 weeks Aug. Bus: C5. Map p 96.*

★★ **Mata 24** ALAMEDA *MODERN/ CREATIVE* This modern, stylish place in Alameda gets great reviews for offerings such as scallops on *salmorejo* sauce with beetroot and potato froth. The menu is also in English. *Plaza de la Mata 24.* ☎ *954 370 586. Entrees 11€–20€. MC, V. Lunch & dinner daily. Closed Sun eve & Mon. Bus: B2, 13, 14. Map p 95.*

★★★ **Mesón Don Raimundo** SANTA CRUZ *ANDALUSIAN* Located in a lovely former convent building on a tiny side alley, the Mesón serves excellent Moorish-influenced Mozarab fare, like wild duck in sherry. Leave room for the delicious desserts. *Argote de Molina 26.* ☎ *954 223 355. www.mesondonraimundo.com. Entrees 16€–25€. DC, MC, V. Lunch & dinner daily. Bus: C5. Map p 96.*

★★ **Modesto** SANTA CRUZ *SPANISH* Good food at reasonable prices: seafood is a specialty. *Cano y Cueto 5.* ☎ *954 416 811. www.modesto restaurantes.com. Entrees 6€–20€. AE, DC, MC, V. Lunch & dinner daily. Bus: 1, C3, C4, 21, 23. Map p 96.*

★★★ **Poncio** TRIANA *ANDALUSIAN/GOURMET* Poncio's chef Willy trained in Paris, but his flavors and styles are far more daring and imaginative than standard French fare. Try, for example, carpaccio of salmon and monkfish with celery and walnut foam. *Victoria 8.* ☎ *954 340 010. Entrees 12€–24€. AE, DC, MC, V. Lunch & dinner Tues–Sat, Lunch Mon. Closed Aug. Bus: C3. Map p 98.*

★★★ **Porta Rossa** ARENAL *ITALIAN* This family-run place does truly excellent Italian cuisine—in fact it's a real favorite among my Sevillian friends. Paco in particular raves about the truffle pasta! More expensive than budget Italian places, but the quality and experience easily justify the prices. *Arenal 3.* ☎ *954 216 139. Entrees 10€–15€. MC, V. Dinner daily. Closed Sun eve, Mon, Aug. Bus: C5. Map p 98.*

★★★ **Pozo Luna** ARENAL *ANDALUSIAN/MODERN* This cool, friendly restaurant serves Andalusian dishes with creative flourishes like finely sliced veal with tarragon and sole spring rolls with dark beer sauce. Good wine list too. *Harinas 20.* ☎ *954 564 059. www.pozoluna. com. Entrees 14€–20€. MC, V. Lunch & dinner daily. Closed Wed, Sun eve July/Aug. Bus: C5 Map p 96.*

★ **Puerta Grande** ARENAL *ANDALUSIAN* A welcoming, traditional family-run restaurant serving classic, good-value Andalusian dishes. It's a stone's throw from the bullring and has an English menu. *Antonia Diaz 33.* ☎ *954 216 896. Entrees 8€–20€. MC, V. Lunch & dinner daily. Closed Sun & Aug. Dining at the bar at Las Piletas. Bus: B2, C4. Map p 98.*

★★ **Restaurante Horacio** ARENAL *ANDALUSIAN* Good service and a friendly atmosphere combine with excellent

cooking here. Favorites include *brocheta de rape con marisco* (monkfish and shellfish kebab) and excellent seafood stew. *Antonia Diaz 9.* ☎ *954 225 385. www. restaurantehoracio.com. Entrees 12€. AE, DC, MC, V. Lunch & dinner daily. Closed 2 weeks Aug. Bus: B2, C4. Map p 96.*

★★★ **Rio Grande** TRIANA *ANDALUSIAN* The best-known restaurant on this side of the river, Rio Grande offers great views of the Giralda—a perfect backdrop for tasty dishes, particularly the seafood. English is spoken here too. *Cl Betis.* ☎ *954 273 956. Entrees 15€–21€. AE, DC, MC, V. Lunch & dinner daily. Dinner only July/Aug. Bus: C3. Map p 98.*

★★ **Robles Placentines** SANTA CRUZ *ANDALUSIAN* Placentines features a similar modern Andalusian menu to famous Casa Robles—one of Seville's finest—but here you can order tapas-sized portions so it's perfect for a lighter, cheaper bite. *Placentines 2.* ☎ *954 213 162. www.casa-robles.com. Entrees 14€–24€. AE, DC, MC, V. Lunch & dinner daily. Bus: C5. Map p 96.*

★★ **Sacristia de Santa Ana** ALAMEDA *ANDALUSIAN/CREATIVE* This attractive restaurant in the hotel of the same name is well above the usual standard of eatery on the Alameda. There are some seriously creative dishes—such as sea bass with pistachios in red wine sauce. *Alameda de Hércules 22.* ☎ *954 915 722. Entrees 8€–11€. AE, DC, MC, V. Lunch & dinner daily. Closed eve Aug. Bus: B2, 13, 14. Map p 95.*

Many restaurants do good-value dishes of the day.

Putting the finishing touches to a dish in Salvador Rojo.

★★★ **Salvador Rojo** SANTA CRUZ *ANDALUSIAN* Relaxed, higher-end dining and great service are complemented with Salvador's innovative and tasty dishes. His *careen de cordero* (slices of lamb with potato puree) was perfect on my visit. *San Fernando 23.* ☎ *954 229 725. Entrees 21€–27€. AE, DC, MC, V. Lunch & dinner Mon–Sat. Closed Aug. Tram: Universidad. Map p 96.*

★★ **San Marco** CENTRO *ITALIAN* Really tasty Italian and French dishes at reasonable prices are served up in this Moorish-style 18th-century palace.There's also a branch on Calle Betis in Triana. *Cuna 6.* ☎ *954 212 440. Pasta 9€, entrees 12€–18€. AE, DC, MC, V. Lunch & dinner daily. Bus: B2, C5. Map p 96.*

★★ **San Marco** TRIANA *ITALIAN* The San Marco group's restaurant on the other side of the river copies the same well-considered formula. Good-value Italian food in a historic setting. *Betis 68.* ☎ *954 280 310. Pasta 9€, entrees 12€–18€. AE, DC, MC, V. Lunch & dinner daily. Bus: C3. Map p 98.*

★★ kids **San Marco Pizzeria** SANTA CRUZ *ITALIAN* Possibly the best of the San Marco group's settings, this one serves slightly less expensive—but very tasty—pizza and pasta dishes in an old Arab bathhouse. The mixed antipasti is a great starter for two. *Mesón del Moro 6.* ☎ *954 564 390. Pizza 6€–10€. AE, DC, MC, V. Lunch & dinner daily. Bus: 1, C3, C4, 23. Map p 96.*

★★★ **Taberna del Alabardero** ARENAL *SPANISH/CREATIVE* With its classically decorated dining rooms in a 19th-century town house, and Seville's cookery school on the premises, you're guaranteed exquisite, carefully presented food. The lunch menu offers outstanding value. *Zaragoza 20.* ☎ *954 502 721. Entrees 20€–30€. Lunch 12.90€. AE, DC, MC, V. Lunch & dinner daily. Closed Aug. Bus: C1, C5. Map p 98.*

★ **Texas Lone Star Saloon** CENTRO *TEX-MEX* This Tex-Mex Bar is owned by a director of a study-abroad program and it's authentically American. Fajitas, burritos and burgers are done well, Budweiser is on tap, and NFL games are televised on Sundays. *Placentines 25.* ☎ *954 210 334. Nachos, burritos & more 7.50€. Burgers 5€. AE, DC, MC, V. Lunch & dinner daily. Closed Mon, Tues July/Aug. Bus: C5. Map p 96.*

Tapas Bars

★ **Ajo Blanco** MACARENA This quirky little place features tacos and burritos on its menu and serves the hottest salsa in Seville. (Spaniards don't generally like spicy dishes.) The owner's a vinyl-record fan and you never know what kind of music he'll be playing. *Alhóndiga 19.* ☎ *954 229 320. Bus: C5. Map p 96.*

★★ **Alcoy 10** ALAMEDA The owner might have lacked imagination when naming his bar (he just chose the address) but the tapas are interesting and the welcome warm. *Alcoy 10.* ☎ *954 905 702. Bus: B2, 13, 14. Map p 95.*

★★ **Bar Alfalfa** CENTRO There's an Italian twist to the tapas in this atmospheric corner bar, with tasty bruschettas being my personal favorite. *Candilejo 1.* ☎ *654 809 297. Bus: C5. Map p 96.*

★★ **Bar Las Teresas** SANTA CRUZ A busy tapas bar in the Barrio Santa Cruz district. Along with tourists there are usually lots of locals, which is always a good sign. Recommended. *Santa Teresa 2.* ☎ *954 213 069. Bus: 1, C3, C4, 23. Map p 96.*

★★ **Bar Santa Ana** TRIANA Right in the heart of Triana, but away from Calle Betis which is increasingly full of expats, this is a friendly neighborhood tapas bar with bullfighting pictures and religious statues behind the bar. *Pureza 82.* ☎ *954 272 102. Bus: C3. Map p 98.*

Bodega Belmonte SANTA CRUZ Just off the more beaten tourist track, this cool bar serves the usual

Taberna del Alabardero serves a great-value lunch.

tapas favorites. It's named after Juan Belmonte, Seville's most famous bullfighter. *Mateos Gaga 24.* ☎ *954 214 014. Bus: C5. Map p 96.*

★ **Bodega Góngora** CENTRO Just a hop from the main shopping streets, Góngora is a great local tapas bar full of atmosphere. Your bill is chalked on the bar. *Albareda 5.* ☎ *954 221 119. Bus: C5. Tram: Plaza Nueva. Map p 96.*

★★★ **Casablanca** CENTRO The King of Spain often tries the tapas here when he's in town. Slightly upmarket and a tad pricey, but absolutely worth it for the great flavors. The daily specials are always good. *Adolfo Rodríguez Jurado 12.* ☎ *954 224 114. Tram: Archivo de Indias. Map p 96.*

Family-Friendly Dining

As you'd expect in a major city, Seville offers plenty of dining options at all prices. A few top-of-the-range establishments aside, the dining philosophy is simple: this is southern Spain, so bring the family and friends and turn your meal into a party—and bring the kids too. Children are expected to be heard as well as seen, so relax, let them run riot and have another glass of wine. If you're looking for picnic food, the produce markets in El Arenal and Triana are good hunting grounds and the basement supermarket in El Corte Inglés (p 75) is reliable.

A busy lunchtime at Bodega Góngora.

Casa Carmelo SANTA CRUZ
ANDALUSIAN Standard tapas fare
is served here, but it's worth a men-
tion because the service is good—a
bit of a rarity in this part of town.
Gloria 6. ☎ *954 225 332. Bus: 1, C3,
C4, 23. Map p 96.*

★★★ Casa Morales ARENAL
This fab old *abacería* (corner shop
and bar) has the tapas menus
chalked on huge old wine barrels. It's
another of my favorites. Try the *montaditos de lomo al Amontillado*—
sandwiches of sherried pork. *Garcia
de Vinnesa 11.* ☎ *954 221 242. Bus:
C5. Tram: Plaza Nueva. Map p 96.*

Inside Casa Placido.

★★ Casa Paco ALAMEDA One of
the best and busiest tapas bars on
the Alameda. I enjoyed the grilled zucchini with cheese. People often wait in
a line for tables, so get here early.
Alameda de Hércules 23. ☎ *954 900
148. Bus: B2, 13, 14. Map p 95.*

★ Casa Placido SANTA CRUZ
One of a handful of genuinely
decent tapas bars in Seville's main
tourist district, this classic old bar
features all the usual fare. *Ximénez
de Enciso 11.* ☎ *954 563 971. Bus: 1,
C3, C4, 23. Map p 96.*

★★ El Ambigu ALAMEDA This
typical local tapas bar with tables on
the pavement is extremely popular
for its creative take on traditional
tapas. You sometimes have to wait at
the bar for a table. *Feria 47.* ☎ *954
381 015. Bus: 13, 14. Map p 95.*

★ El Paladar ALAMEDA Tapas
with a North African twist are the
house specialty here. Try the couscous and the falafel—both are very
good and reasonably priced. *Lum-
breras 14. No phone. Bus: B2, 13, 14.
Map p 95.*

★★★ El Rinconcillo MACARENA
Legend has it tapas were first created in this ancient bar. It's full of
atmosphere and staff are really
friendly. Tapas are a tad predictable,

but you have to go at least once for the experience. *Gerona 40.* ☎ *954 223 183. Bus: C5, 20, 24, 32. Map p 96.*

★★ **Estrella** SANTA CRUZ   A seriously authentic tapas bar and small restaurant tucked down a side street. The tapas menu is available in English and includes traditional favorites and a few more exotic dishes. Try the avocado stuffed with large prawns. *Estrella 3.* ☎ *954 561 426. Bus: 1, C3, C4, 23. Map p 96.*

★★★ **Europa** CENTRO   My friend Luis raves about the tapas here, and rightly so—they are simply delicious. The menu is in English too. My favorite is the deep-fried langoustine—with just a hint of lime in the batter and the aroma of fresh mint in the *alioli. Siete Revueltas 35.* ☎ *954 217 908. Bus: C5. Map p 96.*

★★★ **Jano** MACARENA   Another stand-out tapas bar serving gorgeous food. Claudia, the owner, trained at Seville's prestigious Alabardero cookery school. She also speaks great English. My favorite dish is honey-stuffed squid in salsa verde. Delicious. *Doña María Coronel 17.* ☎ *954 214 804. Bus: C5, 20, 24, 32. Map p 96.*

★★ **La Alacena de San Eloy** CENTRO   More of a wine bar than a tapas bar, the Alacena serves excellent wines by the glass and fabulous serrano ham and cheese. *San Eloy 31.* ☎ *954 215 580. Bus: B2, C5. Map p 96.*

★★★ **La Bodega** CENTRO   The best *montaditos* in town in my opinion. These are small sandwiches with delicious fillings like pork marinated in sherry. Easy to buy too—just point to what you like the look of! *Plaza de Alfalfa 4.* ☎ *954 214 252. Bus: C5. Map p 96.*

★★★ **La Cava del Europa** SANTA CRUZ   This place is getting a real reputation for taking tapas to the next level—with house specials like *wan-tun con chanfaina*—spiced noodles with onion, eggplant, zucchini and fried leek. *Santa María La Blanca 40.* ☎ *954 531 652. Bus: 1, C3, C4, 23. Map p 96.*

La Fresquita SANTA CRUZ   Check out the pictures and cuttings of the famous Semana Santa parades on the walls here! José's specialties are spinach with chickpeas and salted cod in *salmorejo,* a cold tomato soup. *Mateos Gago 29.* ☎ *954 226 010. Bus: 1, C3, C4, 23. Map p 96.*

El Rinconcillo is thought to be the birthplace of tapas.

Delicious tapas at Europa.

★★★ La Giganta MACARENA
Great tapas, a warm atmosphere and excellent house red wine. This is a real find, and a favorite of my Sevillian friends John and Christine. *Alhóndiga 6.* ☎ *954 210 975. Bus: C5, 20, 24, 32. Map p 96.*

★★ La Huerta Mediterránea
MACARENA   The best of the three little places on this plaza, La Huerta does deliciously tangy *salmorejo*—a thick chilled tomato soup. *Plaza de los Terceros 9.* ☎ *954 216 346. Bus: C5, 20, 24, 32. Map p 96.*

★ La Ilustre Victima ALAMEDA
A funky Alameda bar on a street corner, particularly good for vegetarians, with a whole meat-free menu section. There's kebabs, couscous and fajitas on the menu too. *Correduría 35.* ☎ *954 389 490. Bus: 13, 14. Map p 95.*

★★ La Madraza ALAMEDA   La
Madraza still pulls in the crowds for its Moorish-style tapas and I love the tagine with prunes. Some of the more standard tapas were a bit disappointing last time I went though.

Peris Mencheta 21. ☎ *954 908 188. Bus: 13, 14. Map p 95.*

Las Columnas ALAMEDA   One of
the busiest places on the Alameda. You order your beers and tapas from the window, which makes life easy if you've not got the hang of getting waiters' attention. *Alameda de Hércules 19.* ☎ *954 388 106. Bus: B2, 13, 14. Map p 95.*

★★ Las Columnas SANTA CRUZ
A classic, traditional tapas bar with people spilling out onto the pavement and friendly staff. It's one of my wife's favorites too! You're best off trying to get a spot at the bar. Deep-fried eggplant with honey is one we always order. *Rodrigo Caro 1.* ☎ *954 213 246. Bus: 1, C3, C4, 23. Map p 96.*

★ Las Golondrinas TRIANA   This
small two-level bar on a side street is renowned for its steak on toast. Veg dishes are a hit too. *Antillano Campos 26.* ☎ *954 331 626. Bus: C3. Map p 98.*

Los Caracoles CENTRO   A classic,
busy Alfalfa tapas place, Los Caracoles does all the usual favorites and a great glass of Rioja. Friendly service too. *Guardamino 1.* ☎ *954 213 172. Bus: C5. Map p 96.*

★★★ Patio San Eloy ARENAL
The patio has a great long bar with piles of *montaditos* (see La Bodega, above) stacked against the wall and a tiered, tiled seating area. Full of atmosphere and great fun. *San Eloy 9.* ☎ *954 221 148. Bus: C5, 43. Map p 96.*

Taberna los Terceros
MACARENA   One of three places on this square, this is a tad pricier, but still pretty good if you can't get a seat at La Huerta across the way. *Plaza de los Terceros 11.* ☎ *954 228 417. Bus: C5, 20, 24, 32. Map p 96.* ●

Nightlife Best Bets

Best Glam Gay Club
★★ Poseidon, *Marqués de Paradas 30 (p 122)*

Best Bar to Impress a Date
★ Bar San Fernando, *Hotel Alfonso XIII, San Fernando 2 (p 116)*

Best Semana Santa Shrine
★★★ El Garlochi, *Boteros 26 (p 117)*

Best Sweaty Late-Night Music Haunt
★★ Fun Club, *Alameda 86 (p 121)* and ★★ Jackson, *Relator 21 (p 121)*

Best Disco for Beautiful People
★ Antique Theatro, *Matemáticos Rey Pastor y Castro (p 121)*

Best Smoky Jazz Bar
★★ Cafe Naima, *Trajano 47 (p 120)*

Best Trendy Lounge Bar
★★ Groucho, *Zaragoza 33 (p 118)*

Best Strawberry Daiquiri
★★ Glassy Lounge, *Cristóbal Colón 5 (p 118)*

Best Funky Disco for (Older) Groovers
★★★ Elefunk, *Adriano 10 (p 121)*

Best Irish Craic
★★ P'Flaherty's, *Alemanes 7 (p 119)*

Best Down-in-One Shooters
★★ La Rebotica, *Pérez Galdós 11 (p 118)*

Best Unscripted Flamenco
★★★ La Carbonería, *Levíes 18 (p 120)*

Best Relaxed Friendly Club
★★★ Obbio, *Trastamara 29 (p 122)*

Best Rooftop Terrace
★★★ Etnia Espacio Universal, *Jesús del Gran Poder 28 (p 118)*

Best Random Live Music Joint
★★★ El Perro Andaluz, *Bustos Tavera 11 (p 120)* and ★★★ Malandar, *Avda Torneo 43 (p 121)*

Best Gay-Friendly Bar
★★★ Café Cuidad Condal, *Alameda de Hércules 94 (p 116)* and ★★★ República, *Alameda de Hércules 27 (p 119)*

Best Mojito
★ La Tertulia, *Betis 13 (p 119)*

Best for Homesick College Kids
★ Fundición, *Pureza 109 (p 118)*

Best for Ice-Cold Beer on a Corner
★★★ El Tremendo, *San Felipe (p 117)*

Best U.S. Sports Bar
★★ Texas Lone Star Saloon, *Placentines 25 (p 119)*

Strawberry Daiquiris at Glassy Lounge.

Previous page: Bar San Fernando at Alfonso XIII Hotel.

Alameda Nightlife

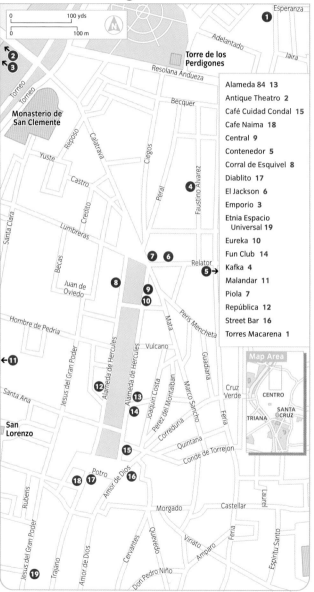

Torre de los Perdigones

Monasterio de San Clemente

Alameda 84 **13**
Antique Theatro **2**
Café Cuidad Condal **15**
Cafe Naima **18**
Central **9**
Contenedor **5**
Corral de Esquivel **8**
Diablito **17**
El Jackson **6**
Emporio **3**
Etnia Espacio Universal **19**
Eureka **10**
Fun Club **14**
Kafka **4**
Malandar **11**
Piola **7**
República **12**
Street Bar **16**
Torres Macarena **1**

Map Area

Cruz Verde

CENTRO

SANTA CRUZ

TRIANA

114

Centro & Santa Cruz Nightlife

Antiguedades **11**
Bar San Fernando **16**
Bokatrapo **1**
Cabo Loco **6**
Catedral **9**
El Garlochi **8**

El Perro Andaluz **2**
El Tamboril **15**
El Tremendo **3**
Entrecalles **14**
La Carbonería **10**
La Rebotica **5**
Nao **7**
P'Flaherty's **12**
Sopa de Ganso **4**
Texas Lone Star Saloon **13**

Triana & Lower Arenal Nightlife

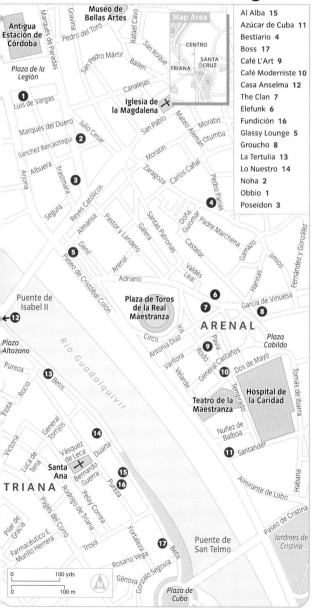

Al Alba **15**
Azúcar de Cuba **11**
Bestiario **4**
Boss **17**
Café L'Art **9**
Café Moderniste **10**
Casa Anselma **12**
The Clan **7**
Elefunk **6**
Fundición **16**
Glassy Lounge **5**
Groucho **8**
La Tertulia **13**
Lo Nuestro **14**
Noha **2**
Obbio **1**
Poseidon **3**

Seville Nightlife A to Z

Bars

Alameda 84 ALAMEDA No prizes for guessing where this narrow, noisy bar is located. Beers on draft and cocktails too, and it gets busy late on. *Alameda de Hércules 84. No phone. Bus: B2, 13, 14. Map p 113.*

★★ **Antiguedades** CENTRO Just down a side street from the cathedral, Antiguedades would make a good place for Halloween considering the weird stuff hanging from the ceiling: bodies, faces and other creepy things. It's good fun and attracts a mixed crowd of locals and tourists. *Argote de Molina 40. No phone. Bus: C5. Map p 114.*

★ **Bar San Fernando** PARQUE MARÍA LUISA The refined environs of the Hotel Alfonso XIII make this place a good bet if money is no object and you have someone along you'd like to impress. This bar is all leather armchairs and dark wood finish, but there's a trendy Martini bar on the terrace too. *San Fernando 2.* ☎ *954 917 000. Bus: AC, B2, C4, 5, 21, 22, 23. Tram: Archivo de Indias. Map p 114.*

Santa Cruz at night.

★ **Bokatrapo** CENTRO If you like dives, this place, owned by a former local musician, fits the bill. Smoky and dark, it draws a mellow crowd for a late-night *copa*. There's a small stage for the occasional music session or live soccer on the big screen. *Bustos Tavera 13. No phone. Bus: C5, 20, 24, 32. Map p 114.*

Cabo Loco CENTRO A little Native American ambience in a little bar, you can try to squeeze in or spill out into the street like most do on Pérez Galdós. A wide variety of shots with a backdrop of 'Indian' artifacts like axes, clothing and more. *Pérez Galdós, 26. No phone. Bus: C5. Map p 114.*

★ **Café Ciudad Condal** ALAMEDA This funky, gay-friendly bar right on the Alameda has a terrace space under the shady trees and it's open all day. *Alameda de Hércules 94.* ☎ *954 903 620. Bus: B2, 13, 14. Map p 113.*

★ **Café L'Art** ARENAL A friendly cafe-bar popular with the cool crowd for early evening drinks and banter. Nice ambience, but often very busy later on. *General Castaños 17. No phone. Bus: C5. Tram: Plaza Nueva. Map p 115.*

★★ **Café Moderniste** ARENAL There's great ambience and a fun crowd in this corner cafe-bar which is vaguely Art Deco in style and usually busy with trendy locals.Gets very crowded at weekends. *Dos De Mayo 28. No phone. Bus C5. Tram Archivo. Map p 115.*

★★ **Central** ALAMEDA One of the most popular places on the Alameda, this has lots of space outside and gets full-on noisy and chaotic later on. Great atmosphere and good beer are a winning combination all the way to 3am. *Alameda de Hércules 62.* ☎ *954 370 999. Bus: B2, 13, 14. Map p 113.*

The Clan ARENAL The only Scottish bar in Seville. This one serves up a decent selection of beers, including special offers like two-for-one Heineken during the week. Televised events include soccer and rugby matches. *Adriano 3. No phone. Bus: C5. Map p 115.*

Corral de Esquivel ALAMEDA A slightly quieter, more local tapas bar on the Alameda, which means it's sometimes a bit easier to get a table outside here. Self-service ordering, so don't wait for a waiter. *Alameda de Hércules 39.* ☎ *954 374 385. Bus: B2, 13, 14. Map p 113.*

★ Diablito ALAMEDA Set right in front of the columns with Hercules and Caesar looking down on you, this is one of my favorite Alameda bars. Friendly and relaxed—but not too grungy. A nice combination. *Alameda de Hércules 7.* ☎ *954 377 461. Bus 13, 14. Map p 113.*

★★★ El Garlochi CENTRO Possibly the quirkiest bar in Seville, this dim drinking den is dripping with religious memorabilia, statues,

Drop by El Tremendo for an ice-cold beer.

artwork, pictures and paintings. It ought to be kitsch but there's so much authenticity to the icons and statues it really does feel like a church. *Boteros 26. No phone. Bus: C5. Map p 114.*

★★★ El Tremendo MACARENA A hole-in-the-wall bar with an undisputed reputation as the place in Seville for the coldest beer. And it's cheap too, with larger glasses of cold Cruzacampo for just 1€. Stand outside (no chairs) with the rest of the crowd where tables are set up along the corner of the street. *San*

The bars overflow into the street in Triana.

Felipe. ☎ 954 214 747. Bus: C5, 20, 24, 32. Map p 114.

★★ Entrecalles SANTA CRUZ
My favorite bar in the tourist district has a relaxed vibe with a mixture of American and Moroccan bits and pieces on the walls and the odd parrot hanging from the ceiling. The guys behind the bar speak some English and are really friendly. *Ximénez de Enciso 14. No phone. Bus: C3, C4, 21. Map p 114.*

★★★ Etnia Espacio Universal
ALAMEDA Take the elevator in the rather unpromising lobby of the Espacio Azahar hotel and be amazed to step out onto a cool rooftop conservatory with hot tub, lounging chairs and twinkling candles. *Jesús del Gran Poder 28.* ☎ *954 384 109. Bus: 13, 14. Map p 113.*

Eureka ALAMEDA You won't have trouble finding this place—it's bigger than the usual Alameda drinking den and has sofas and chairs. Open very late. *Alameda de Hércules 64. No phone. Bus: B2, 13, 14. Map p 113.*

★ Fundición TRIANA You'll feel like you've walked into a college bar in the U.S. here. Pool tables, Budweiser, beer pong on a Tuesday

night, and Sweet Home Chicago on the sound system. Friendly atmosphere, but few locals would set foot in the place. *Pureza 105. No phone. Bus: C3. Map p 115.*

★★ Glassy Lounge ARENAL
A trendy place with white and pink color schemes, and a good cocktail list. Nizar makes the best strawberry Daiquiri in Seville. The English bar menu is perfect if you're tired of tapas, with nachos, nuggets and satay. *Cristóbal Colón 5.* ☎ *954 223 636. Bus: B2, C5. Map p 115.*

★★ Groucho ARENAL One of
central Seville's coolest bars, Groucho is full of gorgeous Sevillians, drinking long drinks and letting their hair down. Live flamenco and disco at weekends. Strict door policy, so dress up smart. *Federico Sánchez Bedoya 30. No phone. www.grouchobar.com. Bus: C5. Tram: Plaza Nueva. Map p 115.*

★★ La Rebotica CENTRO If *chupitos*, or shots, are what you're looking for, this is the place. A hole-in-the-wall bar, it has a list of over 50 shots, some named after celebrities (Harrison Ford, Kim Basinger—the names show the bar opened in the mid-1980s), while others are a

P'Flaherty's is the place for a pint of Guinness.

bit more inspired, like Pipi de Burro, Moco and Cerebrito. *Pérez Galdós 11.* ☎ *679 111 703. Bus: C5. Map p 114.*

★ **La Tertulia** TRIANA   In the middle of buzzing Calle Betis, this place gets really busy later on, but it's worth fighting your way to the bar for their *mojitos* and *caipirinhas*. Sharp and herb-laden, they're just how they should be. *Betis 13.* ☎ *954 333 285. Bus: C3. Map p 115.*

★ **Nao** CENTRO   Another of the bars on busy Pérez Galdós, this joint is a bit classier, with air-con, a long bar and a good-looking selection of spirits. It also gets going later than the smaller bars nearby and stays open until the last person leaves. *Pérez Galdós 28.* ☎ *954 227 276. Bus: C5. Map p 114.*

Noha ARENAL   A trendy bar with DJ turntables and the occasional live music session later on. Major soccer matches are often shown on the big screen here too. *Marqués de Paradas 53. No phone. Bus: B2, B5. Map p 115.*

★★ **P'Flaherty's** CENTRO Seville's first Irish bar now has several imitators, but it's still the place to come for Irish pub food and smooth Guinness. There's live sport of all sorts on the big screens. It's a stone's throw from the cathedral and can get really busy at night. *Alemanes 7.* ☎ *954 210 451. www.paddyflaherty. com. Bus: C5. Map p 114.*

★ **Piola** ALAMEDA   This is a classic Alameda bar, noisy and fun, with a slightly international range of tapas on offer and cocktails too. *Alameda de Hércules 57.* ☎ *954 377 191. Bus: B2, 13, 14. Map p 113.*

★★★ **República** ALAMEDA   This cool cafe-bar is a notch up from the usual Alameda drinking haunts, all white walls and dark furniture. There are great cakes on offer too,

Seville has a buzzing latenight scene.

plus free Wi-Fi and friendly staff who speak good English. Another of Alameda's gay-friendly spots. *Alameda de Hércules 27.* ☎ *954 909 435. Bus: B2, 13, 14. Map p 113.*

★★★ **Sopa de Ganso** CENTRO Offering tapas as well as drinks, this bar gets louder as the night goes on. Music varies but they play more rock and Spanish pop than anything else. Being a *bar de copas* the beverages of choice are mixed drinks, but there's beer here too. *Pérez Galdós 8.* ☎ *954 212 526. Bus: C5. Map p 114.*

★★ **Texas Lone Star Saloon** CENTRO   This Tex-Mex Bar shows all the U.S. sport you could want: live NFL games, NBA games and the NCAA basketball final. Local and European soccer games are also often shown. Check out the chalkboard outside where they post which games they'll have that day. *Placentines 25.* ☎ *954 210 334. Bus: C5. Map p 114.*

Flamenco Bars

★ **Casa Anselma** TRIANA   One of the best-known bars of the Triana flamenco scene, where you'll often see locals dancing. But it's Anselma, the larger-than-life owner, who's

Nightlife in Seville, as in most Spanish cities, starts seriously late. It's quite normal to go out for dinner at 10pm. Bars stay open until 3am and nightclubs don't really liven up until at least then, staying open until 7am. So if you're planning a serious night out, don't expect to get to bed before daylight.

perhaps the biggest attraction. *Pagés del Corro 49. No phone. Bus: B2, C3. Map p 115.*

El Tamboril SANTA

CRUZ   Located on one of my favorite Santa Cruz squares, this place is famous for its statue of the Virgin of Rocío. There's a mix of musical styles played here, from flamenco to salsa. You'll often see locals dancing the *sevillana*. *Plaza de Santa Cruz.* ☎ *954 561 590. Bus: 1, C3, C5, 23. Map p 114.*

★★★ La Carboneria SANTA

CRUZ   Well known and definitely worth the trip. A real mix of people, from cool to earthy and from Spanish to every nationality imaginable, enjoy the free music in the covered back terrace. The front bar with a more rustic, winter pub atmosphere includes a piano, wooden tables and fireplaces. *Levíes 18.* ☎ *954 229 945. Bus: C5. Map p 114.*

★ Lo Nuestro TRIANA   A fixture

on Calle Betis for years, Nuestro is a great place for a little flamenco with a group playing just about every night. Very convenient for the nightlife along the river, this gets much praise, with good reason. *Betis 31A. No phone. Bus: C3. Map p 115.*

★★ Torres Macarena MACARENA

One of the most important *peñas* or local halls in Andalusia, Torres is about as traditional and authentic as you can get. There's a small stage and bar area and a patio with a stage too. Shows are often impromptu, but always of the best 'old school flamenco' quality. *Torrijiano 29.* ☎ *954 372 384. Bus: C1, C2, C3, C4, 13, 14. Map p 113.*

Live Music

Azúcar de Cuba ARENAL   Right before the bridge to Los Remedios, this is the place in town to take in some live Cuban music, sip a Daiquiri and smoke a Cuban cigar. Dinner and lunch are also served—an authentic Cuban dining experience. *Paseo de las Delicias 3.* ☎ *954 228 668. www.azucardecuba.com. Bus: B2, C4. Map p 115.*

★★ Cafe Naima ALAMEDA   In

this relaxed, small bar on a street corner in Alameda, you can catch live jazz from time to time. It's named after the first wife of John Coltrane and has walls full of pictures of jazz legends. *Trajano 47.* ☎ *954 382 485. www.naimacafejazz.com. Bus: B2, 13, 14. Map p 113.*

★ Contenedor MACARENA   This

boho and friendly cafe-bar is really popular with the local San Luis crowd. Film nights, art exhibitions and acoustic sets, chilled vibes and tasty food are the order of the day (and night). *San Luis 50.* ☎ *954 916 333. www.contenedorcultural.com. Bus: 13,14. Map p 113.*

★★★ El Perro Andaluz CENTRO

Rock, blues, flamenco, country-rock, reggae—they do a little of everything in this recently renovated bar, frequented by local actors and artists, in the heart of Santa Catalina.

Open from 11pm. *Bustos Tavera 11. No phone. Bus: C5, 20, 24, 32. Map p 114.*

★★ **Fun Club** ALAMEDA A long-running fixture on the live music scene, grungy Fun Club has everything from rock to electronica and doesn't get going until late, staying open and sweaty until dawn. *Alameda 86.* ☎ *650 489 858. www.salafunclub.com. Bus: B2, 13, 14. Map p 113.*

★★ **Malandar** ALAMEDA Funk, rock, pop, jazz, flamenco: there's all kinds of interesting stuff going on here. Definitely one of the most progressive live-music places in Seville, but you need to stay up late. Most nights don't start 'til past midnight. See website for more info. *Avda Torneo 43.* ☎ *954 221 417. www.malandar.net. No cards. Bus: B2, C3, C4, B5, 6. Map p 113.*

★ **Street Bar** ALAMEDA In this small, friendly bar just off the Alameda, you can catch live music Thursdays, Fridays and Sundays—usually just a guy with a guitar playing jazz, blues or flamenco, often with a South American flavor. *Amor de Dios 64.* ☎ *955 091 515. Bus: 13, 14. Map p 113.*

Nightclubs

★ **Al Alba** TRIANA With its modern, monochrome decor and a smattering of local celebs, this flamenco disco is another favorite for young Sevillian sophisticates, writhing and spinning and dancing *sevillianas*. *Betis 41A. www.alalbasevilla.com. Bus: C3. Map p 115.*

★ **Antique Theatro** CARTUJA If you're into celeb-spotting, this is the place: actors, and soccer players are sometimes seen here. It's been completely renovated and is fit to please the most avid disco-goer. Dress to impress to get in. *Matemáticos Rey Pastor y Castro.* ☎ *954 462 207. www.antiquetheatro.com. Bus: C1, C2. Map p 113.*

★★ **Bestiario** ARENAL More of a lounge club than a full-on disco, Bestiario features a slightly older, more sophisticated crowd. There's a DJ spinning house and Spanish pop and a small dance floor for shaking your thing. Another one with a snooty door policy so dress well. *Zaragoza 33.* ☎ *954 213 475. Bus: C5. Tram: Plaza Nueva. Map p 115.*

Boss TRIANA Boss has four bars on different levels and a very large, stadium-type dance area. It's a favorite of many for the late-night scene but the door policy is pretty arrogant. Dress well and go in small groups but be prepared to be turned away if you're not cool enough. *Betis 67.* ☎ *954 990 104. Bus: C3. Map p 115.*

★ **Catedral** CENTRO A smaller disco located just down the street from Plaza Alfalfa, Catedral offers *copas* and dancing until late at night, playing the latest house, R'n'B and hip-hop tunes to a young and international crowd. Small, quite glam, good fun, young. *Cuesta del Rosario 12.* ☎ *954 219 029. Bus: C5. Map p 114.*

★★ **El Jackson** ALAMEDA Funk and soul are the order of the day in this converted house on a side street just off the end of the Alameda. Laid back and friendly, as you'd expect for Alameda. Free entry and good-value drinks too. *Relator 21. No phone. Bus: 13, 14. Map p 113.*

★★★ **Elefunk** ARENAL An older, less glam crowd gathers here for the relaxed vibe.

Elefunk is a friendly laid-back nightclub.

There's always a friendly crowd at Obbio.

No snooty doormen or beautiful people, just a genuinely friendly place with eclectic sounds from funk to hip-hop to electronica. *Adriano 10.* ☎ *954 222 581. Bus: C5. Map p 115.*

★★ **Emporio** CARTUJA Almost anything goes at this glam, funky mixed club. Regular Planeta Coneja nights (usually on Sundays) attract a rainbow crowd in all sorts of finery. Dress code—as outrageous as you dare. Music—techno. *Avda Marie Curie.* ☎ *954 433 169. www. myspace.com/emporiosevilla. Bus: C1, C2. Map p 113.*

★★ **Kafka** ALAMEDA A small, smokey joint on a side street with stacks of atmosphere, Kafka attracts a fairly young crowd with an eclectic mix of music: Funky house in the main, but reggae nights on Wednesdays too. *Faustino Álvarez 27. No*

phone. www.myspace.com/kafkaclub. No cards. Bus: 13, 14. Map p 113.

★★★ **Obbio** ARENAL Wear what you want and be what you want. Indie, soul and funk with a friendly crowd makes this one of my favorite late-night spots. Art-house movies are shown Monday through Wednesday. Club nights are Fridays and Saturdays. *Trastamara 29. No phone. www.myspace.com/salaobbio No cards. Bus: B2, B5. Map p 115.*

★★ **Poseidon** ARENAL Seville's grand old dame of the gay scene is back after several years of absence, and it's just as fab. It caters to a glam mixed crowd these days. Drag acts and general late night craziness guaranteed. From 11pm nightly. *Marqués de Paradas 30. No phone. Bus: B2, B5. Map p 115.* ●

A Moving Feast

Seville's best nightspots vary by season. In winter and spring the thronging bars around Plaza Alfalfa and the Alameda are busy all night long, spilling out onto the streets. When the weather gets really hot in July the action moves to the riverbank and parks where it's cooler. Here you'll often find late-night, open-air summer bars— *terrazas de verano*—springing up. Check with your hotel for locations, as they vary. The bars along the riverbank on Calle Betis in Triana are also popular in summer.

AUDITORIO MUNICIPAL

ROCIO

Arts & Entertainment Best Bets

Best **Organ Recital Venue**
★★ Hospital de los Venerables,
Plaza de los Venerables 8 (p 129)

Best **English-Language Movie
House**
★★ Avenida 5 Cines, *Avda Marqués
de Paradas 15 (p 129)*

Best **Opera Hall**
★★★ Teatro de la Maestranza,
Paseo de Colón 22 (p 129)

Best **Independent Art Gallery**
★★★ Concha Pedrosa, *Fernán
Caballero 11 (p 127)*

Best **Fine Art Gallery**
★★★ Museo de Bellas Artes, *Plaza
del Museo 9 (p 128)*

Best **Bullfights**
Plaza de Toros, *Adriano 37
(p 131)*

Best for **Mainstream Theater
(in Spanish)**
★★ Teatro Lope de Vega, *Avda
Maria Luisa (p 132)*

Best **Contemporary Theater
(in Spanish)**
★★ Teatro Central, *José de Gálvez
(p 132)*

Best **Alternative Theater
(in Spanish)**
★★ Sala la Imperdible, *Plaza del
Duque (p 132)* and ★ Sala Ocero,
Sol 5 (p 132)

Best **Setting for Choral Music**
★★★ Catedral de Sevilla, *Plaza
Virgen de los Reyes (p 129)*

Best **Contemporary Dance**
★★ Endanza *Centro de las Artes de
Sevilla, Torneo 18 (p 131)*

Best **Open-Air Pop Venue**
★★★ Auditorio Municipal Rocío
Jurado, *Isla de la Cartuja (p 129)*

Best **All-Singing, All-Dancing
Flamenco Show**
★ El Palacio Andaluz, *Maria Auxili-
adora 18 (p 130)*

Best **Authentic Flamenco Show**
★★★ Casa de la Memoria, *Ximénez de Enciso 28 (p 130)*

Best **Soccer Stadium**
★ Estadio Sánchez Pizjuán (Sevilla
FC), *Avda Eduardo Dato (p 131)*

Best **Theater for Kids (in
Spanish)**
★★ Teatro Municipal Alameda,
Credito 11 (p 132)

Seville's bullring is one of Spain's finest.

Previous page: Auditorio Municipal Rocío Jurado stages major pop and rock concerts.

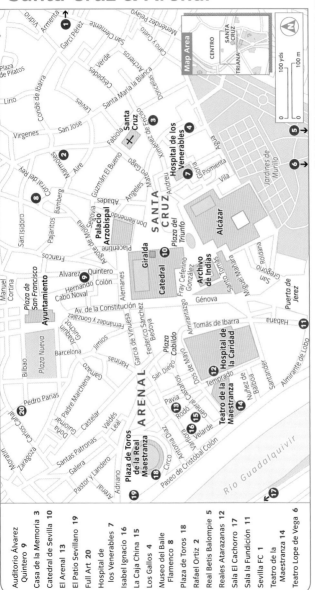

Santa Cruz & Arenal

Auditorio Álvarez Quintero **9**
Casa de la Memoria **3**
Catedral de Sevilla **10**
El Arenal **13**
El Patio Sevillano **19**
Full Art **20**
Hospital de los Venerables **7**
Isabel Ignacio **16**
La Caja China **15**
Los Gallos **4**
Museo del Baile Flamenco **8**
Plaza de Toros **18**
Rafael Ortiz **2**
Real Betis Balompie **5**
Reales Atarazanas **12**
Sala El Cachorro **17**
Sala la Fundición **11**
Sevilla FC **1**
Teatro de la Maestranza **14**
Teatro Lope de Vega **6**

Alameda, Macarena & Centro

Auditorio Municipal Rocío Jurado **22**
Avenida 5 Cines **16**
CAAC **23**
Centro de las Artes de Sevilla **9**
Cine Alameda **11**
Cine Cervantes **12**
Concha Pedrosa **14**
El Palacio Andaluz **2**
Endanza **10**
Espacio Escala **17**
Estadio Olímpico **20**
Félix Gomez **5**
Galería Nuevoarte **18**
Iglesia de San Luis **1**
Museo de Bellas Artes **15**
Sala Apolo **4**
Sala Joaquín Turina **7**
Sala la Imperdible **13**
Sala Ocero **3**
Sanvicente 31 **19**
Teatro Central **21**
Teatro Municipal Alameda **8**
Teatro Quintero **6**

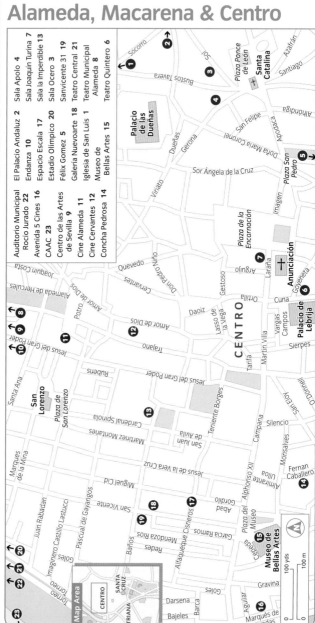

Arts & Entertainment A to Z

Art Galleries

★★ CAAC CARTUJA Andalusia's Contemporary Art Museum (p 25) resides in the cloisters of the old Cartuja monastery, featuring major exhibitions by international artists. *Américo Vespucio 2.* ☎ *955 037 070. www.caac.es. 3.01€; free for E.U. passport holders on Tues. Oct–Mar Tues–Fri 10am–8pm, Sat 11am–8pm, Sun 10am–3pm. Apr–Sept open till 9pm weekdays. Closed Mon. Bus: C1, C2. Map p 126.*

★★ Centro de las Artes de Sevilla ALAMEDA This small, airy exhibition space is a real hive of activity, housing regularly changing contemporary art exhibitions, video installations, theater and more. It's also the temporary home of the Endanza dance troupe (see Theater, Dance & Ballet, p 126). *Torneo 18. No phone. Tues–Sat 11am–2pm, 6–9pm. Closed Sun, Mon. Bus: 2, C1, C2. Map p 126.*

★★★ Concha Pedrosa CENTRO Concha's mission is to provide a space for new local artists to display and sell their work. And she only works with the best: the art on show here is usually really impressive. It's one of my favorite galleries. *Fernán Caballero 11.* ☎ *954 226 536. www.conchapedrosa.com. Tues–Fri noon–2pm, 6–9pm, Sat noon–2pm. Bus: B2, C5, 43. Map p 126.*

★★ Espacio Escala CENTRO One of Spain's largest banks, Cajasol isn't short of some spare cash to spend on art. Items from the bank's 5,000-piece collection, worth 13 million euros, are displayed here. Usually contemporary in style, exhibitions change every couple of months. All disciplines are featured. *Cisneros 5.* ☎ *954 373 241. Mon–Fri 11am–2pm, 5–9pm, weekends 11am–2pm. Bus: B2, C5. Map p 126.*

Félix Gomez CENTRO Tucked away at the end of what looks like a blind alley, Felix's gallery exhibits paintings, sculpture, collages and, in particular, murals. Each temporary exhibition lasts about 20 days. *Moreria 6.* ☎ *954 225 320. Mon–Fri 11am–1:30pm, 6–8:30pm, Sat 11am–2pm. Bus: B2, C5. Map p 126.*

Seasonal Variations

Seville is an artistically diverse city and there's always lots going on. Entertainments vary by season and the same venue is often used for many disciplines. So, while the Teatro de la Maestranza is known primarily as an opera house, it's also an important venue for the Seville Royal Symphony Orchestra. In the hot summer months, entertainments move outside to the open spaces. Your first stop should be the helpful tourist information office in Plaza de San Francisco which publishes a detailed weekly What's On list. They can help with reservations too. Altenatively, ask at your hotel reception. Look out too for local listings magazines *El Giraldillo* (Spanish), the Sevilla Institute for Culture and Arts' (ICAS) *Sevilladc* (Spanish) and *The Tourist* (English). Also www.whatsonwhen.com is worth checking out. Virtually all theatrical productions are only in Spanish.

128

The Best Arts & Entertainment

Full Art CENTRO   This two-room gallery on the ground floor (first door to the right inside the front door) hosts seven exhibitions a year of modern art by contemporary Spanish artists. Works are primarily painting, sculpture and photography, and most are for sale. *Madrid 4.* ☎ *954 221 613. www.fullart.net. Mon–Fri 11am–2pm, 6–9pm, Sat 11am–2pm. Bus: C5. Tram: Plaza Nueva. Map p 125.*

Galería Nuevoarte CENTRO Another one-room local gallery that displays drawings and paintings by local artists. All are for sale, typically costing 400€ per piece. *San Vicente 32.* ☎ *954 915 668. Mon–Fri 5:30–9pm, Sat 11am–2pm. Bus: C3, C4. Map p 126.*

Isabel Ignacio ARENAL   A small, one-room gallery, close to the bullring, which hosts contemporary art exhibitions from up-and-coming artists—painting, sculpture installations, video. Works are for sale. *Velarde 9.* ☎ *954 562 555. www. galeriaisabelignacio.com. Mon*

San Juan Evangelista *by Juan Montañés at Museo de Bellas Artes.*

6–9pm, Tues–Fri 11am–1:30pm, 6–9pm, Sat 11am–2pm (closed Sat June–Aug). Bus: B2, C4, C5. Map p 125.

★ **La Caja China** ARENAL   The contemporary works by Andalusian artists here include sculpture, painting and photography. Exhibitions change regularly. More information on the website. *General Castaños 30.* ☎ *954 219 358. www.lacajachina. net. Tues–Fri 10:30am–1:30pm, 6–9pm, Sat noon–2pm, Mon 10:30am–1:30pm. Bus: B2, C4, C5. Map p 125.*

★★★ **Museo de Bellas Artes** CENTRO   Housed in the former Convento de la Merced Calzada, Seville's Fine Arts Museum (p 126) houses one of Spain's finest collections of the 17th-century Seville School of artists. There are some great medieval paintings and sculptures too. *Plaza del Museo 9.* ☎ *954 221 829. 1.50€; free for E.U. passport holders. Tues 3–8pm; Wed–Sat 9am–8pm, Sun 9am–2pm. Closed Mon. Bus: B2, C5. Map p 126.*

Rafael Ortiz SANTA CRUZ   Fairly off-the-wall modern paintings and sketches are on display at this gallery in an old town house. Don't forget to climb the steep stairs up to the small additional exhibitions space on the second floor. *Mármoles 12.* ☎ *954 214 874. www. galeriarafaelortiz.com. Mon 6–9pm, Tues–Fri 11am–1:30pm, 6–9pm, Sat 11am–1:30pm. Bus: C5. Map p 125.*

★ **Sanvicente 31** ALAMEDA   On a street corner just opposite Galería Nuevoarte, this one tends to exhibit works by just one artist at a time. When I last visited there were attractive oils of modern Sevillian life on display. Exhibitions change regularly and works are for sale. *San Vicente 31.* ☎ *954 908 424. Mon–Fri 11am–2pm, 5:30–9pm, Sat 11am–2pm. Bus: C3, C4. Map p 126.*

Classical Music & Opera

★★★ Catedral de Sevilla SANTA
CRUZ   The largest Gothic cathedral
in the world makes a memorably apt
setting for choirs and classical concerts, usually featuring music with a
religious theme. *Plaza Virgen de los
Reyes. (Details from the tourist office,
Plaza de San Francisco 19.* ☎ *954
595 288.) Tram: Archivo de Indias.
Bus: C5. Map p 125.*

★★ Hospital de los Venera-
bles SANTA CRUZ   There are regular organ recitals in winter in the
baroque church here, which houses
one of Europe's finest 20th-century
church organs—made by German
organ-maker Gerhard Grenzing in
1991. *Plaza de los Venerables 8.*
☎ *954 562 696. www.focus.abengoa.
es. Bus: 1, C3, C4, 23. Map p 125.*

★ Iglesia de San Luis MACARENA
This fantastically ornate old church is
now owned by the municipality and
makes a great venue for occasional
classical music productions and classical theater. *San Luis.* ☎ *954 550
207. Bus: 13, 14. Map p 126.*

★★ Sala Apolo MACARENA   The
Seville Royal Symphony Orchestra
often performs in the Teatro de la
Maestranza (see below), but its per-
manent home is here. This smaller,
modern concert hall is an acousti-
cally impressive venue. *Gerona 25.*
☎ *954 217 579, 954 561 536. www.
rossevilla.com. Bus: C5, 20, 24, 32.
Map p 126.*

★★★ Teatro de la Maestranza
ARENAL   Seville's modernist opera
house is one of the world's premier
venues. The focus is on works inspired
by Seville, such as Mozart's *The Mar-
riage of Figaro*, although jazz, classical
music—performed by the Seville Symphony Orchestra—and even Spanish
zarzuelas (operettas) are also staged
here. *Paseo de Colón 22.* ☎ *954 226
573. www.teatromaestranza.com.
Bus: B2, C4. Map p 125.*

*Avenida 5 Cines is good for English-version
movies.*

Film & Cinema

★★ Avenida 5 Cines CENTRO
The best for original-soundtrack pictures, with larger screens and
almost always at least one English-
version movie. Conveniently close
to the center too. *Avda Marqués de
Paradas 15.* ☎ *954 293 025. Online
ticket sales: www.cinentradas.com.
Bus: B2, 43. Map p 126.*

★ Cine Alameda ALAMEDA
Tucked away in a small shopping
arcade at the bottom of the Alameda, this four-screen theater shows
the usual mainstream movies, in
Spanish only. *Alameda de Hércules
9.* ☎ *954 915 762. Online ticket
sales: www.cineciudad.com. Bus: 13,
14. Map p 126.*

Cine Cervantes ALAMEDA
Another that sometimes shows
films in the original language—not
just English, but French, Italian and
more, all subtitled of course in Spanish. It's located just toward Alameda. *Amor de Dios 33.* ☎ *954 915
681. Online ticket sales: www.cine
ciudad.com. Bus: 13, 14. Map p 126.*

Flamenco Shows

★★ Auditorio Álvarez Quin-
tero CENTRO   A small, intimate
and authentic flamenco venue. The

Flamenco at El Palacio Andaluz.

music and dance are good, but the is room rather cramped. Shows start at 9pm, so arrive in good time to get a good seat. *Álvarez Quintero 48.* ☎ *954 293 949. www.avlarez quintero.com. Tickets 16€. Tram: Archivo de Indias. Bus: C5. Map p 125.*

★★★ Casa de la Memoria

SANTA CRUZ   I think this is the best trade-off between an organized performance and the spontaneity of flamenco. Young local artists sing and dance nightly in an intimate patio. It's great value for money compared to other *tablaos* (shows). *Ximénez de Enciso 28.* ☎ *954 560 670. www. casadelamemoria.es. Tickets 15€. Bus: 1, C3, C4, 23. Map p 125.*

★★ El Arenal ARENAL   A *tablao*

that's been around for years, situated in a renovated 17th-century building. Choose from a show with dinner or with just a drink (less expensive) in a cozy atmosphere where you'll get a close view of the show, which is consistently good. *Rodo 7.* ☎ *954 216 492. www.tablaoelarenal.com. Bus: B2, C4, C5. Map p 125.*

★ El Palacio Andaluz CENTRO

Lights, luxury and a big venue: this is one the most upscale *tablaos* in Sevilla. Another place to choose dinner or just a drink with the show. It's more of a razzle-dazzle musical than a flamenco show, but good entertainment nonetheless. *Maria Auxiliadora 18.* ☎ *954 534 720. www.elpalacioandaluz.com. Tickets 36€–74€. Bus: 1, C1, C2, C3, C4. Map p 126.*

★ El Patio Sevillano ARENAL

Formed in 1952 and moved to its current location in 1973, El Patio is one of the first *tablaos* in Sevilla. Flamenco shows take place in a typically Andalusian patio, and the building is located right next to the Plaza de Toros (bullring) and the river. Choose show with dinner or with just a drink. *Paseo de Colón 11A.* ☎ *954 214 120. www.elpatio sevillano.com. Tickets 37€–70€. Bus: B2, C4, C5. Map p 125.*

★ Los Gallos SANTA CRUZ

Founded in 1966, this little club has launched some of the biggest names in today's flamenco circuit, and founder Don José Luis Núñez de Prado has done much to resurrect flamenco as an art form. The twice-nightly shows offer a more intimate *flamenco puro* performance than Patio or Palacio, but they're pricer than Memoria or Quintero. *Plaza de Santa Cruz 11.* ☎ *954 216 981. www.tablaolosgallos.com. Tickets 30€. Bus: 1, C3, C4, 23. Map p 125.*

★★ Museo del Baile Flamenco

SANTA CRUZ   Seville's flamenco museum also has shows on Fridays and Saturdays and given the heritage of the place—legendary dancer

Cristina Hoyos is artistic director—you can be assured of authenticity. The show starts at 7:30pm. *Manuel Rojas Marcos 3,* ☎ *954 340 311. www.museoflamenco.com. Tickets 25€. Bus: 1, C3, C4, 23. Map p 125.*

Rock & Pop
★★★ Auditorio Municipal Rocio Jurado CARTUJA This
open-air arena is Europe's largest, with a capacity of 6,000. It's Seville's primary venue for international rock concerts. *Isla de la Cartuja.* ☎ *689 020 627. Bus: C1, C2. Map p 126.*

Estadio Olímpico CARTUJA
Built for the 1992 Expo, Seville's huge Olympic stadium hosts major rock concerts and sporting events. *Sector Norte, Isla de la Cartuja.* ☎ *954 489 400. Bus: C2. Map p 126.*

Spectator Sports
Plaza de Toros ARENAL Some say a bullfight is *the* quintessential Sevillian spectator sport, others that it's a bloodthirsty spectacle. If you go, get a seat in the shade half-way back and get advice on who to see—some matadors are far better than others. *Adriano 37.* ☎ *954 501 382. Sun, Easter to Oct; Thurs eve July/Aug. Daily during Feria de Abril (p 160). www.plazadetorodelamaestranza. com. Tickets 10€–80€ from the ticket office (despacho de entradas). Bus: B2, C4, C5. Map p 125.*

Real Betis Balompié PARQUE MARÍA LUISA Seville's two soccer teams enjoy intense rivalry. You can sometimes watch reserve games for free on Sunday mornings. *Estadio Ruiz de Lopera, Avda de Heliopolis.* ☎ *954 610 340. www.realbetis balompie.es. Bus: 6, 34. Map p 125.*

★ **Sevilla FC** NERVION At the time of writing Sevilla were one of Spain's highest-flying teams. Soccer matches in Spain are usually played September to May on Sunday afternoons. *Estadio Sanchez Pizjuán, Avda Eduardo Dato.* ☎ *902 501 901. www.sevillafc.es. Bus: C1, C2, 5, 22, 23, 32. Map p 125.*

Theater, Dance & Ballet
★ **Endanza** ALAMEDA For now they're performing on other people's stages, but the Endanza troupe's commitment to adventurous contemporary dance and drama remains as passionate as ever. Check with the tourist office for the latest venue news. *Centro de las Artes de Sevilla, Torneo 18.* ☎ *954 904 034. www. endanza.net. Bus: 2, C1, C2. Map p 126.*

Reales Atarazanas ARENAL Several of the vaulted spaces that were docks in the old royal shipyards have been converted into modern performance spaces which make great settings for occasional theater. *Temprado 1. Closed for renovation at time of writing.*

Sala El Cachorro TRIANA This small, quirky venue is the home of the Viento Sur theater school. It's a local theater space where all kinds of stuff goes on: contemporary drama, music, puppetry and more. Ask at the tourist office for the latest information. *Procurador 19.* ☎ *954 339 747. www.salaelcachorro.com. Bus: B2, C3, 5, 42. Map p 125.*

kids **Sala Joaquín Turina** CENTRO This cultural space, sponsored by Spanish banking giant Cajasol, has music, flamenco and workshops for kids. Check with the tourist board for the latest performances. *Laraña 4.* ☎ *954 484 848. Bus: B2, C5, 20, 24, 32. Map p 126.*

★ **Sala la Fundición** ARENAL Fun contemporary modern theater is performed here in the building that was the old foundry for the Royal Mint in the 17th century. *Habana 18.* ☎ *954 225 844.*

www.fundiciondesevilla.es. Bus: B2, C4, 5, 21, 22, 23. Map p 125.

★★ Sala la Imperdible ALAM-
EDA   This fab little community theater stages some of Seville's best contemporary drama, usually put on by local troupes. They're building a brand-new theater and are temporarily resident at the building below. Check website or tourist office for latest news. *Plaza del Duque, s/n.* ☎ 954 905 458. *www.imperdible. org.* Bus: B2, 13, 14. Map p 126.

kids Sala Ocero MACARENA
This funky venue has recently been renovated and provides an intimate space with room for around 150 people. It specializes in contemporary comedy and experimental theater as well as workshops for kids in the mornings. *Sol 5.* ☎ 954 225 165. *www.salacero.com.* Bus: C5, 20, 24, 32. Map p 126.

★★ Teatro Central CARTUJA
A mixed bag of top-notch entertainment takes place at Seville's main theater. Performances are arranged into themed seasons featuring a whole range of disciplines: dance, pop, jazz, classical music or flamenco. *José de Gálvez.* ☎ 955 037

200 (box office). *www.teatrocentral. com.* Bus: C1, C2. Map p 126.

★★ Teatro Lope de Vega
PARQUE MARÍA LUISA   The *teatro* was built for the 1929 Exposition, forming part of the public dance halls. Today, having been thoroughly remodeled, it stages ballet and other musical and theatrical performances. *Avda María Luisa.* ☎ 955 472 822. *www.teatrolopedevega.org.* Bus: 1, C1, C2, 5, 33, 34. Map p 125.

★★ kids Teatro Municipal Alameda ALAMEDA   This local theater often has plays and puppet shows for kids as well as contemporary local theatrical productions. It's on the corner and entrance is actually in Calle Calatrava. *Crédito 11.* ☎ 954 900 164. Bus: 13, 14. Map p 126.

★★ Teatro Quintero CENTRO
This swanky venue contains the studios for Spanish TV star Jésus Quintero's weekly chat show, and you can get tickets to see 'The madman on the hill' live. There are also big-budget dramatic productions staged here in the 300-seat theater. *Cuna 15.* ☎ 954 500 292. Bus: B2, C5, 20, 24, 32. Map p 126. ●

A Big Song & Dance

Flamenco seems to be everywhere in Seville: as a soundtrack in bars, drifting from open windows, being performed, impromptu, by anyone from pre-teen girls to barmen, and at organized tourism events. Old hands tend to sneer at these flamenco *tablaos* (shows) as rehearsed nonsense, a million miles from spontaneous true flamenco, but they offer an easily accessible and entertaining night out. Artists range from the nationally to internationally known, and the dress and costumes are flamboyantly colorful. Many shows offer dinner or just a drink as part of the deal. Real purists, however, will prefer the more traditional, spontaneous songs and dances late at night in the *peñas* (flamenco bars) of the Triana and Macarena districts. The best of these are listed in the Nightlife section (p 111).

Lodging Best Bets

Best for **Friendly Service**
★★ Hotel Alminar $$ *Álvarez Quintero 52 (p 140)*

Best **Value Hotel**
★★★ Hotel Murillo $$ *Lope de Rueda 7–9 (p 142)*

Best **Location**
★★ Hotel Inglaterra $$$ *Plaza Nueva 7 (p 141)*

Best for **Comfortable Elegance**
★★★ Casa Romana $$$ *Trajano 15 (p 138)*

Best **Affordable Design**
★★ Petit Palace Santa Cruz $$ *Ega 5 (p 143)*

Best **Cheap & Cheerful Hotel**
★ Hotel Goya $ *Mateos Gago 31 (p 141)*

Best **Hotel with Moorish Charm**
★★ Alcoba del Rey $$ *Bécquer 9 (p 138)*

Best **Sophisticated Hideaway**
★★★ Hospes Las Casas del Rey de Baeza $$$ *Plaza Jesús de la Redención 2 (p 140)*

Best **In-Hotel Dining**
★★★ Taberna del Alabardero $$ *Zaragoza 20 (p 144)*

Best **Refined & Intimate Townhouse Hotel**
★★ Corral del Rey $$$ *Corral del Rey 12 (p 139)*

Best **Apartment with a View**
★★ Puerta Catedral Apartments $$ *Alemanes 15 (p 144)*

Best **Luxury Apartment**
★★★ Suite Alcázar $$$ *Santo Tomas 1 (p 144)*

Best **Value Apartments**
★★★ Sevilla5 $ *Feria 80 (p 144)*

Most **Charming Hotel**
★★★ Las Casas de la Judería $$$ *Callejón de Dos Hermanas 7 (p 142)*

Best **Hotel with a Terrace**
★★ Vincci La Rábida $$$ *Castelar 24 (p 144)* and ★ Hotel Doña María $$ *Don Remondo 19 (p 141)*

Best for **Music Lovers**
★★ Amadeus La Música $$ *Farneso 6 (p 138)*

Best for **No Expense Spared**
★ Hotel Alfonso XIII $$$ *San Fernando 2 (p 140)*

Best for **Cheapskates**
★★ Pension Doña Trinidad $ *Archeros 7 (p 143)*

Best **Backpacker Hostel**
★ Urbany Hostel $ *Doña María Coronel 12 (p 144)*

Best **Groovy Roof Terrace**
★★ Espacio Azahar $$ *Jesús del Gran Poder 28 (p 139)*

Best **Family Hotel**
★ Hotel Bécquer $$ *Reyes Católicos 4 (p 140)*

Best **Business Hotel**
★ Barceló Renacimiento $$$ *Isla de la Cartuja (p 138)*

Best **Out-of-Town Hotel**
★★★ Hacienda Benazuza/El Bulli Hotel $$$ *Calle Virgen de las Nieves, Sanlúcar la Major (p 139)*

Previous page: Moorish-style decor at the hotel Alcoba del Rey.

Alameda & Macarena Lodging

Alcoba del Rey **2**

Barceló Renacimiento **1**

Casa Romana **8**

Casa Sacristia Santa Ana **6**

Espacio Azahar **7**

Hotel Casona de San Andrés **9**

Hotel San Gil Seville **3**

Patio de la Alameda
Aparthotel **4**

Sevilla5 Apartments **5**

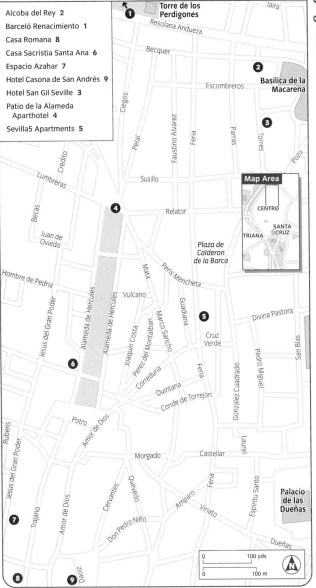

Centro, Arenal & Santa Cruz

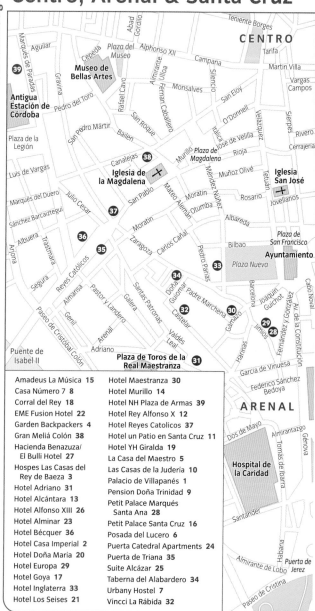

Amadeus La Música **15**
Casa Número 7 **8**
Corral del Rey **18**
EME Fusion Hotel **22**
Garden Backpackers **4**
Gran Meliá Colón **38**
Hacienda Benazuza/
 El Bulli Hotel **27**
Hospes Las Casas del
 Rey de Baeza **3**
Hotel Adriano **31**
Hotel Alcántara **13**
Hotel Alfonso XIII **26**
Hotel Alminar **23**
Hotel Bécquer **36**
Hotel Casa Imperial **2**
Hotel Doña María **20**
Hotel Europa **29**
Hotel Goya **17**
Hotel Inglaterra **33**
Hotel Los Seises **21**

Hotel Maestranza **30**
Hotel Murillo **14**
Hotel NH Plaza de Armas **39**
Hotel Rey Alfonso X **12**
Hotel Reyes Catolicos **37**
Hotel un Patio en Santa Cruz **11**
Hotel YH Giralda **19**
La Casa del Maestro **5**
Las Casas de la Judería **10**
Palacio de Villapanés **1**
Pension Doña Trinidad **9**
Petit Palace Marqués
 Santa Ana **28**
Petit Palace Santa Cruz **16**
Posada del Lucero **6**
Puerta Catedral Apartments **24**
Puerta de Triana **35**
Suite Alcázar **25**
Taberna del Alabardero **34**
Urbany Hostel **7**
Vincci La Rábida **32**

Lodging

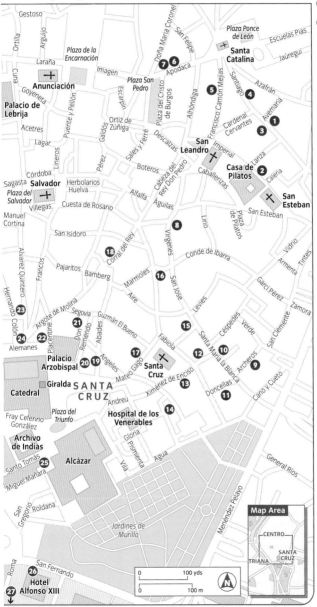

Gestoso
Ortilla
Arguijo
Cuna
Goyeneta
Laraña

Plaza de la
Encarnación

Doña María Coronel
San Felipe

Plaza Ponce
de León

Escuelas Pías
Jáuregui

✚ Santa
Catalina

Anunciación ✚

Palacio de
Lebrija

Acetres
Puente y Pellón
Lineros
Lagar

Imagen

Plaza San
Pedro

Escarpín

Ortiz de
Zúñiga

Galdós

Plaza del Cristo
de Burgos

Apodaca

Alhóndiga

Francisco Carrión Mejías

Santiago

Azafrán

Ave María

Cardenal-
Cervantes

⑦⑥

⑤

④

❶

❸

Córdoba
Sagasta

Salvador

Pérez
Sales y Ferré
Descalzas
Boteros

San Leandro ✚

Imperial

Casa de
Pilatos ❷

Lanza

Calería

Plaza del
Salvador ✚

Herbolarios
Huelva

Cabeza del
Rey Don Pedro

Caballerizas

San
Esteban ✗

Manuel
Cortina
Villegas

Cuesta de Rosario

Alfalfa

Águilas

San Esteban

Plaza
de Pilatos

Vidrio

San Isidoro

❽

Vírgenes

Lirio

Armenta
Tintes

Álvarez Quintero
Francos
Pajaritos

Bamberg

⑱

Marmoles

⑯

Conde de Ibarra

San José

Garcí Pérez

Zamora

Hernando Colón
Alemanes

㉓

㉔

㉒

㉑

Argote de Molina
Bermudo

Segovia
Don

Guzmán El Bueno

Aire

Levíes

Santa María la Blanca

Céspedes

Verde

San Clemente

Palacio
Arzobispal

⑳⑲

⑰

Abades
Ángeles

Mateo Gago

Fabiola

⑮

⑫

⑩

Archeros

❾

Giralda

SANTA
CRUZ

Santa
Cruz ✗

Ximénez de Enciso

⑬

Doncellas

⑪

Cano y Cueto

Catedral

Fray Ceferino
González

Andreu

Plaza del
Triunfo

Hospital de los
Venerables

⑭

Archivo
de Indias

Santo Tomás

Miguel Mañara

㉕

Alcázar

Gloria
Pimienta

Agua

Vila

General Ríos

San Gregorio
Roldana

Jardines de
Murillo

Menéndez Pelayo

Roma

San Fernando

Hotel
Alfonso XIII

㉖

㉗

| 0 | 100 yds |
| 0 | 100 m |

Ⓝ

Map Area

CENTRO

TRIANA

SANTA
CRUZ

Seville Hotels **A to Z**

★★ **Alcoba del Rey** MACARENA
The rooms feel like a sultan's palace in this delightful Moorish-style boutique hotel—all twinkling lamps, drapes and horseshoe arches. Jacuzzis in some rooms. There's a roof terrace with Jacuzzi too. The only downside is the location, a long way from the old center. *Bécquer 9.* ☎ *954 915 800. www.alcobadelrey. com. 15 units. 119€–195€. AE, DC, MC, V. Bus: C1, C2, C3, C4, 13, 14. Map p 135.*

★★ **Amadeus La Música** SANTA CRUZ   This charming small hotel is a family affair. María Guerrero and her daughters keep it in immaculate condition, and service is of the highest standard. The musical theme permeates the hotel, with instruments lining the walls and pianos in some rooms. *Farnesio 6.* ☎ *954 501 443. www.hotelamadeussevilla.com. 19 units. Doubles 82€–145€. DC, MC, V. Bus: 1, C3, C4, 21. Map p 136.*

★ **Barceló Renacimiento** TRIANA/CARTUJA   This modern garden hotel overlooking the river has large, comfortable rooms, a sauna and an outdoor pool. Food and service in the restaurant are faultless. Good value considering its luxury, but a 10-minute cab ride from the

center. *Isla de la Cartuja.* ☎ *954 462 222. www.barcelo.com. 295 units. Doubles 225€. AE, DC, MC, V. Bus: C1, C2, E5. Map p 135.*

★ **Casa Número 7** SANTA CRUZ
This *casa* is immaculately decked out with antiques, oil paintings and oriental rugs. The six rooms are tranquil, if rather formal—a little pricey for what they are. The roof terrace has views over the Giralda. *Vírgenes 7.* ☎ *954 221 581. www.casanumero7.com. 6 units. 177€–275€. AE, MC, V. Bus: C5. Map p 136.*

★★★ **Casa Romana** CENTRO
A delightful boutique hotel with bright, spacious, comfortable rooms furnished with fresh flowers daily. The sundeck and Jacuzzi on the roof terrace will mean you'll struggle to leave. *Trajano 15.* ☎ *954 915 170. www.hotelcasaromana.com. 27 units. Doubles 120€–275€. AE, DC, MC, V. Bus: 13, 14. Map p 135.*

★★ **Casa Sacristía Santa Ana** ALAMEDA   This stylish casa on the Alameda has a pleasantly relaxed interior patio with wooden ceilings and fountain, and good-sized rooms, each with a slightly different theme. A real notch up on anything else nearby, there's a good restaurant

Moorish-style decor at the hotel Alcoba del Rey.

Corral del Rey.

too. *Alameda de Hércules 22.* ☎ *954 915 722. www.hotelsacristia.com. 25 units. Doubles 60€–291€. AE, DC, MC, V. Bus: 13, 14. Map p 135.*

★★ Corral del Rey SANTA CRUZ This 17th-century palace house has been stylishly converted into a comfortable hideaway, located moments from the hubbub of Santa Cruz. Nice roof terrace with plunge pool too. The Reid family also owns the gorgeous Hacienda de San Rafael just out of town. *Corral del Rey 12.* ☎ *954 227 116. www.corraldelrey. com. 6 units. Doubles 280€–380€. AE, DC, MC, V. Bus: C5. Map p 136.*

EME Fusion Hotel CENTRO Brilliant location right next to the cathedral, stunning roof terrace and achingly cool, award-winning interior design is let down by hopelessly snooty service. It all feels oddly out of place in a city like Seville. *Alemanes 27.* ☎ *954 560 000. 63 units. www.emecatedralhotel.com. Doubles 150€–250€. Tram: Plaza Nueva. Bus: C5. Map p 136.*

★★ Espacio Azahar ALAMEDA Reception looks rather unpromising, but the 14 rooms with a Moorish edge are light and cool, with plasma TVs. The building was designed by Aníbal González, architect of the Plaza de España. There's a groovy roof terrace too. *Jesús del Gran Poder 28.* ☎ *954 384 109. 14 units. www.espacioazahar.com. Doubles 90€–130€. Bus: 13, 14. Map p 135.*

★ Garden Backpackers SANTA CRUZ There are backpacker places springing up all over town. This one opened in October 2009 and it's well located, with a nice garden. Clean and well run, with bike rental and free Wi-Fi, it can get a little noisy—or it's great for social life, depending on your viewpoint. *Santiago 19.* ☎ *954 223 866. www.thegarden backpacker.com. Beds 15€–20€. MC, V. Bus: C5. Map p 136.*

★★ Gran Meliá Colón ARENAL The recent makeover of this grand old dame has been a success. It's still a big, slightly soulless five-star hotel, but rooms are tastefully designed and genuinely comfortable. All manner of upgrade options available if budget's not an issue. *Canalejas 1.* ☎ *954 505 599. www. gran-melia-colon.com. 211 units. Doubles 270€–345€. AE, DC, MC, V. Bus: AC, B2, C5, 43. Map p 136.*

★★★ Hacienda Benazuza/El Bulli Hotel SANLÚCAR LA MAYOR Near the hamlet of Sanlúcar la Mayor, 19km (12 miles) south of Seville, this is the place to stay if you're a foodie and have time to spend a night out of town. The kitchen at this stylish and intimate hotel is under the direction of Ferran Adrià, the Catalan chef whose El Bulli restaurant is regularly voted best in the world. The 33-course tasting menu makes an unforgettable eating experience. *Virgen de las Nieves, Sanlúcar la Major.* ☎ 955 703 344. *www.elbullihotel.com.* 44 *units. Doubles 340€–425€. AE, DC, MC, V. From Seville, follow the signs for Huelva & head south on the A-49, taking exit 16. Map p 136.*

★★★ Hospes Las Casas del Rey de Baeza SANTA CRUZ

This antique house is a real gem, with stone floors and 19th-century Andalusian architecture, an interior patio surrounded by a cozy coterie of stylishly comfortable rooms, a cool rooftop pool and soothing spa. *Plaza Jesús de la Redención 2.* ☎ 954 561 496. *www.hospes.es.* 41 *units. Doubles 160€–200€. AE, DC, MC, V. Bus: 1, C3, C4, C5, 10, 24, 27. Map p 136.*

★ Hotel Adriano ARENAL

A good-value hotel, well located, with a small roof terrace, the Adriano has spacious, clean rooms with amenities like minibar and safe. *Adriano 12.* ☎ 954 293 800. *www.adrianohotel.com.* 34 *units. Doubles 80€–130€. MC, V. Bus: C5. Map p 136.*

★★ Hotel Alcántara SANTA CRUZ

An attractively furnished, tranquil hotel in a great location, the Alcántara has one of the best flamenco patios right next door (but no noise problems). *Ximénez de Enciso 28.* ☎ 954 500 595. *www.hotelalcantara.net.* 21 *units. Doubles 73€–145€. AE, DC, MC, V. Bus: 1, C3, C4, 23. Map p 136.*

★ Hotel Alfonso XIII PARQUE MARÍA LUISA

Part of Starwood Hotels' Luxury Collection, Seville's most opulent hotel is a stately palace. The large rooms are Moorish and Castilian in style, with all the amenities you'd expect and prices to match. *San Fernando 2.* ☎ 954 917 000. *www.luxurycollection.com.* 149 *units. Doubles 455€–598€. AE, DC, MC, V. Bus: AC, B2, C4, 5, 21, 22, 23. Tram: Universidad. Map p 136.*

★★★ Hotel Alminar CENTRO

Consistently No 1 at TripAdvisor and rightly so: Francisco and his friendly team are in my opinion the most helpful in Seville. Small reception area, but rooms are well sized, with hi-fi systems and the usual amenities. *Álvarez Quintero 52.* ☎ 954 293 913. *www.hotelalminar.com.* 13 *units. Doubles 95€–125€. AE, DC, MC, V. Bus: C5. Map p 136.*

★ Hotel Bécquer ARENAL

This friendly, family-owned hotel is modern and functional in style, offering good value for such amenities, including a rooftop terrace and pool. There's a small spa and it's easily accessible by car. *Reyes Catolicos 4.* ☎ 954 228 900. *www.hotelbecquer.com.* 137 *units. Doubles 85€–210€. AE, DC, MC, V. Bus: AC, B2, C5, 43. Map p 136.*

★★ Hotel Casa Imperial SANTA CRUZ

This Sevillian palace, set away from the busy-ness of Santa Cruz, houses a luxury hotel with elegant rooms around four tranquil patios. Service is particularly good here. *Imperial 29.* ☎ 954 500 300. *www.casaimperial.com.* 24 *units. 214€–449€. AE, DC, MC, V. Bus: C5, 24, 27. Map p 136.*

Hotel Casona de San Andrés CENTRO

The San Andrés is located in an atmospherically renovated 19th-century palace with dark wood furniture and wrought-iron balustrades. There are two pretty patios and a roof terrace with sun loungers, and some rooms have balconies overlooking the square and San Andrés Church. *Daóiz 7.* ☎ 954 915 253. *www.casonadesanandres.com.* 25 *units. Doubles 100€. MC, V. Bus: 13, 14. Map p 135.*

One of Hotel Inglaterra's comfortable suites.

★ **Hotel Doña María** SANTA CRUZ A rooftop pool with lovely views of the Giralda is the main incentive here. The slightly twee but good-value and comfortable rooms are well furnished; some have four-poster beds. *Don Remondo 19.* ☎ *954 224 990. www.hdmaria.com. 68 units. Doubles 100€–222€. AE, DC, MC, V. Bus: C5. Map p 136.*

★★ **Hotel Europa** ARENAL Rooms here are basic and a little tired, but it's well located, close to the center and well priced. A pretty good deal if you're on a budget, with a triple and a quadruple room too. *Jimios 5.* ☎ *954 500 443. www. hoteleuropasevilla.com. Doubles 52€–89€. MC, V. Bus: C5. Tram: Plaza Nueva. Map p 136.*

★ **Hotel Goya** SANTA CRUZ A modestly priced option in the center of the tourist district, the Goya's 19 rooms are simply furnished, clean and with TV and air-conditioning. *Mateos Gago 31.* ☎ *954 211 170. www.hostalgoyasevilla.com. 19 units. Doubles 75€–95€. MC, V. Bus: C5. Map p 136.*

★★ **Hotel Inglaterra** CENTRO Ideally located on Plaza Nueva, a step away from the sights and the shopping, the Inglaterra is Seville's oldest hotel. Recently renovated, it offers spacious, quite formal but comfortable rooms and suites. Service is attentive and helpful. *Plaza Nueva 7.* ☎ *954 224 970. www. hotelinglaterra.es. 86 units. Doubles 130€–200€. AE, DC, MC, V. Bus: C5. Tram: Plaza Nueva. Map p 136.*

Hotel Los Seises SANTA CRUZ Right in the center of Seville, this 16th-century former archbishop's palace has a rooftop pool with views over the Giralda. The stylish rooms are well equipped, but common areas are a little tired and it has a reputation for poor service. *Segovia 6.* ☎ *954 229 495. www.hotel losseises.com. 43 units. Doubles 158€–286€. AE, DC, MC, V. Bus: C5. Map p 136.*

★★★ **Hotel Maestranza** ARENAL Bright, simple, but comfortable accommodations, in an attractive old town house, well located for the center, are coupled with friendly service at this good-value, family-run hotel. *Gamazo 12.* ☎ *954 561 070. www.hotelmaestranza.es. 18 units. Doubles 57€–115€. MC, V.*

Bus: C5. Tram: Plaza Nueva. Map
p 136.

★★★ Hotel Murillo SANTA CRUZ

Hidden in the heart of Santa Cruz,
the Murillo is a welcoming, good-
value hotel in a great location.
Reception has an antique carved
ceiling and rooms are attractively
furnished. The rooftop terrace has
views of the Giralda. Apartments also
available. *Lope de Rueda 7–9.* ☎ *954
216 095. www.hotelmurillo.com. 57
units. Doubles 75€–100€. AE, DC,
MC, V. Bus: 1, C3, C5. Map p 136.*

★ Hotel NH Plaza de Armas

ARENAL   A sleek, curvaceous building, the Plaza has a rooftop pool
with riverside views and stylish,
modern rooms. It's a 10-minute
walk from the center, but well
placed for the art museums. *Marqués de Paradas.* ☎ *954 901 992.
www.nh-hotels.com. 262 units. Doubles 122€–222€. AE, DC, MC, V. Bus:
B2, C3, C4, 6. Map p 136.*

★ Hotel Rey Alfonso X SANTA

CRUZ   A modern, stylish hotel in a
good location with easy access for
taxis, the Rey's rooms are sleek and
understated and the staff friendly
and helpful. Guests can use the
swimming pool at the Fernando III
opposite. *Ximénez de Enciso 35.*
☎ *954 210 070. www.reyalfonsox.
com. 35 units. Doubles 166€–218€.
AE, DC, MC, V. Bus: 1, C3, C4, 21.
Map p 136.*

Hotel Reyes Catolicos ARENAL

A fairly standard hotel in an easily
accessible location, the Reyes has
large, clean, modern rooms and is
well located for shopping and the
museums. *Gravina 57.* ☎ *954 211
200. www.hotelreyescatolicos.info.
26 units. Doubles 95€–160€. AE,
DC, MC, V. Bus: AC, B2, C5, 43. Map
p 136.*

★ Hotel San Gil Seville

MACARENA   Set amid palm trees,
the San Gil has an interior garden
with tinkling fountains and pretty
mosaics. There's every modern
amenity, including a lovely rooftop
swimming pool. *Parras 28.* ☎ *954
906 811. www.hotelsangil.com. 60
units. Doubles 101€–213€. AE, DC,
MC, V. Bus: C3, 2, 13, 14. Map p 135.*

★ Hotel un Patio en Santa Cruz SANTA CRUZ

Well located in
Santa Cruz, the Patio has a modern,
functional interior in a traditional old
Sevillian house. Several rooms have
balconies, while two third-floor
rooms have direct access to the
hotel's roof terrace, with views of
the Giralda. Triple room available
too. *Doncellas 15.* ☎ *954 539 413.
www.patiosantacruz.com. 13 units.
Doubles 68€–128€. AE, DC, MC, V.
Bus: 1, C3, C4, 21. Map p 136.*

★★ Hotel YH Giralda SANTA

CRUZ   This attractively furnished,
comfortable small hotel is well
located in Santa Cruz. Rooms and
bathrooms are to a high standard
and Lourdes and her small team are
really friendly and helpful. There's no
lift or breakfast room. *Abades 30.*
☎ *954 228 324. www.yh-hoteles.
com. 14 units. Doubles 70€–85€. AE,
DC, MC, V. Bus: 1, C3, C5. Map p 136.*

★★ La Casa del Maestro

SANTA CRUZ   This house belonged
to famous guitarist Niño Ricardo
and the tastefully decorated rooms
are full of the maestro and other flamenco greats. Rooms are comfortable, with big beds and fluffy
pillows, and there's an attractive
patio. *Almudena 5.* ☎ *954 500 007.
www.lacasadelmaestro.com. 11
units. Doubles 110€–130€. AE, DC,
MC, V. Bus: C5, 10, 11, 12, 20, 24, 27,
32. Map p 136.*

★★★ Las Casas de la Juderia

SANTA CRUZ   A luxurious warren
of ancient houses and patios connected by underground tunnels, the

Casas is one of Seville's most attractive hotels. Each room is unique, some fantastically opulent. There's an enticing rooftop pool and spa, and service is excellent. *Santa Maria la Blanca 5.* ☎ *954 415 150. www. casasypalacios.com. 116 units. Doubles 140€–175€. AE, DC, MC, V. Bus: 1, C3, C4, 21. Map p 136.*

★ **Palacio de Villapanés** SANTA CRUZ   Set in a huge palace house, the Palacio has been renovated in luxuriously modern style with lots of dark wood and white upholstery. The five-star rooms are really spacious. There is a pool and terrace on the roof and a fine-dining restaurant in the vaulted cellars. *Santiago 31.* ☎ *954 502 063. www.almasevilla. com. 55 units. Doubles 162€–520€. AE, DC, MC, V. Bus: 1, C3, C4, C5, 10, 24, 27. Map p 136.*

Patio de la Alameda Aparthotel ALAMEDA   Right on the Alameda, with several cool bars and cafes on the doorstep, these simply furnished, small but well-appointed apartments offer good value for money. *Alameda de Hércules 56.* ☎ *954 904 999. www.patiodela alameda.com. 21 units. Doubles 85€–99€. AE, DC, MC, V. Bus: 13, 14. Map p 135.*

★★ **Pension Doña Trinidad** SANTA CRUZ   A great option if you're on a budget. Well located on a quiet side street in Santa Cruz, the Pension is housed in an old Sevillian house with a cool tiled patio. Rooms are simple and clean. Service is friendly. *Archeros 7.* ☎ *954 541 906. www.donatrinidad.com. 16 units. Doubles 48€–60€. MC, V. Bus: 1, C3, C4, 21. Map p 136.*

★★ **Petit Palace Marqués Santa Ana** ARENAL   Another in the chain of High Tech hotels (Seville has three with a fourth on the way), the Petit Palace Santa Cruz features the same attractive formula: sleek modern lines and furniture in a renovated, airy palace. *Jimios 9.* ☎ *954 221 812. www.hthoteles.com. 57 units. Doubles 75€–160€. AE, DC, MC, V. Bus: C5. Tram: Plaza Nueva. Map p 136.*

★★ **Petit Palace Santa Cruz** SANTA CRUZ   Part of the High Tech chain (see above), the Petit Palace features smooth lines, muted tones and modern decor inside a nicely renovated 17th-century palace. LCD TVs and hydro-massage showers in most rooms. *Muñoz y Pabón, 18.* ☎ *954 221 032. www.hthoteles. com. 46 units. Doubles 90€–160€. AE, DC, MC, V. Bus: C5. Map p 136.*

Las Casas de la Judería is set in fragrant courtyards.

Posada del Lucero CENTRO

This modern, stylish hotel features dark wood furniture and cream upholstery. Bathrooms have slate floors and black granite surrounds. Avoid rooms at the front as the road is quite noisy. *Almirante Apodaca 7.* ☎ *954 502 480. www.hotelposada dellucero.es. 39 units. Double 166€– 218€. AE, DC, MC, V. Bus: C5, 20, 24 32. Map p 136.*

★★★ Puerta Catedral Apartments CENTRO

With probably the best roof terraces in Seville, offering spectacular views of the cathedral, these stylish, comfortable apartments are furnished to a high standard and make a great base for exploring Seville. *Alemanes 15.* ☎ *954 216 912. www.puerta catedral.com. 10 units. Double 190€. MC, V. Tram: Plaza Nueva. Bus: C5. Map p 136.*

★ Puerta de Triana CENTRO

This budget hotel, built in the early 1970s, is 5 minutes from the cathedral. Antique styles are mixed with modern features, and the interior is surprisingly elegant. The hotel offers simply but comfortably furnished rooms. *Reyes Católicos 5.* ☎ *954 215 404. 65 units. Doubles 90€– 130€. AE, DC, MC, V. Bus: AC, B2, C5, 43. Map p 136.*

★★★ Sevilla5 Apartments

MACARENA   Located in the traditional neighborhood of Macarena, 15 minutes from the center, these modern, bright apartments are great value. The top-floor studio has a huge roof terrace. Sevilla5 has lots more nice apartments available in all price brackets. *Feria 80.* ☎ *954 387 550. www.sevilla5.com. Doubles 60€. MC, V. Bus: 13,14. Map p 135.*

★★★ Suite Alcázar SANTA CRUZ

If money's no object then this luxury villa, run by the Casa Romana Hotel, is right next to the Alcázar with a sun terrace offering stunning views and Jacuzzi. Finished to a high standard, it has all the usual amenities. *Santo Tomás 1.* ☎ *954 915 170. www.suitealcazar.com. 1 unit. 1,000€. AE, DC, MC, V. Tram: Archivo de Indias. Map p 136.*

★★★ Taberna del Alabardero

CENTRO   With the catering academy next door, the Taberna offers some of Seville's finest dining. They've now added seven guest rooms to this restored 19th-century mansion, all with antique furniture and whirlpool baths. *Zaragoza 20.* ☎ *954 502 721. 7 units. 110€–235€. AE, DC, MC, V. Bus: AC, C5, 43. Map p 136.*

★ Urbany Hostel CENTRO

This clean, modern backpacker hostel has two-, four-, six- and eight-person rooms. Breakfast is included. There's a small, modern lounge area, free Wi-Fi and no curfew. *Doña Maria Coronel 12.* ☎ *954 227 949. www.sevillaurbany.com. Beds 12€– 25€. Bus: C5, 10, 11, 12, 20, 24, 27, 32. MC, V. Map p 136.*

★★ Vincci La Rábida CENTRO

This stylishly restored 18th-century town house palace, part of the excellent Vincci chain, is both luxurious and comfortable. Its terrace restaurant also offers some of the best rooftop views in Seville. *Castelar 24.* ☎ *954 501 280. www.vinccihoteles. com. 81 units. Doubles 165€–320€. AE, DC, MC, V. Bus: AC, C5 43. Map p 136.* ●

Itálica

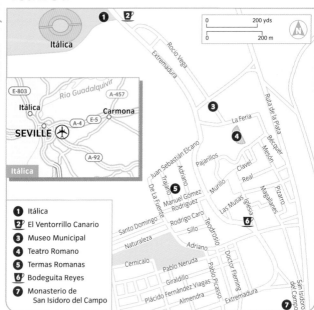

1. Itálica
2. El Ventorrillo Canario
3. Museo Municipal
4. Teatro Romano
5. Termas Romanas
6. Bodeguita Reyes
7. Monasterio de San Isidoro del Campo

Apart from the odd re-used pillar, Seville's Roman history isn't too evident. But the Romans were here and left their mark five miles north at Itálica, which was once the third-largest city in the Roman empire. The ruins here make an interesting day trip, a reminder that great civilizations preceded the Moors. There's also a spectacular restored monastery nearby. **START: Catch the M172 bus to Santiponce from the bus station at Seville's Plaza de Armas. Get off at the last stop, right opposite the entrance to the ruins. Buses run every 10 to 20 minutes.**

1 ★★★ Itálica. Founded in 206 B.C., Itálica rose to prominence during the reign of Hadrian in the 2nd century A.D. Hadrian was one of three Roman emperors born here (the others were his father Trajan and Theodosius). He expanded the city of his birth to the point where its population grew to half a million. The signed route takes you through the old city walls onto wide streets arranged at right angles to one another. There are remains of villas with mosaics, in particular in the House of Neptune and the House of the Birds, where a mosaic depicts 30 bird species in surprising detail. There's another fine mosaic, of the deities of the seven days of the week, in the **House of the**

Previous page: Patio Naranjos.

Fine mosaics in the House of the Planetarium.

Planetarium. Other excavations include the baths, but the star of the show is the huge amphitheater, which retains its distinct oval shape, tiered seating galleries, and pits where animals and gladiators waited before entering the arena. It's a hugely evocative walk around the tunnels on the ground floor. From their narrow doorways there are views into the huge arena which offer a real sense of the sheer scale of the place. It once seated 25,000. Make sure to bring a hat, water and sunscreen on hot days as there's not much shade. ⏱ *1 hr. Avda de Extremadura 2, Santiponce.* ☎ *955 622 266. 1.50€; free for E.U. passport holders. Tues–Sat 9am–5:30pm (8:30pm in summer), Sun 10am–3pm, closed Mon.*

2 El Ventorrillo Canario. This local bar almost opposite the entrance to the ruins serves cool drinks and tapas. The restaurant to the right of the hotel entrance does good meat dishes if you want a bigger bite. *Avda de Extremadura 13.* ☎ *955 996 700. $.*

3 Museo Municipal (Municipal Museum). Santiponce isn't the most inspiring of towns, despite the wealth of Roman remains here. The tourist information office is hidden on a back street off the main road. The staff are helpful and have maps of the town and of local driving trails. The small municipal museum here features changing art installations. *La Feria.* ☎ *955 998 028. Free. Tues–Sun 10am–2pm (also 4:30–7:30pm in winter), closed Mon.*

4 ★★ Teatro Romano (Roman Theater). This theater is just across from the tourist office. Unfortunately you can't gain access to the site, but have to be content merely to look through a fence. However, there's a viewpoint (*mirador*) further into town which gives a better impression. To reach it from the tourist office, return to the main road, walk up the short hill round a bend and take a left past the small park. Work your way round to the site along Calle Siete Revueltos—it's signposted. From above there's a good view of the semicircle of

Itálica's vast amphitheater once seated 25,000 people.

banked seats and stage. The theater could accommodate around 1,000 spectators. The seating area has been restored and in the past it's been used to stage local concerts and plays. ⏱ *10 min. Siete Revueltos. Free. Tues–Sat 9am–2pm (viewpoint).*

⑤ Termas Romanas (Roman Baths). This smaller bath site predates the larger bath buildings at Itálica. Along with the Teatro it's evidence of the smaller provincial town that stood here before the period of expansion under Emperor Hadrian. There are several deep trenches and brick foundations but not a great deal else. It's a 10-minute walk to the site. As at the Teatro you look through a fence; visiting inside is not possible. If you have a car it's worth a quick detour; if you are

on foot you might choose not to. ⏱ *5 min. Trajano. Free.*

⑥★ Bodeguita Reyes. This traditional local cellar makes a good resting point if you are on foot (it's a bit of a walk to the next stop on this tour). Tapas include grilled prawns and sirloin in whisky. *Avda de Extremadura 34.* ☎ *955 998 368. $.*

⑦ ★★★ Monasterio de San Isidoro del Campo. The San Isidoro monastery was founded in 1301. It's part of a huge monasterial complex. A 12-year renovation project has restored the two churches, several rooms and the peaceful central courtyard. It's a spectacular achievement. Two Gothic churches house ornately decorated

A Roman ruin at Santiponce.

Hop on the Bus

It's a bit of a walk from the Roman ruins to the Monasterio de San Isidoro del Campo—about 40 minutes in total. If you time it right you can jump on the bus to get between the sites. Buses run every 20 to 30 minutes depending on the time of day. There are three bus stops in Santiponce on the M172 line and you'll see them as you come through town on the way to start this tour at the Itálica ruins. The first stop is close to the monastery, the second is on the main avenue at the junction of the Teatro viewpoint, and the last stop is Itálica itself. The bus follows the same route on its return.

altarpieces, one carved by the celebrated local sculptor Martínez Montañés (1568–1749) with San Isidoro at its center and biblical scenes around it. It took Montañés 18 months to complete, and he lived in the monastery while he crafted it. Down the ages different orders inhabited the monastery and decorated it in various ways—clearly evident in the cloister with its combination of Mudéjar-style tiles and Hieronymite murals. Rooms leading from it include the refectory, which houses exhibits from elsewhere in the monastery, the vestry, with mirrors on the walls to help the monks robe for services, and other function rooms. Almost all are painted with beautifully colored murals showing details of monastic life and depictions of saints. Most date from the 15th century and are some of the finest and most complete in Spain. ⏱ *1 hr. Avda San Isidoro del Campo 18.* ☎ *955 624 400. 2€. Wed–Sat 10am–2pm, 4–7pm. Sun 10am–3pm. Closed Mon & Tues. Summer hours vary.*

The Monasterio de San Isidoro del Campo has been beautifully restored.

Carmona

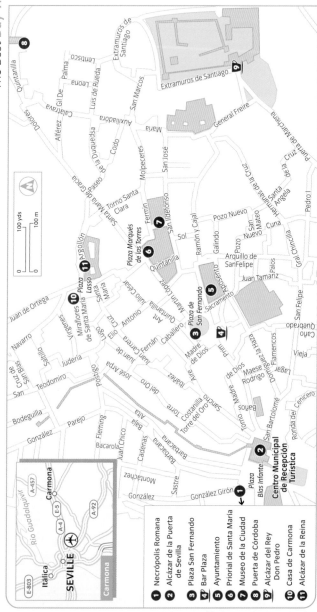

1 Necrópolis Romana
2 Alcázar de la Puerta de Sevilla
3 Plaza San Fernando
4 Bar Plaza
5 Ayuntamiento
6 Priorial de Santa Maria
7 Museo de la Ciudad
8 Puerta de Cordoba
9 Alcázar del Rey Don Pedro
10 Casa de Carmona
11 Alcázar de la Reina

Carmona is a beautifully preserved fortified town situated 39km (24 miles) east of Seville. One of the oldest settlements in Spain, today it's a prosperous, refined place. Inside its old walls you'll find a dense concentration of mansions, churches, cobbled streets and palaces. If you have time, consider an overnight stay as there are several delightful hotels and good restaurants too (see box on p 153). START: **If you have a car, drive to the Roman Necropolis on the outskirts of town (Avda Jorge Bonsor). If you take the bus, start at ② and restrict your tour to the walled town, which is easily walkable. Buses (around one per hour) leave from Seville's main bus station at Prado de San Sebastian.**

① ★★ Necrópolis Romana.

Carmo, as the Romans called the city, was a major crossroads on the Via Augusta and an important outpost in the vast Roman empire. During the 1st and 2nd centuries A.D., higher-ranking citizens were customarily buried here, outside the city walls, in specially constructed tombs, on the site of earlier burial grounds. This burial complex is the only one of its kind in Spain. You can step down into several rock tombs. There's also a small, nicely laid-out museum exhibiting finds from the

Tomb of the Elephant at Necrópolis Romana.

tombs—including the strange statue of an elephant that gave one tomb its name. Walk up the steps at the side of the building to get a sense of the scale of the complex from up on the roof. Across the road are the sizeable remains of a Roman amphitheater built in the 1st century BC. *Avda Jorge Bonsor 9.* ☎ *954 140 811. 2€; free for E.U. passport holders. Tues–Fri 9am–6pm. Weekends 9am–3:30pm (closes 2pm in summer).*

② ★★★ kids Alcázar de la Puerta de Sevilla. The city's

most prominent sight is the solid old fortress and fortified gateway into the old town. Its origins are Carthaginian, but through the ages the Romans, Moors and Christians expanded and revised it. It now houses a helpful tourist information office, and you can visit many of the rooms, some of which house exhibits. It's well worth watching the informative DVD (available in English) about the town's history, in the first (audiovisual) room. From here you climb up into the battlements, crossing above the two huge gateways where you see the shutes down which boiling liquids were poured to repel invaders. Further up there's an elevated patio, and on up the tower there are views in all directions. *Arco de la Puerta de Sevilla.* ☎ *954 190 955. 2€. Mon–Sat 10am–6pm, Sun 10am–3pm.*

Plaza San Fernando.

❸ Plaza San Fernando. This square is the center of the old town and in Roman times was the forum, where the main east–west and north–south roads intersected. It remains the focus of the old town today, lined with trees and ancient wood-beamed houses. Kids kick soccer balls around while old men sit in the shade watching the world go by.

❹ ★★ Bar Plaza. My favorite of the tapas bars here has tables at the side of the plaza. Salmorejo, a cool, thick tomato soup with lashings of garlic and lemon juice, is a regional specialty, and they do a delicious one here. *Plaza San Fernando.* ☎ 954 190 067. $.

❺ ★★ Ayuntamiento. The town hall is an 18th-century building with an imposing Renaissance facade. It houses municipal offices, but you can also sneak inside to admire the Roman mosaic in the main courtyard, with Gorgona Medusa at its center and goddesses representing the four seasons in each corner. Originally part of the Roman baths in Calle Pozonuevo, a street nearby, it was uncovered in 1923 during excavation work and subsequently moved here. *Salvador 2.* ☎ 954 140 011. Free. Mon–Fri 8am–3pm.

❻ ★★ Priorial de Santa María. Built on the site of the city's main mosque after the Christian reconquest in the 15th century, this is the finest of the town's churches. You enter through the shady orange-tree-lined patio that was originally the mosque's ablutions patio. The church has a huge Gothic vaulted ceiling, carved choirstall, ornate statue of the Virgin of the Grace (from around 1300) and exquisite golden altarpiece—one of the best examples of Plateresque carving in the region. Up a narrow spiral staircase in the corner of the courtyard there's a small museum displaying silver chalices, the sword of Inigo de Loyola (St. Ignatius, 1491–1556, founder of the Jesuit Order), ceremonial clothing and—stars of the show—12 strikingly realistic paintings of the apostles by Zurbarán. *Plaza Marqués de las Torres.* ☎ 954 141 330. 3€. Mon–Fri 9am–2pm, 5:30–7pm, Sat 9am–2pm, closed Aug 20–Sept 20.

❼ ★★★ Museo de la Ciudad. Carmona's city museum, although small, deserves a visit. Housed on two floors of an attractive baroque town house, it traces the history of the city through the ages, with

The Priorial de Santa María bell tower.

some signage in English. Arrow-heads, tools and ceramics from the Carthaginian, Roman and Moorish eras are on display, along with the Saltillo Collection—several virtually complete Tartessian earthenware pots from around the 6th century B.C., decorated with oriental scenes. Exhibits continue to the present day, with contemporary paintings and displays on current digs. Confusingly, some maps have the museum marked as the Museo Casa Palacio del Marqués de las Torres. *San Ildefonso 1.* ☎ *954 140 128. 2€ (free Tues). 11am–7pm daily except closed Tues pm. Summer hours vary.*

The Museo de la Ciudad is housed in an attractive baroque town house.

8 ★★★ **Puerta de Córdoba.** A 10-minute walk from the museum past the Plaza de Santiago, with its cross and church, this second surviving gate from the Roman era, where the Via Augusta continued to Córdoba, has been altered several times through the ages. With no houses on either side, and built in a natural hollow, it's a striking sight. The gate was originally two octagonal towers with three archways between them—a large one in the center for carriages and two smaller ones either side for pedestrians. The smaller openings were closed up in the 2nd century. Carmona architect José de Echamorro gave the gate its romantic Renaissance facade between 1786 and 1800.

Tours: book at tourist office. ☎ *954 140 128. 2€. Tues, Sat, Sun 11:30am, 12:30pm & 1:30pm.*

9 ★★★ **Alcázar del Rey Don Pedro.** This imposing 14th-century palace overlooking the plains is now a parador—a historic hotel. Paradors offer some of the most delightful accommodations in Spain and, with its lovely patio, vaulted dining hall and sweeping views, this one is no exception (see above). Non-residents are welcome to use the bar and patio for a relaxing drink or tapas. *Alcázar.* ☎ *954 141 010. www.parador.es. $$.*

Stay a While

Carmona boasts several first-rate hotels so, if you have time, stay a while. The parador Alcázar del Rey Don Pedro (above) is the height of luxury in a beautiful setting. The hotel **10** **Casa de Carmona** (Plaza de Lasso 1. ☎ 954 191 000. www.casadecarmona.com) and the **11** **Alcázar de la Reina** (Plaza de Lasso 2. ☎ 954 196 200. www.alcazar-reina.es) are both elegant, tranquil and homely and offer great service. It's highly advisable to book ahead. All three offer excellent dining.

Córdoba

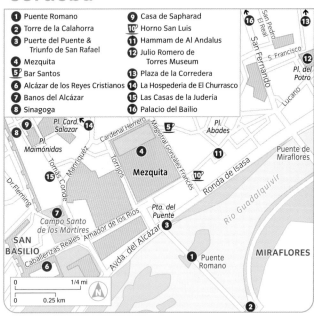

1. Puente Romano
2. Torre de la Calahorra
3. Puerte del Puente & Triunfo de San Rafael
4. Mezquita
5. Bar Santos
6. Alcázar de los Reyes Cristianos
7. Banos del Alcázar
8. Sinagoga
9. Casa de Sapharad
10. Horno San Luis
11. Hammam de Al Andalus
12. Julio Romero de Torres Museum
13. Plaza de la Corredera
14. La Hospederia de El Churrasco
15. Las Casas de la Judería
16. Palacio del Bailio

Córdoba is one of Andalucia's gems. In the 10th century it was the western capital of the Islamic empire—a place of learning, sophistication and wealth. Today its historic center is a lovely maze of whitewashed houses and restaurants, ideal for strolling. At its heart lies one of the most extraordinary buildings in Europe—the magical Mezquita. There's plenty for a day trip, and I'd recommend an overnight stay if you have time. START: **Catch the train from Seville's main railway station Santa Justa (45 min; see p 165). By car, take the fast A6 road direct to Córdoba.**

1 ★★ Puente Romano. Córdoba is best known for its Moorish heritage but, long before the Moors, it was an important Roman provincial capital. The much-restored bridge is the most potent reminder of the city's Roman past. Walk across for great views of the old town, with the vast bulk of the Mezquita dominating the skyline.

2 ★ Torre de la Calahorra. The Calahorra Tower was one of the defensive gates of the Islamic city. It now houses displays explaining Córdoba's history and introducing key characters who influenced it through the ages. It's a little pricey for what it is and the audio headsets are a tad quirky, but it is recommended if you want to understand the sights in context. ⏲ *45 min.*

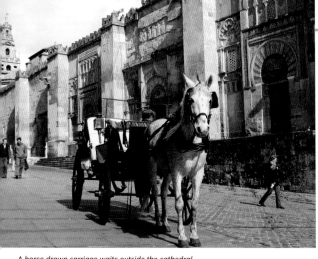

A horse-drawn carriage waits outside the cathedral.

Puente Romano. ☎ *957 293 929. www.torrecalahorra.com. 4.50€, concessions 3€. Daily 10am–6pm (Oct–April); 10am–2pm, 4:30–8:30pm (May–Sept).*

❸ Puerte del Puente & Triunfo de San Rafael.

Returning across the bridge you pass under another of the old city gates—Puerte del Puente (Bridge Gate), being restored as a museum at the time of writing. Once through, you'll see a statue on a tall column. This is San Rafael (St. Raphael), the city's patron saint. It was crafted by the sculptor Miguel Verdiguier in 1756 as thanks to the saint for having saved the city from a great earthquake.

❹ ★★★ Mezquita (cathedral).

The clue is in the name. It's been the city's cathedral since 1236, but locals still call it 'the mosque' (*mezquita*). Step inside and you see why: first impressions are dominated by its Islamic history—a forest of over 400 red-and-white-striped Moorish double arches supported on marble columns. The impact is breathtaking. Begun by Emir Abd al Rahman I in 785, the mosque was built in stages, but each addition followed the same architectural principles. Unusually, it was oriented toward Damascus—the Emir's homeland—rather than toward Mecca. Wander further and you reach the beautiful *mihrab* on the south wall—a horseshoe-shaped prayer niche smothered in intricate golden decoration. Following the recapture of Córdoba by King Ferdinand III in 1236, the mosque was reconsecrated as a cathedral. Sensitive additions in the form of small chapels—among them the Mudéjar-style Capilla de Villaviciosa (1377)—were added at first, but there was no compromise with the vast cathedral, which Bishop Alonso Manrique started in 1523. Plonked slap in the middle of the mosque, it certainly makes a statement—an extravagant edifice of Renaissance domes and baroque altar vaults. Flooded with light from the high windows, it's in complete contrast to the darkness of the surrounding mosque. The most remarkable thing about this unique building? It works. This brutal combination of religious styles has a symmetry that is oddly beguiling and immensely satisfying. ⏱ *1½ hr. Torrijos.* ☎ *957 470 512.*

8€ adults, 4€ concessions. Mar–Oct Mon–Sat 10am–7pm, Sun & holidays 8:30–10:15am, 2–7pm. Nov–Feb Mon–Sat 10 am–6pm, Sun & holidays 8:30–10:15am, 2–6pm.

5 ★ **Bar Santos.** This little bar has a big reputation for its huge tortilla. Not to be confused with the corn-flour snack, a Spanish tortilla is a thick potato omelet, and none come thicker than Francisco Santos', made using just olive oil, potatoes and eggs. A slice costs 1.50€ and a cold beer is the perfect accompaniment. *Magistral González Francés 3.* ☎ *957 479 360.* $.

6 **Alcázar de los Reyes Cristianos.** The Alcázar was the site of the Moorish Caliph's palace, but when the city was recaptured by the Christians it was virtually destroyed. King Alfonso XI elected to create a new palace here in 1328 as a counterpoint to the mosque and a demonstration of the victors' new religion and economic prosperity. It was from here that Catholic monarchs Fernando II and Isabella

later plotted the reconquest of Granada and the final ousting of the Moors from the Spanish peninsula. The palace later housed the Spanish Inquisition; more recently it was the town's prison. The interior rooms contain impressive mosaics rescued from the Plaza de la Corredera (**13**) but little else of merit. The palace's real pleasure is its fragrant, water-filled gardens, which offer cool respite on hot summer days and evenings. ⏱ *30 min. Caballerizas Reales.* ☎ *957 420 151. 4€ adults, 2€ concessions; free Wed. Summer (June 16–Sept 15) 9:30am–2:30pm daily; gardens open 8pm–midnight. Winter (Sept 16–June 15) 8:30am–7:30pm Tues–Fri, 9:30am–4:30pm Sat; 9:30am–2:30pm Sun. Closed Mon.*

7 ★ **Banos del Alcázar.** The Caliph's private baths featured marble-decked rooms and heated pools. Several meters below modern-day ground level, they've been nicely excavated, and there are interesting descriptions in English. The introductory film is available in English. From the baths, walk out the top left corner of the square, along Cairuan,

The interior of the breathtaking Mezquita.

Córdoba's relaxing Moorish-style baths.

and turn right into the Jewish quarter (Judería) through the Puerta de la Luna (Moon Gate). As in Seville, the city's Jewish quarter retains its narrow, whitewashed lanes and is a delight to wander. 🕐 *30 min. Campo Santo de los Martires. No phone. 2€ adults, 1€ concessions; free Wed. Same opening hours as the Alcázar above.*

8 ★ Sinagoga (synagogue). For most of the Moorish era, the city's Jewish population flourished, contributing much to its intellectual and cultural life. But after the forced exile of Jews in the 15th century, few traces remained. This small synagogue is one of just three that remain in Spain from this era. Built in 1315, its small prayer room is decorated in the same Mudéjar style as Christian palaces of the time. But look closely and you'll see that the inscriptions are in Hebrew. After the expulsion of the Jews, it was used as a hospital and a nursery school. 🕐 *10 min. Judios 20. ☎ 957 202 928. .30€; free for E.U. passport holders. Tues-Sat 9:30am–2pm & 3:30–5:30pm. Sun 9:30am–1:30pm. Closed Mon.*

9 ★★ Casa de Sapharad. While the Synagogue doesn't offer much detail about Córdoba's Jewish history, this vibrant little museum fills the gap. Spanish Jews were known as *Sephardim*—hence the name of this restored 14th-century house, which contains five rooms with collections of clothing and jewelry from Jewish families of that era, and detailed descriptions in English. New rooms being added will provide information about famous Sephardic scholars of the time, in particular the hugely influential physician and philosopher Maimonides. 🕐 *30 min. Corner Judios & Averroes. ☎ 975 421 404. www.casadesefarad.com. Adults 4€, concessions 3€. Mon–Sat 10am–6pm; Sun 11am–2pm.*

10 Horno San Luis. After a wander round the Jewish quarter, return to Mezquita square. If you fancy a coffee and a pastry, this traditional bakery on a corner comes as a pleasant surprise after the touristy cafes nearby. Try pastel córdobes—a traditional Córdoba cake made with puff pastry and sweet pumpkin. *Cardinal González 71. No phone. $.*

Find the fine arts museum on Plaza del Potro.

⓫ ★ Hammam de Al Andalus.

If you're in need of some relaxation, a warm wallow and a massage in an Arabic-style bathhouse is ideal. These bathing rooms are wonderfully atmospheric, taking their theme from the ornate arches of the Mezquita. Reservations recommended. ⏱ *1 hr. Corregidor Luis de la Cerda 51.* ☎ *957 484 746. www.hammamspain.com/cordoba. Bath and massage from 33€. Daily 10am–midnight.*

⓬ ★★ Julio Romero de Torres Museum.

Córdoba's most famous 20th-century painter, Julio Romero de Torres (1874–1930), was born in this house. He experimented with many styles, but his depictions of classically dark-skinned Córdoban girls in various states of undress are perhaps his most famous. The large canvas entitled *Look How Lovely She Was* (1895) on the ground floor features a deathbed scene with the artist himself among the mourners. The city's Fine Arts Museum is just across the courtyard. ⏱ *45 min. Plaza del Potro 1.* ☎ *957 491 909. Adults 4€, concessions 2€; Wed free. Tues–Sat 10am–2pm, 5:30–7:30pm (4:30–6:30pm Oct–May). Sun & holidays 9:30am–2:30pm. Closed Mon & afternoons in July/Aug.*

⓭ ★ Plaza de la Corredera.

This fine Castilian-style, 17th-century arcaded square was originally the setting for bullfights and other public events. It has an air of gentle dilapidation nowadays, with a jumble of antiques shops and cafes housed in the cloisters. In the evenings it's a pleasant place for a leisurely drink, away from the touristy chaos of the historic center. ●

Stay a While

If you fancy making a break of it, nice places to stay include ⓮ **La Hospederia de El Churrasco** (Romero 38. ☎ 957 294 808. www.elchurrasco.com), a small, nine-room hotel attached to one of Córdoba's best restaurants; the excellent and perfectly located ⓯ **Las Casas de La Judería** (Tomás Conde 10. ☎ 957 20 20 95. www.casasypalacios.com); and the Hospes chain's lovely ⓰ **Palacio del Bailio** (Ramírez de las Casas Deza 10. ☎ 957 498 993. www.hospes.com), a 15-minute walk from the historic center.

The
Savvy Traveler

Before You Go

Spanish Government Tourist Board Offices

In the U.S.: New York: 666 Fifth Ave., 35th Floor, New York, NY 10103 ☎ 212 265 8822; Chicago: 845 N. Michigan Ave., Ste. 915E, Chicago, IL 60611 ☎ 312 642 1992; Los Angeles: 8383 Wilshire Blvd., Ste. 956, Beverly Hills, CA 90211 ☎ 323 658 7188; Miami: 1395 Brickell Ave., Ste. 1130, Miami, FL 33131 ☎ 305 358 1992.

In Canada: 2 Bloor St. W., Ste. 3402, Toronto, ON M4W 3E2 ☎ 416/961 3131.

In the U.K.: 79 New Cavendish St., 2nd Floor, London W1W 6XB ☎ 020 7486 8077.

The Best Times to Go

Late spring and fall are the perfect times to visit. In late April and early May the scent of orange blossom perfumes the air and the sun is warm but not too hot. The weather gets increasingly hot as the summer progresses. June is usually quite bearable but July and August are baking and best avoided. Late September and October offer sunny days and mild nights. Visiting Seville during the main festival season for Semana Santa (Holy Week) and the Feria de Abril (late March and early April; see Festivals, below) provides an unforgettable experience, but the city is packed out, accommodations are hard to find and prices are correspondingly high. November to March can have some pleasant sunny weather but chilly nights and wet days. Some hotel rooms can feel very cold, but you can benefit from bargain room rates, and the tourist numbers drop appreciably.

Festivals & Special Events

SPRING. Seville's two biggest annual events take place around Easter. During **Semana Santa** (Holy Week), from Palm Sunday to Easter Sunday, flamboyant processions take place across the city, parading effigies of Christ and the Virgin Mary through the streets accompanied by morbid-looking, white-hooded *nazarenos* (Nazarenes). Holy Week also kicks off the **bullfighting** season. The **Feria de Abril** follows, around two weeks after Easter. The sombre mood of Semana Santa is forgotten and people celebrate spring, donning traditional flamenco costume. A large fair comes to town, the streets are jammed and virtually no one goes to bed before dawn.

SUMMER. May heralds the beginning of the month-long **Festival Internacional de Teatro y Danza** (International Theater and Dance Festival), where world-class companies perform in the city's main concert hall, the Teatro de la Maestranza, and at Itálica. Seville's Patron **Saint Ferdinand** is honored on May 30 with celebrations in the cathedral. **Corpus Christi** is celebrated a week or so later with a procession of the enormous silver monstrance and branches of rosemary strewn around the streets. In August, when it's seriously hot, **evening events** are organized outdoors, with theater in the Alcázar gardens and outdoor movies. Across the river in Triana, the **Velada de Santa Ana** takes place, with food stalls and plank-walking competitions.

Previous page: San Pablo Airport, Seville.

SEVILLE'S AVERAGE MONTHLY TEMPERATURE & RAINFALL

	JAN	FEB	MAR	APR	MAY	JUNE
Daily Temp. (°C)	15°	18°	21°	24°	27°	32°
Daily Temp. (°F)	59°	64°	70°	75°	81°	90°
Avg. Rainfall (mm)	70	61	64	52	36	14
Avg. Rainfall (inch)	2.8	2.4	2.5	2.1	1.4	0.6

	JULY	AUG	SEPT	OCT	NOV	DEC
Daily Temp. (°C)	36°	38°	32°	26°	20°	16°
Daily Temp. (°F)	97°	100°	90°	79°	68°	61°
Avg. Rainfall (mm)	1	5	17	57	77	76
Avg. Rainfall (inch)	0	0.2	0.7	2.3	3.1	3.0

FALL. Fall is particularly good for arts and entertainment in Seville. The **Bienal de Arte Flamenco** (www.bienal-flamenco.org) takes place during the last two weeks of September every two years, in even-numbered years. World-class artists perform to rapturous crowds. There's also the annual **Sevilla en Otoño** season—a variety of cultural events which takes place throughout the city during the months of September, October and November, including dance, theatrical and musical performances. In early November, the **Festival Internacional de Jazz** takes place, attracting stars from around the world. And later in the month the **Seville Film Festival** offers arthouse and contemporary European cinema.

WINTER. The Christmas period dominates festivals in winter. Parents dress their children up in 16th-century costumes and take them to church to sing and dance before the main altar in celebration of the day of the **Immaculate Conception** on December 8. Wandering minstrels take to the streets around Plaza del Triunfo and Santa Cruz. Parades take place throughout Andalusia on January 6. **Día de los Reyes** (Three Kings Day) marks the eve of the festival of Epiphany. Three kings ride through town in a procession, throwing sweets to the onlooking children.

The Weather

Seville's climate varies depending on the season. Spring and fall are delightful, with warm, long, sunny days. It rarely falls to freezing in winter, but it's often damp and cool. Locals moan about the humidity. Surrounding hills get chilly, even snowy. July and August are best avoided as Seville boils under the summer sun, regularly notching up the highest temperatures in Spain. Temperatures of 38°C (100°F) are common. Many places shut as locals head for the coast to escape the heat.

Useful Websites

- **www.okspain.org** The well-organized Spanish Tourist Board portal is packed with useful information. Select your country of departure from the drop-down menu.

- **www.exploreseville.com** Jeff Spielvogel is an American who loved the city so much he married a local and stayed here. His website is packed with useful information.

- **www.sevilla5.com** Very helpful local accommodations agency. Their site offers good-value hotel and apartment accommodations and they speak English too.

- **www.turismosevilla.org** The portal for Seville city and regional tourism. Click the Sevilla Tourism box to visit the Seville city tourist board site, and the Tourism of the Province of Seville box to visit the regional tourist board site. Both have English-language versions.

- **www.renfe.es** The Spanish rail website offers routes, schedules and booking. English version available.

- **www.tussam.es** The Seville urban transport network site (Spanish only) has bus routes and times, and information about the latest tramway and subway developments.

Cellphones (móviles)

Like all of Europe, Spain uses the GSM system. If you have a multi-band GSM cellphone, you can make and receive calls from Spain. Call your cellphone operator and ask for 'international roaming' to be activated. You pay to receive as well as to make calls, and the cost can be high. If you plan to stay a while, consider purchasing a local SIM card, which gives you a Spanish phone number and will mean you don't pay to receive calls. You can also rent or buy GSM phones before you go, through www.onspanishtime.com, which offers a good-value, efficient service and will deliver to your hotel. Other options in North America include InTouch USA (☎ 800 872 7626, www.intouchglobal.com) and RoadPost (☎ 888 290 1616 or 905 272 5665, www.roadpost.com).

Car Rentals

Avis (U.S. ☎ 800 331 1212, www.avis.com; U.K. ☎ 08445 818181, www.avis.co.uk), Hertz (U.S. ☎ 800 654 3001, www.hertz.com; U.K. ☎ 08708 44 88 44, www.hertz.co.uk) and Budget (U.S. ☎ 800 527 0700, www.budget.com; U.K. ☎ 08701 56 56 56, www.budget.co.uk).

Getting **There**

By Plane

San Pablo Airport (☎ +34 954 449 000; +34 954 672 981) is 10km (6 miles) northeast of the city center on the A-4. There's a convenient and inexpensive half-hourly bus service (6:15am–11pm), marked EA on bus maps. It runs to the city center (2.30€) and takes about 30 minutes. It terminates at the main bus station, Prado de San Sebastián (see By Bus, below), which is a bit of a walk from most hotels if you have luggage so you'll probably need to jump in a taxi or take the tram to complete your journey. The bus also stops at Santa Justa, the main railway station (see By Train, below). A taxi from the airport into town costs about 22€.

By Car

Seville is 217km (135 miles) northwest of Málaga, 252km (140 miles) from Granada, 97km (60 miles) from Jerez de la Frontera, 129km (80 miles) from Cadiz and 192km (120 miles) from Algeciras, and is well connected by road.

By Train

Seville has 23 trains a day connecting it with Córdoba. Trains arrive at Santa Justa station (Avda de Kansas City ☎ 902 400 202). The high-speed AVE train takes just 45 minutes, and considerably less expensive ordinary trains make the trip in 1 hour 20 minutes. There are six trains daily to Málaga (3 hr) and four to Granada (4 hr). The station is a fairly long and rather dull 20- to

30-minute walk from the historic city center, so it's best to take a bus (C1 or C2) or taxi.

By Bus
Buses mostly run from Prado de San Sebastián (Calle José María Osborne 11 ☎ 954 417 111). Routes to Córdoba take (2½ hr), Málaga (3½ hr) and Granada (4 hr). Some long-distance services depart from the bus station (Plaza de Armas ☎ 954 908 040). There are useful timetables at www. andalucia.com/travel/bus/seville.htm.

Getting **Around**

By Car
Seville's narrow streets are badly congested and the one-way system maddening. Driving in town is not recommended.

By Taxi
Taxis are plentiful and generally drivers use the meter and don't overcharge. Local firms include Tele Taxi (☎ 954 622 222), Radio Taxi Giralda (☎ 954 675 555) and Radio Taxi (☎ 954 580 000/954 571 111). Taxi ranks are well located at Plaza Nueva outside the Hotel Inglaterra, Calle Alemanes right next to Starbucks, and Puerta de Jerez outside Hotel Alfonso XIII.

By Bus
Urban bus services operated by the town transport system Tussam (www.tussam.es) are frequent but most don't enter the old city's narrow streets. However the C5 line, often serviced by an electric microbus, does go into the old city and it's quite handy for getting around, stopping at many of the tourist sights. C1, C2, C3, C4 also do useful clockwise and counterclockwise circuits of the perimeter. Single-journey tickets (1.2€) can be bought on board. Ten-journey multi-tickets (bónobus) can be bought from newsstands (kioscos). One- and three-day passes are available from the Tussam office at the bus station (see By Bus, above) and Tussam

kiosks at Plaza Ponce de Léon and Puerta de Jerez.

By Streetcar (Tram)
Seville's first streetcar line is a modest affair of just four stations, but it's very handy, connecting Prado de San Sebastián, where the airport bus terminates, with the historic center. Line 1 of Seville's much-awaited subway (metro) is now open, but it's not particularly useful for tourists as it bypasses the historic center.

On Foot
Seville's old center is compact and easily navigated on foot. Much of it is pedestrianized too.

By Bike
Sevillans are really getting into cycling. Cycle lanes have been laid down on main routes and there are plenty of racks to lock your bike. The recent introduction of the new Sevici urban cycle program has been a big success. Visitors can use the Sevici bikes too, and they're a great way to get around (see Bike Rentals, p 164).

By Horse & Carriage
You don't have to look far for a horse and carriage in Seville. They await custom at Plaza Virgen de los Reyes, Plaza del Triunfo, Avenida de la Constitución, Puerta de Jerez, Torre de Oro, Plaza de España and

Plaza de América. There's a standard tour that lasts an hour and should cost 36.06€ per carriage. (43.27€ during Holy Week and 86.54€ during April Fair Week).

Stand your ground if the carriage driver tries to charge you more. I've had one try to make me pay 50€ for a standard tour.

Fast **Facts**

APARTMENT RENTALS Set up by a German and an American, **Sevilla 5** (☎ 954 387 550, www.sevilla5.com) has well-managed, well-located accommodations to cover most price requirements. **Apartments Sevilla** (☎ 954 216 912, www.apartmentssevilla.com) has several high-standard apartments in the center. Staff speak good English and are very helpful.

ATMS Seville has plenty of banks and almost all have ATMs that accept Visa, MasterCard and American Express.

BIKE RENTALS The city's bike hire program, **Sevici,** has now been extended to visitors. Just register with your credit card at one of the many cycle-stand booths. You're given a unique user ID and select a PIN code which you input each time you take a bike. The first 30 minutes are completely free, the next hour costs 1€ and subsequent hours 2€ (see www.sevici.es for more info in English). They are generally well maintained, but check your selected bike is in good order before setting off. During rush hour it's sometimes hard to find a bike or, conversely, to find a free parking stand.

If you want longer-term hire, specialist bikes or guided cycling tours, **Rentabikesevilla** (☎ 619 461 491, www.rentabikesevilla.com) is recommended and can deliver to your hotel. Folding bikes cost 12€ per day, 9€ for each subsequent day or 50€ per week. Mountain bikes are also available.

BUSINESS HOURS **Banks** are open Monday through Friday from 8:30am to 2pm. Most **offices** are open Monday through Friday from 9am to 6 or 7pm. In July, opening times are 8am to 3pm, and in August, businesses are on skeleton staff if not closed altogether. At restaurants, lunch is usually from 1:30 or 2 to 4pm and dinner from 9 to 11:30pm or midnight. **Major stores** open Monday through Saturday from 9:30 or 10am to 8pm. Most **smaller establishments,** however, close for siesta in mid-afternoon, doing business from 9 or 10am to 2pm, and 5pm to 8 or 8:30pm.

CAR RENTALS Car-hire desks are on the ground floor of the airport terminal building as you exit arrivals. The cheapest by far is local company **Auriga/Crown** (☎ 954 516 808, en.aurigacrown.com). **Avis** (☎ 954 449 121), **Europcar** (☎ 954 254 298) and **Hertz** (☎ 954 514 720) also have airport hire desks. The downtown location for car hire is the main Santa Justa station on Avenida de Kansas City.

CLIMATE (see Weather).

CONCIERGE SERVICES Eduardo Blanco at **Different Spain** (☎ 606 009 521, www.differentspain.com) offers bespoke personal travel and support services and is recommended.

CONSULATES & EMBASSIES In Seville most nations only have consulates, which means passport replacement involves a long trip to the nearest embassy in Madrid or Málaga. Seville contact numbers are: **U.S. Consulate** ☎ 954 218 571; **Canada Consulate** ☎ 954 296 819; **Ireland Consulate** ☎ 954 216 361; **U.K. Consulate** ☎ 954 228 874/952 352 300.

ELECTRICITY Like the rest of central Europe, Spain operates on 220 volts AC (50 cycles) using plugs with two round pins.

EMBASSIES (see Consulates and Embassies).

EMERGENCIES The 911/999 equivalent in Spain is ☎ **112.** You can also dial ☎ 061 for ambulances. The nearest emergency care center to the old quarter is Centro de Urgencia el Porvenir, just across from the Jardines Murillo (Marqués de Paradas 35, ☎ 955 017 300). The two main hospitals with emergency centers are: Hospital Universitario Virgen del Rocio (Avda Manuel Siurot, ☎ 955 012 000) and Hospital Universitario Virgen Macarena (Avda Dr. Fedriani, ☎ 955 008 000).

EVENT LISTINGS The helpful main tourist office on Plaza de San Francisco posts a detailed list of events each week on its noticeboard. Monthly *El Giraldillo* carries cultural listings of all sorts, but it's only in Spanish. Two handy publications in English are *The Tourist* and *Welcome & Olé*, available at tourist offices and hotel reception areas.

FAMILY TRAVEL *Mediterranean Spain with Your Family,* also published by Frommer's, has detailed advice and information about holidaying in Seville with children in tow. See www.frommers.com.

GAY & LESBIAN TRAVELERS Seville and urban Spain generally are gay- and lesbian-friendly places. The free *Gay and Lesbian Seville Guide,* available from the tourist office, was out of print at the time of writing. The main nightlife area is around the Alameda.

HOLIDAYS Holidays observed include: January 1 (New Year's Day), January 6 (Feast of the Epiphany), March/April (Good Friday and Easter Monday), May 1 (May Day), May/June (Whit Monday), June 24 (Feast of St. John), August 15 (Feast of the Assumption), October 12 (National Day), November 1 (All Saints' Day), December 6 (Constitution Day), December 8 (Feast of the Immaculate Conception), December 25 (Christmas) and December 26 (Feast of St. Stephen).

HOSPITALS (see Emergencies).

INSURANCE Check your existing insurance policy before you buy travel insurance to cover trip cancellation, lost luggage, medical expenses or car rental insurance. **U.S. Travelers:** For travel overseas, most U.S. health plans (including Medicare and Medicaid) do not provide coverage, and the ones that do often require payment up front for services. For additional medical insurance, try MEDEX Assistance (☎ 410 453 6300, www.medexassist.com) or Travel Assistance International (☎ 800 821 2828, www.travelassistance.com; for general information on services, call their Worldwide Assistance Services, Inc., ☎ 800 777 8710). **U.K. Travelers:** Travelers from the U.K. should carry their European Health Insurance Card (EHIC) as proof of entitlement to free/reduced-cost medical treatment in Spain (☎ 0845 606 2030; www.ehic.org.uk). The EHIC only covers 'necessary medical treatment,' and for repatriation costs, lost money, baggage or cancellation, travel insurance from a reputable company should be sought.

INTERNET ACCESS Wi-Fi access is increasingly available in hotels, though there's sometimes a cost involved. The **tourist office** on Plaza de San Francisco has 10 terminals offering free access, but you may have to wait your turn.

LOST PROPERTY Call credit card companies the minute you discover your wallet has been lost or stolen, and file a report at the nearest police precinct (see Police, below). Your credit card company or insurer may require a police report number or record. **Spanish emergency numbers:** Visa ☎ 900 991 124; American Express ☎ 902 375 637; MasterCard ☎ 900 971 231.

MAIL & POSTAGE The Central Post Office (Correos y Telegrafos) is at Avenida de la Constitución 2 ☎ 954 224 760. It's open Monday to Friday 8:30am to 8:30pm, Saturday 9am to 2pm. Stamps (sellos) can also be bought at tobacconists (estancos).

MONEY Spain is part of the single European currency and uses the euro (€), divided into 100 cents. For current rates check the currency converter website www.xe.com/ucc.

PARKING Underground parking lots in the old town can be found at Plaza Nueva, Plaza de la Concordia, Plaza de la Magdalena, Plaza Ponce de León, Marqués de Paradas, Calle Sor Ángela de la Cruz and Paseo de Colón. Parking for 24 hours normally costs around 20€.

PASSPORTS As E.U. citizens, U.K. passport holders do not require a visa for visiting Spain. Visas are not required for U.S. or Canadian

visitors to Spain providing their stay does not exceed 90 days. Australian visitors do need a visa. If your passport is lost or stolen, contact your country's embassy or consulate immediately; see Consulates & Embassies, above. Before leaving home, make a copy of your passport's critical pages and keep it separate from your passport.

PHARMACIES *Farmacias* are plentiful and can give advice about minor ailments. Many pharmacists speak some English too. Typical opening times are 9am to 2pm and 5 to 8:30pm. Each district runs a **rota system** to cover siesta and the night shift: ask your hotel or call ☎ 902 522 111.

POLICE The national police emergency number is ☎ **091.** For local police, call ☎ **092.**

POST OFFICE (See Mail & Postage).

SAFETY Like any big city, petty crime does take place in Seville, but it's generally a pretty safe place. Alameda, with its more down-at-heel vibe, is a little less secure at night. Avoid dangling cameras or purses and leaving possessions visible on table tops or in empty cars.

SMOKING A law banning smoking in public places, including on public transport and in offices, hospitals and some bars and restaurants, was enacted in 2006. Non-smoking sections in restaurants are beginning to appear but they remain relatively rare. Expect this to change as Spaniards adapt. If you feel strongly about avoiding second-hand smoke, ask to sit in the *no fumadores* (non-smoking) section.

TAXES Sales tax (known in Spain as IVA) ranges from 7% to 33%, depending on the commodity. Food, wine and basic necessities are taxed at

7%, most goods and services (including car rentals) at 13%, luxury items (jewelry, all tobacco, imported liquors) at 33% and hotels at 7%. Non-E.U. residents are entitled to reimbursement of IVA tax paid on most purchases worth more than 90€ made at shops offering tax-free or global-refund shopping. Forms, obtained from the store where you made your purchase, must be stamped at Customs on departure. See www.globalrefund.com.

TELEPHONES For national telephone information, dial ☎ 1003. For international telephone information, call ☎ 025. To make an international call, dial ☎ 00, wait for the tone, and dial the country code, area code and number. If you're making a local or national call, dial the two-digit city code first (☎ 95 in Seville) and then the seven-digit number. The best-value way to call home is to use a **telephone card** purchased from a newsstand or tobacconist. Most offer a toll-free number which you dial, followed by a pin number and the number you're calling. The central post office has calling booths in a room to the left as you enter the main gates. Using coins at a telephone booth or calling direct from a hotel room will always be the most expensive option.

TIPPING Service charges of around 10% are often added to restaurant bills. Spaniards as a rule don't tip a great deal. It's typical to leave a few cents or round up the bill to the nearest euro.

TOILETS Public toilets (*los servicios*) were once a rarity, but modern, generally well-serviced cubicles (*aseos*) have appeared around town and cost 20 cents to use. Bars are legally obliged to let you use their toilets, and I think nothing of just walking in and asking to use them. *D* (*damas*) or *S* (*señoritas*) stands for ladies and *C* (*caballeros*) for men.

TOURIST OFFICES IN SEVILLE The excellent main **city tourist office** is

Seville on the Cheap

Aside from accommodations, which can be pricey, Seville is good value compared to many European cities. If you're looking to save money, be selective about which days you visit places and, if you hold an E.U. passport or ID card, remember to carry it with you. **Free to all**: Museo Histórico Militar (p 91); Costurero de la Reina Museum (p 90); Castillo de San Jorge Museum (p 60); Archivo de Indias (p 29); Convento de Santa Clara (p 64); Torre del Oro, Tuesdays only (p 17); Hospital de Los Venerables, 4pm to 8pm Sundays only (p 47); Casa de la Condesa Lebrija, 10:30am to 12:30pm Wednesdays only (p 54).

   Free for E.U. passport holders: Museo de Bellas Artes (p 25); Museo Arqueológico (p 91); Museo de Artes y Costumbres Populares (p 92); Casa de Pilatos, Tuesdays 1pm to 5pm only (p 13); Monasterio de la Cartuja and Centro Andaluz de Arte Contemporáneo, Tuesdays only (p 25).

   And to get from one place to another, use the **Sevici** city bikes (p 164) for no more than half an hour at a time, and that's free too!

at 19 Plaza de San Francisco (☎ 954 595 288). There's another at 21 Avenida de la Constitución (☎ 954 757 578). There's also a desk in the museum at the Basílica de la Macarena (☎ 954 901 896) and another in the arrivals hall at the airport (☎ 954 449 128). If you want to explore more of the region, the helpful **tourist office for the province** is at Plaza del Triunfo 1, just after the exit from the Alcázar (☎ 954 210 005).

TOURS If you're looking for really interesting **walking tours** to less-discovered parts of the old town, David Cox and Luis Salas's **Really Discover tours** (☎ 645 350 750/ 955 113 912; www.reallydiscover. com) are highly recommended. They also offer tours around, and day trips to, Granada and Córdoba. Ever-popular hop-on-hop-off **bus tours** around the perimeter of the old city are also available from **Sevillatour** (☎ 902 101 081, www.sevillatour. com) and **Sevirama** ☎ 954 560 693. 16€ adults, 7€ children (Sevillatour and Sevirama).

TRAVELERS WITH DISABILITIES Many higher-standard hotels and restaurants now cater for wheelchair users and others with reduced mobility. The city tourist office (Plaza de San Francisco) has a guide in English called **Seville Open to Everybody** (Sevilla Para Todos), which lists wheelchair-friendly sites, itineraries, accommodations and restaurants.

WEATHER (See Climate).

Seville: **A Brief History**

500 B.C. Southern Spain ruled by the Carthiginians.

206 B.C. Scipio Africanus defeats the Carthiginans. Romans found the town of Itálica.

45 B.C. Julius Caesar designates Hispalis (Seville) a Roman colony.

A.D. 409 End of Roman rule. Hispalis sacked by Vandals.

500 Visigoth Christian kingdom and culture established.

711 Muslim invasion. Isibilia (Seville) is mainly ruled from Córdoba. Period of stability and cultural flourishing.

1031 The Muslim Caliphate fragments and splinter Moorish states rule in small, sometimes warring kingdoms.

1086 Almoravids from North Africa invade Al Andalus.

1147 Almohade Muslim dynasties rule. During their reign the Giralda is built.

1248 Christian King Ferdinand III reconquers Seville.

1364 Pedro I orders construction of the Alcázar.

1391 Jews in Seville are persecuted.

1481 Spanish Inquisition is established in Seville.

1492 Catholic kings Ferdinand and Isabella conquer Granada, the last Muslim kingdom in Spain. Columbus sights America. Jews expelled from Spain.

1503 Seville granted monopoly on trade with the Indies. Huge expansion of the city.

1580 Seville becomes Spain's largest and richest city.

1609 Expulsion of remaining Moors.

1649 Plague decimates Seville's population, killing one in every three people.

1717 Silting up of Guadalquivir river means monopoly on trade with the Indies passes to Cadiz.

1771 Royal Tobacco Factory in Seville is completed.

1810–12 French forces take Seville. Bonaparte is King of Spain.

1814 Spain's American colonies begin struggle for independence.

1929 Ibero-American Exhibition in Seville.

1936–39 Spanish civil war. Franco becomes Head of State.

1975 Death of Franco; establishment of democracy.

1982 Andalusia becomes an autonomous region, with Seville as regional capital.

1986 Spain joins the European Community (now the European Union).

1992 Seville's Universal Exposition.

2002 Spain adopts the euro.

Seville's **Architecture**

Positioned with North Africa to the south and central Europe to the north, Seville has been conquered and reconquered, named and renamed over the ages. These different cultural influences can be seen today in the city's wealth of architecture.

Roman (2nd C. B.C.–4th C. A.D.)
Apart from reused Roman pillars in all sorts of unexpected places, there are few reminders of Roman Hispalis today. The site of Itálica, north of Seville (p 146), is the place to see Roman ruins. At the peak of its glory, Itálica was the third-largest city in the world, surpassed only by Rome and Alexandria.

Moorish (8th–15th C.)
North African Muslims, known as Moors, subdued Andalusia in the early 8th century, and their influence remains today, not just in architecture but in the language and customs too. Instead of depicting the human form, Moorish art and architecture focused on intricate, lacy patterns and on Arabic calligraphy, and was typified by intricate, flowing details and abstract, geometric designs. These new conquerors built a wall

around Isbiliya (as they called Seville) to protect it. Sections can still be seen, most notably in the Macarena area. Over 100 towers were built along the walls; the most notable, the 12-sided Torre del Oro, remains today along with several smaller towers. The city's best example of Moorish architecture is, however, Seville's signature building, the Giralda. Now the tower of the cathedral, it was originally the minaret of the Great Mosque, completed in 1198.

Mudéjar or Post-Moorish (mid-14th to late 15th C.)
After the Muslims were ousted by the Christian King Fernando III in 1248, many churches in Seville were built on the sites of former mosques. Often original Moorish architectural motifs were incorporated into them, such as ornamental brickwork in relief, alternating with stone,

archways and even roof tiles. Some Muslims were allowed to stay on after the reconquest and were employed to build churches and palaces. This produced a new hybrid style of architecture known as Mudéjar. The word literally means 'those who were permitted to stay.' One of the best examples of the Mudéjar style is the Alcázar, a palace built for a Christian king but which looks for all the world like a Muslim fortress. The Salón de Embajadores here is a stunning achievement, surmounted by a wooden dome and flanked

Torre del Oro.

with double windows. Dozens of churches in Seville also retain Mudéjar architectural motifs, particularly in the form of geometrical ceiling carvings, towers that were originally minarets, horseshoe-shaped arches and geometrically patterned wall tiles. Iglesia de San Marcos in Macarena is just one example.

Gothic (13th–16th C.)

When the Christian reconquerors turned their attention to the city's largest building, the Great Mosque, they wanted to replace it with a building of equally vast proportions. The result is the Gothic cathedral, characterized by massive columns that hold up mammoth arches. Its spectacularly elaborate vaulting is in the Flamboyant Gothic style and rises 56m (184 ft.). Most of this structure was constructed between 1401 and 1507, with exotic buttresses supporting the huge, pointed arches. By the end of the 15th century, Spain had developed its unique style of Gothic architecture, calling it Isabelline in honor of the Catholic Queen Isabella I (1451–1504). This style's exuberant decoration covered entire facades of buildings, its rich, even lavish, ornamentation coming in the form of lace-like carvings and heraldic motifs.

Renaissance (16th C.)

Renaissance-style architecture in Spain had local elements worked into it. Early Renaissance architecture continued the flamboyance of the Isabelline style and was termed Plateresque (platero means silversmith) because

La Giralda before and after the Reconquista.

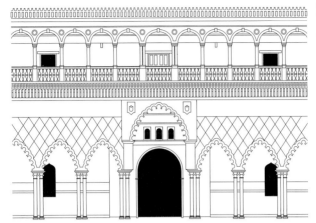

The Alcázar.

its fine detailing evoked the ornate work of silversmiths. The best example of the Plateresque style in Andalusia is Seville's Ayuntamiento (town hall). Completed in 1534, its east side is a feast of detailed, intricate carving featuring famous people in the city's history. At the end of the 16th century Plateresque increasingly gave way to the Herreran style, named after Juan de Herrera (1530–97), the greatest figure of Spanish classicism. Herrera's buildings were less flamboyant, grand but austere as well as geometric. The best example of his work can be seen at the Archivo de Indias, completed in 1598.

Baroque (17th-18th C.)

'Baroque' suggests flamboyance but early Spanish baroque was more austere. In the 17th century a family of architects led by José de Churriguera (1665–1725) pioneered a type of architecture noted for its dense concentrations of ornamentation covering entire facades of buildings, which became known as Churrigueresque. The Palacio de San Telmo's ornately carved portal on Avenida de Roma, completed in 1734, is a good

example. Later in this period, the baroque style blossomed in Spain, particularly in Andalusia. Seville has more baroque churches per square kilometer than any city in the world. Outstanding examples are the Capillita de San José and the extraordinarily ornate Iglesia de San Luis.

Modern (20th C.)

Modern architectural achievement in Seville owes much to the two great exhibitions the city hosted in the 20th century. The Ibero-American Exhibition of 1929 allowed the talents of local architect Aníbal González to shine. He drew on earlier Mudéjar and Renaissance styles to create unique, romantic buildings—in particular the grandiose Spanish pavilion known as the Plaza de España. A new term was coined for this style: Regionalist. More recently, Expo 92 provided another spurt of innovation. Its best legacy was five new bridges spanning the Guadalquivir river, the most exceptional being Santiago Calatrava's harp-shaped Puente del Alamillo, and the Puente de la Barqueta, a suspension bridge held by a single curved overhead beam.

Useful **Phrases**

Useful Words & Phrases

ENGLISH	SPANISH	PRONUNCIATION
Good day	Buenos días	bweh-nohs dee-ahs
How are you?	¿Cómo está?	koh-moh es-tah
Very well	Muy bien	mwee byehn
Thank you	Gracias	grah-thee-ahs
You're welcome	De nada	deh nah-dah
Goodbye	Adiós	ah-dyos
Please	Por favor	por fah-vohr
Yes	Sí	see
No	No	noh
Excuse me	Perdóneme	pehr-doh-neh-meh
Where is . . . ?	¿Dónde está . . . ?	dohn-deh es-tah
To the right	A la derecha	ah lah deh-reh-chah
To the left	A la izquierda	ah lah ees-kyehr-dah
I would like . . .	Quisiera	kee-syeh-rah
I want . . .	Quiero	kyeh-roh
Do you have . . . ?	¿Tiene usted?	tyeh-neh oo-sted
How much is it?	¿Cuánto cuesta?	kwahn-toh kwehs-tah
When?	¿Cuándo?	kwahn-doh
What?	¿Qué?	keh
There is (Is there . . . ?)	(¿)Hay (. . . ?)	aye
What is there?	¿Qué hay?	keh aye
Yesterday	Ayer	ah-yehr
Today	Hoy	oy
Tomorrow	Mañana	mah-nyah-nah
Good	Bueno	bweh-noh
Bad	Malo	mah-loh
Better (Best)	(Lo) Mejor	(loh) meh-hohr
More	Más	mahs
Less	Menos	meh-nohs
Do you speak English?	¿Habla inglés?	ah-blah een-glehs
I speak a little Spanish	Hablo un poco de español	ah-bloh oon poh-koh deh es-pah-nyol
I don't understand	No entiendo	noh ehn-tyehn-doh
What time is it?	¿Qué hora es?	keh oh-rah ehss
The check, please	La cuenta, por favor	lah kwehn-tah pohr fah-vohr
The station	La estación	lah es-tah-syohn
A hotel	Un hotel	oon oh-tehl
The market	El mercado	ehl mehr-kah-doh
A restaurant	Un restaurante	oon rehs-tow-rahn-teh
The toilet	El baño	ehl bah-nyoh
A doctor	Un médico	oon meh-dee-koh
The road to . . .	El camino a . . .	ehl kah-mee-noh ah
To eat	Comer/menjar	ko-mehr

ENGLISH	SPANISH	PRONUNCIATION
A room	Una habitación	*oo-nah ah-bee-tah-syohn*
A book	Un libro	*oon lee-broh*
A dictionary	Un diccionario	*oon deek-syoh-nah-ryoh*

Numbers

NUMBER	SPANISH	PRONUNCIATION
1	uno	*(oo-noh)*
2	dos	*(dohs)*
3	tres	*(trehs)*
4	cuatro	*(kwah-troh)*
5	cinco	*(theen-koh)*
6	seis	*(says)*
7	siete	*(syeh-teh)*
8	ocho	*(oh-choh)*
9	nueve	*(nweh-beh)*
10	diez	*(dyehth)*
11	once	*(ohn-theh)*
12	doce	*(doh-theh)*
13	trece	*(treh-theh)*
14	catorce	*(kah-tohr-theh)*
15	quince	*(keen-seh)*
16	dieciséis	*(dyeh-thee-says)*
17	diecisiete	*(dyeh-thee-syeh-teh)*
18	dieciocho	*(dyeh-thee-oh-choh)*
19	diecinueve	*(dyeh-thee-nweh-beh)*
20	veinte	*(bayn-teh)*
30	treinta	*(trayn-tah)*
40	cuarenta	*(kwah-rehn-tah)*
50	cincuenta	*(theen-kwehn-tah)*
60	sesenta	*(seh-sehn-tah)*
70	setenta	*(seh-tehn-tah)*
80	ochenta	*(oh-chehn-tah)*
90	noventa	*(noh-behn-tah)*
100	cien	*(thyehn)*

Menu **Terms**

Decoding the Menu

SPANISH	ENGLISH
A la brasa	Charcoal-grilled
A la plancha	Grilled
Al horno	Baked
Asado	Roasted
Estofado	Stew
Frito	Fried
Hervido	Boiled
Medio hecho	Medium
Muy hecho	Well done

SPANISH	ENGLISH
Picante	Spicy
Poco hecho	Rare
Salsa	Sauce

Classic Tapas

SPANISH	ENGLISH
Aceitunas (rellenas)	Olives (stuffed)
Albóndigas	Meatballs
Boquerones	Anchovies
Calamares (en su tinta)	Squid (cooked in its ink)
Champiñones al ajillo	Mushrooms in garlic
Chorizo (al vino)	Spicy sausage (in wine)
Croquetas	Potato croquettes (often stuffed)
Ensaladilla rusa	Russian salad (vegetables in mayonnaise)
Gambas al ajillo	Prawns in garlic
Gambas a la plancha	Grilled prawns
Jamón serrona	Cured ham
Patatas ali oli	Potatoes in garlic mayonnaise
Patatas bravas	Potatoes in spicy tomato sauce
Pimientos fritos	Deep-fried peppers
Pincho moruno	Grilled meat brochette
Revuelto	Scrambled eggs
Riñones al jerez	Kidneys in sherry
Salmorejo	Thick creamy cold tomato soup
Tortilla	Thick Spanish omelet with onion and potato

Meat, Sausages & Cold Cuts

SPANISH	ENGLISH
Bistec	Steak
Buey	Beef
Carne	Meat
Cerdo	Pork
Chorizo	Spicy sausage
Conejo	Rabbit
Cordero	Lamb
Hígado	Liver
Jamón	Ham
Jamón york	Cooked ham
Jamón serrano	Cured ham
Pato	Duck
Pollo	Chicken
Riñones	Kidneys
Salchicha	Sausage
Solomillo	Sirloin
Ternera	Veal

Seafood & Shellfish

SPANISH	ENGLISH
Anchoa	Anchovy (salted)
Atún	Tuna

SPANISH	ENGLISH
Bacalao	Cod
Boquerón	Anchovy (fresh)
Caballa	Mackerel
Calamar	Squid
Cangrejo	Crab
Gamba	Prawn
Jibia	Cuttlefish
Langosta	Lobster
Lenguado	Sole
Lubina	Bass
Mejillón	Mussel
Merluza	Hake
Pescado	Fish
Pez espada	Swordfish
Pulpo	Octopus
Rape	Monkfish
Salmón	Salmon
Sardina	Sardine

Vegetables & Legumes

SPANISH	ENGLISH
Berengena	Eggplant (aubergine)
Calabacín	Pumpkin
Cebolla	Onion
Col	Cabbage
Ensalada	Salad
Espinaca	Spinach
Garbanzo	Chickpea
Habas	Fava beans (broadbeans)
Lechuga	Lettuce
Lenteja	Lentil
Lombarda	Red cabbage
Patata	Potato
Puerro	Leek
Seta	Mushroom
Tomate	Tomato
Verduras	Vegetables
Zanahoria	Carrot

Drinks

SPANISH	ENGLISH
Café solo	Espresso-style coffee
Café con leche	Coffee with milk
Agua (sin gas)	Still mineral water
Agua (con gas)	Sparkling mineral water
Cerveza	Beer
Vino tinto	Red wine
Vino blanco	White wine
Vino rosado	Rosé wine

Index

See also Accommodations and Restaurant indexes, below.

A

Accommodations. *See also* Accommodations Index
  best bets, 134
  maps, 135–137
Airports, 162
Al Alba nightclub, 121
Alameda de Hércules, 64
Alameda 84 bar, 116
Alameda neighborhood, 62–65
Alcázar, 10–11
Alcázar de la Puerta de Sevilla, 151
Alcázar de los Reyes Cristianos, 156
Alfarería, 61
Ambigú tapas bar, 39
Antigua Fundición Real, 30–31
Antiguedades bar, 116
Antiques stores, 73
Antique Theatre nightclub, 121
Apartment rentals, 164
Aquópolis Sevilla, 44
Arab Bathhouse (Baños Árabes), 14
Archivo de Indias, 29, 167
Art galleries and museums, 22–27, 127, 128
  Centro Andaluz de Arte Contemporáneo, 25, 87, 127, 167
  Centro de las Artes de Sevilla, 65, 127
  Concha Pedrosa, 24, 124, 127
  El Patio del Arte, 48
  Espacio Escala, 25, 127
  Félix Gomez, 127
  Full Art, 24, 128
  Galería Nuevoarte, 25, 128

Hospital de la Caridad, 18, 23
Hospital de los Venerables, 47
Isabel Ignacio, 24, 128
Julio Romero de Torres Museum, 158
La Caja China, 24, 128
Monasterio de la Cartuja, 25
Museo de Bellas Artes, 20, 25, 26, 124, 128
Museo Municipal, 147
Painters studios, 48
Pasarela de la Cartuja, 25
Rafael Ortiz, 128
Santa Isglesia Catedral (Seville Cathedral), 7
Sanvicente 31, 25, 128
ATMs, 164
Auditorio Álvarez Quintero, 129–130
Auditorio Municipal Rocío Jurado, 124, 131
Avenida 5 Cines, 124, 129
Ayuntamiento, 52–53, 152
Azúcar de Cuba, 120

B

Ballet, 131–132
Bank, Cajasol, 25
Baños Árabes (Arab Bathhouse), 14
Baños del Alcázar, 156–157
Bar Alfalfa, 37–38, 107
Barber of Seville (Gioachino Rossini), 49
Barrio Santa Cruz, 9, 46–51
Bars, 116–122. *See also* Tapas bars
Bar San Fernando, 116
Basílica de la Macarena, 68
Bestiario nightclub, 121
Bicycling, 82–88, 91, 163, 164, 167
Bienal de Arte Flamenco festival, 161
Boating, 42
Bokotrapo bar, 116
Boss nightclub, 121
Bullfighting, 19, 20, 124, 131, 160
Buses and bus tours, 15, 43, 44, 149, 163
Business hours, 9, 164

C

CAAC. *See* Centro Andaluz de Arte Contemporáneo
Cabo Loco bar, 116
Café Cuidad Condal bar, 116

Café L'Art bar, 116
Café Moderniste bar, 116
Cafe Naima bar, 120
Cajasol Bank, 57
Calatrava, Santiago, 86
Callejón del Agua, 48
Camera stores, 73, 74
Capilla de los Marineros, 60
Capillita del Carmen, 60
Capillita de San José, 53
Carmona, 150–153
Car rentals, 162, 164
Casa Anselma flamenco bar, 119, 120
Casa de la Condesa Lebrija, 54–55, 167
Casa de la Memoria, 49, 124, 130
Casa de la Moneda, 30
Casa de Murillo, 50
Casa de Pilatos, 13, 167
Casa de Sapharad, 157
Casa Paco, 39, 108
Cash machines, 164
Castillo de San Jorge Museum, 60–61, 167
Catedral de Sevilla, 124, 129
Catedral nightclub, 121
Cellphones, 162
Central bar, 116–117
Centro Andaluz de Arte Contemporáneo (CAAC), 25, 87, 127, 167
Centro de las Artes de Sevilla, 65, 127
Ceramics, 74–75
Cervantes, Miguel de, 47, 49, 55–57
Chapel of the Ancient Virgin, 7
Chapel of St. Andrew, 7
Chapel of St. Anthony, 7
Chapter House, 7
Children, activities for, 40–44, 165
  dining, 99, 106, 107
  monuments and attractions, 91
  museums, 59, 91–92
  outdoors, 11, 91
  shopping, 75
  sports, 131, 132
  theater, 132
  theme parks, 86
  towers and fortresses, 8, 17, 18, 31, 65, 151
Churches and religious sites, 32–35
  Basílica de la Macarena, 68
  Capilla de los Marineros, 60

Capillita del Carmen, 60
Capillita de San José, 53
Convento de Santa
    Clara, 33, 64–65
Convento de Santa
    Paula, 34
Iglesia de los
    Terceros, 34
Iglesia del Salvador, 56
Iglesia de San Juan de la
    Palma, 35
Iglesia de San Luis de
    los Franceses, 67
Iglesia de San Marcos,
    35
Iglesia de San Pedro,
    32–33
Iglesia de Santa Ana,
    59–60
Iglesia de Santa Marina,
    67–68
La Magdalena, 20, 54
Mezquita cathedral,
    155–156
Monasterio de la
    Cartuja, 86–87
Monasterio de San
    Clemente, 65
Monasterio de San
    Isidoro del Campo,
    148, 149
Palacio de las
    Dueñas, 33
Parroquia de Nuestra
    Señora de la O, 61
Priorial de Santa María,
    152
Santa Iglesia Catedral
    (Seville Cathedral),
    6–8
Sinagoga (synagogue),
    157
Templo de Nuestro
    Padre Jesús del Gran
    Poder, 63
Cine Alameda, 129
Cine Cervantes, 129
Cinema, 124, 129
Clan bar, 117
Climate, 160, 161
Clubs, 121–122
Colón, Cristóbal. See Colum-
    bus, Christopher
Columbus, Christopher,
    7, 28–30
Concha Pedrosa, 24, 124,
    127
Concierge services, 164
Consulates, 165
Contenedor bar, 120

Convento de Santa Clara, 33,
    64–65, 167
Convento de Santa Paula, 34
Córdoba, 154–158
Corpus Christi festival, 160
Corral de Esquivel bar, 117
Cortés, Hernando, 29, 30
Cosmetics stores, 75
Costurero de la Reina
    (Queen's Sewing Box)
    Museum, 84, 90, 167
Cradle Street, 55
Cruises, 42
Currency, 166

D
Dance, 124, 131–132
Day trips, 146–158
    Carmona, 150–153
    Córdoba, 154–158
    Itálica, 146–149
Department stores, 75–76
Diablito bar, 117
Día de los Reyes festival, 161
Dining. See also Restaurant
    Index
    best bets, 94
    maps, 95–98
Disabilities, travelers with,
    168
Driving, 162, 163

E
El Arenal, 130
Electricity, 165
Elefunk nightclub, 121–122
El Garlochi bar, 117
El Giraldillo entertainment
    listing, 127
El Jackson nightclub, 121
El Palacio Andaluz, 124, 130
El Patio del Arte, 48
El Patio Sevillano, 130
El Perro Andaluz bar,
    120–121
El Rinconcillo, 33, 38, 39,
    108–109
El Tamboril flamenco bar,
    120
El Tremendo bar, 117–118
Embassies, 165
Emergencies, 165
Emporio nightclub, 122
Endanza, 124, 131
Entertainment. See Perform-
    ing arts and
    entertainment
Entrecalles bar, 118
Espacio Escala, 25, 127
Estadio Olímpico, 131

Estadio Sánchez Pizjuán, 124
Estrella tapas bar, 14, 37,
    109
Etnia Espacio Universal bar,
    118
Eureka bar, 118
Europa tapas bar, 37, 55, 94,
    109
Event listings, 165
Exhibition Pavilions, 86,
    89–90
Explorers, 29, 30

F
Family travel, 165. See also
    Children, activities for
Fashion, 76–77, 79, 80
Félix Gomez art gallery, 127
Feria de Abril festival, 160
Festival Internacional de
    Jazz, 161
Festival Internacional de
    Teatro y Danza, 160
Festivals, 160, 161
Flamenco bars, 119–120,
    132
Flamenco shows, 49, 124,
    129–132
Free attractions, 167
Fuente de los Leones, 91
Full Art, 24, 128
Fun Club nightclub, 121
Fundición bar, 118

G
Galería Nuevoarte, 25, 128
Gardens
    Alcázar, 10–11
    Alcázar de los Reyes
        Cristianos, 156
    Casa de Pilatos, 13
    Jardines de Murillo,
        15, 49
    Monasterio de la
        Cartuja, 86–87
    Palacio de San
        Telmo, 89
    Parque Maria Luisa,
        90, 91
Gay and lesbian travelers,
    112, 165
Gift stores, 77–78
Giralda (cathedral tower),
    8, 42, 51
Glassy Lounge bar, 118
Glorieta de la Infanta (Monu-
    ment to the Princess), 90
González, Aníbal, 60, 85, 91
Goya, Francisco, 7
Groucho bar, 118

H

Hammam de Al Andalus, 157–158
Historical sites and museums, 68
  Alcázar de la Puerta de Sevilla, 151
  Alcázar de los Reyes Cristianos, 156
  Antigua Fundición Real, 30–31
  Archivo de Indias, 29
  Ayuntamiento, 152
  Banos del Alcázar, 156–157
  Casa de la Condesa Lebrija, 54–55
  Casa de la Moneda, 30
  Casa de Sapharad, 157
  Castillo de San Jorge Museum, 60–61
  Hospital de Cinco Llagas, 68
  Itálica, 54, 92, 146–147
  Judería, 51
  Las Reales Atrazanas, 31
  Monasterio de la Cartuja, 86–87
  Monasterio de San Isidoro del Campo, 148, 149
  Monolitos Romanos, 14
  Murales, 46–47
  Museo Arqueológico, 85, 91–92
  Museo de Artes y Costumbres Populares, 92
  Museo de Carruajes, 59
  Museo Histórico Militar, 91
  Necrópolis Romana, 151
  Plaza de la Corredera, 158
  Plaza del Triunfo, 46
  Plaza San Fernando, 152
  Priorial de Santa María, 152
  Puente de Isabel II, 60
  Puerta de Córdoba, 153
  Puerte del Puente, 155
  Sinagoga (synagogue), 157
  Termas Romanas (Roman Baths), 148
  Torre de la Calahorra, 154–155
  Torre del Oro, 17, 18, 41–42, 84

Holidays, 165
Holy Week (Semana Santa), 160
Horse-drawn carriage rides, 11, 42–43, 163–164
Hospital de Cinco Llagas, 68
Hospital de la Caridad, 18, 23
Hospital de Los Venerables, 47, 124, 129, 167
Hotels. See Accommodations
House of the Planetarium, 146–147

I

Ibero-American Exposition, 10, 86, 89–90
Iglesia de los Terceros, 34
Iglesia del Salvador, 56
Iglesia de San Juan de la Palma, 35
Iglesia de San Luis, 129
Iglesia de San Luis de los Franceses, 67
Iglesia de San Marcos, 35
Iglesia de San Pedro, 32–33
Iglesia de Santa Ana, 59–60
Iglesia de Santa Catalina, 33–34
Iglesia de Santa Marina, 67–68
Immaculate Conception festival, 161
Insurance, 165–166
Internet access, 166
Isabel Ignacio, 24, 128
Isla Mágica, 44, 86
Isleta de los Patos, 91
Itálica, 54, 92, 146–149

J

Jano tapas bar, 39, 94, 109
Jardines de Murillo, 15, 49
Jewelry stores, 78
Judería, 51
Julio Romero de Torres Museum, 158

K

Kafka nightclub, 122

L

La Alacena de San Eloy, 54
La Bodega, 38, 109
La Caja China, 24, 128
La Carbonería flamenco bar, 120
La Giganta, 39, 110
La Macarena neighborhood, 66–68

La Magdalena, 20, 54
La Rebotica bar, 118–119
Las Columnas, 9, 10, 37, 110
Las Reales Atrazanas, 31
La Tertulia bar, 119
Leatherware stores, 80
Lodging. See Accommodations
Lo Nuestro flamenco bar, 120
Los Gallos, 130–131
Lost property, 166

M

Magellan, Ferdinand, 29, 30
Malandar nightclub, 121
Mañara, Miguel de, 23
Markets, 61, 68, 80, 107
Mercadillo de la Feria, 68
Mercado de Triana, 61
Mesa, Juan de, 63
Mezquita (cathedral), 155–156
Monasterio de la Cartuja, 25, 86–87, 167
Monasterio de San Clemente, 65
Monasterio de San Isidoro del Campo, 148, 149
Monolitos Romanos, 14
Montañés, Juan Martínez, 56, 64, 149
Monte Gurugu, 91
Monumento a la Tolerancia, 85
Monument to the Princess (Glorieta de la Infanta), 90
Morales Ortega antique store, 47
Mudéjar architecture, 10
Murales, 46–47, 68
Murillo, Bartolomé Estéban, 7, 18, 20, 23, 24, 49, 50, 54
Museo Arqueológico, 85, 91–92, 167
Museo Casa Palacio del Marqués, 152–153
Museo de Artes y Costumbres Populares, 85, 92, 167
Museo de Bellas Artes, 20, 25, 26, 124, 128, 167
Museo de Carruajes, 59
Museo de la Ciudad, 152–153
Museo del Baile Flamenco, 13, 14, 130
Museo Histórico Militar, 91, 167
Museo Municipal, 147

Museums. *See* Art galleries and museums; Historical sites and museums
Music, 79, 120–121, 124, 129, 131

N

Nao bar, 119
Necrópolis Romana, 151
Neighborhood walks, 46–68
    Alameda, 62–65
    Centro, 52–57
    La Macarena, 66–68
    Santa Cruz, 46–51
    Triana, 58–61
New World Adventures tour, 28–31
Nightlife, 112–122
    bars, 116–119
    flamenco bars, 119–120
    live music, 120–121
    maps, 113–115
    nightclubs, 121–122
NO8DO (Seville's motto), 17
Noha bar, 119

O

Obbio nightclub, 122
One-day tours, 6–20
Opera, 124, 129
Optical stores, 79
Outdoor activities, 82–92
    bicycling, 82–88
    parks and pavilions, 89–92

P

Painters studios, 48
Palaces
    Alcázar, 10–11
    Alcázar de los Reyes Cristianos, 156
    Casa de Pilatos, 13
    Palacio de las Dueñas, 33
    Palacio de San Telmo, 84, 89
    Torre de Don Fadrique, 64–65
Parking, 166
Parks, 89–92
Parque de las Delicias, 84–85
Parque María Luisa, 41, 90, 91
Parroquia de Nuestra Señora de la O, 61
Pasarela de la Cartuja, 25
Passports, 166

Patio de Banderas, 51
Patio de Naranjas, 8
Performing arts and entertainment, 124–132
    art galleries, 127, 128
    classical music and opera, 129
    film and cinema, 129
    flamenco shows, 129–131
    maps, 125–126
    rock and pop, 131
    spectator sports, 131
    theater, dance and ballet, 131–132
Perfume stores, 75
P'Flaherty's bar, 119
Pharmacies, 166
Photo developing, 73, 74
Piola bar, 119
Plaza Alfaro, 48
Plaza de América, 85, 91
Plaza de España, 15, 60, 85, 90
Plaza de Jesús de la Pasión, 55
Plaza de la Alianza, 47
Plaza de la Corredera, 156, 158
Plaza del Altozano, 60
Plaza de las Cruces, 49
Plaza del Salvador, 56
Plaza del Triunfo, 46
Plaza de San Francisco, 57
Plaza de San Lorenzo, 63
Plaza de Toros, 124, 131
Plaza de Toros de la Real Maestranza, 19, 20
Plaza Doña Elvira, 48
Plaza Refinadores, 49
Plaza San Fernando, 152
Plaza Santa Cruz, 50
Plaza Virgen de los Reyes, 6
Police, 166
Poseidon nightclub, 122
Post offices, 166
Pottery, 74–75
Priorial de Santa María, 152
Puente de Cachorro, 86
Puente de Isabel II, 60, 85–86
Puente de la Barqueta, 86
Puente de la Cartuja, 87
Puente de Los Remedios, 84
Puente de San Telmo (San Telmo Bridge), 84
Puente de Triana, 85–86
Puente Romano, 154
Puerta de Córdoba, 153
Puerte del Puente, 155

Q

Queen's Sewing Box. *See* Costurero de la Reina Museum

R

Rafael Ortiz art gallery, 128
Real Betis Balompie, 131
Reales Atarazanas, 131
Religious sites. *See* Churches and religious sites
República bar, 119
Rinconete y Cortadillo (Miguel de Cervantes), 55
Rodrigo de Triana Monument, 59
Roldán, Pedro, 23, 35, 61
Roman Baths (Termas Romanas), 148
Rossini, Gioachino, 49
Royal Chapel, 7
Royal Tobacco Factory, 28–29

S

Sacristy of the Chalices, 7
Safety, 166
St. Peter's Chapel, 7
Saint Ferdinand festival, 160
Sala Apolo, 129
Sala El Cachorro, 131
Sala Joaquín Turina, 131
Sala la Fundición, 31, 131–132
Sala la Imperdible, 124, 132
Sala Ocero, 132
Santa Cruz neighborhood, 9, 46–51
Santa Iglesia Catedral (Seville Cathedral), 6–8
San Telmo Bridge (Puente de San Telmo), 84
Sanvicente 31, 25, 128
Semana Santa (Holy Week), 160
Sevici, 87, 164, 167
Sevilladc entertainment listing, 127
Sevilla en Otoño festival, 161
Sevilla FC, 131
Seville
    architecture of, 169–171
    history of, 168–169
    motto of, 17
Seville Cathedral (Santa Iglesia Catedral), 6–8
Seville Film Festival, 161
Seville Royal Symphony Orchestra, 127, 129

Shoe stores, 80
Shopping, 70–80
  antiques, 73
  best bets, 70
  books, 73
  cameras, 73, 74
  in Centro neighborhood, 55, 57
  ceramics and pottery, 74–75
  with children, 75
  department stores and shopping centers, 75–76
  fashion and accessories, 76–77, 79, 80
  gifts and souvenirs, 77–79
  jewelry, 78
  music, 79
  in Triana neighborhood, 61
Siesta, 9
Sinagoga (synagogue), 157
Smoking, 166
Soccer, 131
Sopa de Ganso bar, 119
Souvenir stores, 77–78
Spanish Government Tourist Board Offices, 160
Spanish language, 14, 172–175
Special events, 160, 161
Special-interest tours, 22–44
  art museums and galleries, 22–27
  for children, 40–44
  churches and convents, 32–35
  New World Adventures, 28–31
  tapas bars, 36–39
Specialty stores, 78–79
Sports, 131
Sports, spectator, 124
Street Bar, 121
Streetcars, 163
Synagogue (sinagoga), 157

T

Tapas, 38, 152
Tapas bars, 36–39, 106–110. See also Restaurant Index
Taxes, 166–167
Taxis, 15, 163
Teatro Central, 124, 132
Teatro de la Maestranza, 124, 127, 129
Teatro Lope de Vega, 124, 132
Teatro Municipal Alameda, 124, 132

Teatro Quintero, 132
Teatro Romano, 147–148
Teen boutiques, 79, 80
Telephones, 167
Templo de Nuestro Padre Jesús del Gran Poder, 63
Termas Romanas (Roman Baths), 148
Texas Lone Star Saloon bar, 119
Theater, 124, 131–132, 147–148
Theme parks, 44, 86
Tipping, 167
Toilets, 167
Torre de Don Fadrique, 64–65
Torre de la Calahorra, 154–155
Torre del Oro, 17, 18, 31, 41–42, 84, 167
Torre de los Perdigones, 44, 65
Torres, Julio Romero de, 158
Torres Macarena flamenco bar, 120
Tourist offices, 167, 168
The Tourists entertainment listing, 127
Tours, 168
  one-day, 6–11
  two-day, 12–15
  three-day, 16–20
Trains, 162–163
Trams, 15, 163
Triana neighborhood, 58–61
Triunfo de San Rafael, 155

U

Universidad (university), 28–29

V

Valdés Leal, Juan de, 18, 23, 24
Velada de Santa Ana festival, 160
Velázquez, Diego, 47, 53

W

Walking, 15, 163. See also Neighborhood walks
Water parks, 44
Weather, 160, 161
Websites, useful, 161–162
What's On entertainment listing, 127

Z

Zurbarán, Francisco de, 7, 24, 25, 53, 152

Accommodations

Alcázar del Reina, 153
Alcázar del Rey Don Pedro, 153
Alcoba del Rey, 134, 138
Amadeus la Música, 134, 138
Bar Alfonso, 17
Barceló Renacimiento, 134, 138
Casa de Carmona, 153
Casa Número 7, 138
Casa Paco, 39
Casa Romana, 134, 138
Casa Sacristía Santa Ana, 138–139
Corral del Rey, 134, 139
El Bulli Hotel, 134, 140–141
EME Fusion Hotel, 139
Espacio Azahar, 134, 139
Garden Backpackers, 139
Gran Meliá Colón, 139
Hacienda Benazuza, 134, 140–141
Hospes Las Casa del Rey de Baeza, 134, 140
Hotel Adriano, 140
Hotel Alcántara, 140
Hotel Alfonso XIII, 134, 140
Hotel Alminar, 134, 140
Hotel Bécquer, 134, 140
Hotel Casa Imperial, 140
Hotel Casona de San Andrés, 140
Hotel Doña Maria, 134, 141
Hotel Europa, 141
Hotel Goya, 134, 141
Hotel Inglaterra, 134, 141
Hotel Los Seises, 141
Hotel Maestranza, 141–142
Hotel Murillo, 134
Hotel NH Plaza de Armas, 142
Hotel Rey Alfonso X, 142
Hotel Reyes Catolicos, 142
Hotel San Gil Seville, 142
Hotel un Patio Santa Cruz, 142
Hotel YH Giralda, 142
La Casa del Maestro, 142
La Hospederia de El Churrasco, 158
Las Casas de la Judería, 134, 142–143, 158
Palacio del Bailio, 158
Patio de la Alameda Aparthotel, 143
Pension Doña Trinidad, 134, 143
Petit Palace Marqués Santa Ana, 143

Petit Palace Santa Cruz,
134, 143
Placio de Villapanés, 143
Posada del Lucero, 144
Puerta Catedral Apartments,
134, 144
Puerta de Triana, 144
Sevilla5 Apartments,
134, 144
Suite Alcázar, 134, 144
Taberna del Alabardero,
134, 144
Urbany Hostel, 134, 144
Vincci la Rábida, 134, 144

Restaurants
Abades Triana, 99
Abantal, 94, 99
Ajo Blanco, 106–107
Alcázar del Rey Don Pedro,
153
Alcoy 10, 107
Almanara, 94, 99
Al-Medina, 99
Al Solito Posto, 94, 99
Ambigú, 39
As Sawirah, 94, 99
Avenida de la Constitución
16, 103
Azúcar de Cuba, 99–100
Az-Zait, 94, 100
Bar Alfalfa, 37–38, 107
Barbiana, 94, 100
Bar Las Teresas, 49–50, 107
Bar Plaza, 152
Bar Santa Ana, 107
Bar Santos, 156
Becerrita, 100
Bobo, 100
Bodega Belmonte, 107
Bodega Góngora, 107
Bodegón Alfonso XII, 20
Bodeguita Reyes, 148
Burladero, 100
Café Moderniste, 23
Cafeteria del Monasterio,
27, 87

Casablanca, 30, 107
Casa Carmelo, 47–48, 108
Casa Cuesta, 61, 100
Casa Manolo, 100
Casa Morales, 94, 108
Casa Paco, 39, 108
Casa Placido, 108
Casa Robles, 94, 100
Contenedor, 67
Cosa Nostra, 101
Diablito, 64
Douchka, 67
Duplex, 101
Egaña-Oriza, 94, 101
El Ambigu, 108
El Corral Del Agua, 101
El Paladar, 108
El Rinconcillo, 33, 38, 39,
108–109
El Ventorrillo Canario, 147
Enrique Becerra, 94, 101
Eslava, 94, 101
Estrella, 14, 37, 109
Europa, 37, 55, 94, 109
Faro de Triana, 101
Foster's Hollywood,
94, 101–102
Gastromium, 94, 102
Horno de San Buenaventura,
24, 42, 94, 103
Horno Monte-Sion, 68
Horno San Louis, 157
Jano, 39, 94, 109
Kiosco de Las Flores, 102
Kiosko Abilio, 85, 92
La Alacena de San Eloy, 109
La Albahaca, 102
La Alicantina, 102
La Bodega, 38, 109
La Campaña, 103
La Cava del Europa, 109
La Cueva, 102
La Fresquita, 109
La Giganta, 39, 110
La Habanita, 94, 102
La Huerta Mediterránea, 110
La Ilustre Victima, 110

La Isla, 94, 102–103
La Judería, 103
La María Bodega, 103
La Mia Tana, 94, 103
La Nieta de Pepa, 103
La Plazoleta, 35
La Raza, 103–104
Las Columnas (Alameda),
110
Las Columnas (Santa Cruz),
9, 10, 37, 110
Las Golondrinas, 110
Las Piletas, 104
Los Caracoles, 110
Luis Barceló, 104
Maccheroni, 104
Mata 24, 104
Mesón Don Raimundo, 104
Modesto, 104
Pastelería Los Angeles, 18
Patio San Eloy, 110
Poncio, 104–105
Porta Rossa, 94, 105
Pozo Luna, 105
Puerta Grande, 105
Rayas, 103
República, 64
Restaurante Horacio, 105
Río Grande, 105
Robles Laredo, 53, 103
Robles Placentines, 105
Sacristia de Santa Ana, 105
Salvador Rojo, 94, 106
San Fernando 27, 94, 101
San Marco, 106
San Marco Pizzeria, 106
Taberna del Alabardero,
94, 106
Taberna los Terceros, 110
Terrace Bar, Hotel Doña
María, 11
Tetería, 103
Texas Lone Star Saloon,
94, 106

Photo **Credits**

Explore over 3,500 destinations.

TOKYO — 7766 miles

LONDON — 3818 miles

TORONTO — 4682 miles

SYDNEY — 5087 miles

NEW YORK — 4947 miles

LOS ANGELES — 2556 miles

HONG KONG — 5638 miles

Frommers.com makes it easy.

Find a destination. ✓ Book a trip. ✓ Get hot travel deals.
Buy a guidebook. ✓ Enter to win vacations. ✓ Listen to podcasts.
Check out the latest travel news. ✓ Share trip photos and memories.
And much more.